hypnotism and psychic phenomena

by
SIMEON EDMUNDS

New truths grow strong amid the rough winds of scorn, opposition, and contumely; it is thus that their vitality is tested. All must be cast into the furnace, and if the fire of trial burns up the hay and the stubble, we have at least the consolation that the gold and the stone shall remain.—1 Cor. iii. 12.

V. C. DESERTIS

Published by
Melvin Powers
WILSHIRE BOOK COMPANY
12015 Sherman Road
No. Hollywood, California 91605
Telephone: (213) 875-1711

First published 1961
© Simeon Edmunds 1961

Printed by
HAL LEIGHTON PRINTING COMPANY
P.O. Box 3952
North Hollywood, California 91605
Telephone: (213) 983-1105

Printed in the United States of America
ISBN 0-87980-077-1

Acknowledgements

Thanks for permission to quote are gratefully extended to the following.

Mrs Eileen J. Garrett, editor of *Tomorrow*, and the Parapsychology Foundation Inc., New York.

The Council of the Society for Psychical Research and the editor of its *Proceedings*, Mr G. W. Fisk.

Professor C. J. Ducasse, author of *A Critical Examination of the Belief in a Life after Death*, and Mr Charles C. Thomas, publisher, Springfield, Illinois.

The Council of the American Society for Psychical Research and the editor of its *Journal*.

Miss Ruby Yeatman, the Council of the College of Psychic Science, and the editor of *Light*, Mr F. Clive-Ross.

Mr Eric Cuddon, author of *Hypnosis, its Meaning and Practice*, and Messrs. Bell and Sons Ltd., London.

Messrs. Ernest Benn Ltd. (Williams and Norgate), London.

The editor and publishers of the *Daily Express*, London.

H.M. Stationery Office.

Drs Gordon Ambrose and G. F. Newbold, authors of *A Handbook of Medical Hypnosis* and Messrs. Baillière, Tindall & Cox Ltd., London.

The editor, Mr H. J. D. Murton, and the publishers of *Prediction*, London.

The author also acknowledges the invaluable assistance given by Mrs Grace M. Caswell and Miss Louise Puller in the preparation of this book.

Contents

Chapter		Page
	INTRODUCTION	ix
1	HISTORICAL SURVEY	1
2	THE NATURE OF HYPNOSIS	11
3	THE TECHNIQUE OF HYPNOTISM	24
4	HYPNOTIC PHENOMENA	37
5	POST-HYPNOTIC PHENOMENA	48
6	AUTO-SUGGESTION AND SELF-HYPNOSIS	56
7	DISSOCIATION AND MULTIPLE PERSONALITY	65
8	PSYCHIC PHENOMENA	78
9	CLAIRVOYANCE	81
10	TELEPATHY	95
11	MEDIUMISTIC PHENOMENA	114
12	REINCARNATION?	130
13	HYPNOTISM AND CRIME	139
14	MISCELLANY	151
15	CONCLUSION	164
	APPENDIX I—THE HYPNOTISM ACT, 1952	167
	APPENDIX II—THE *Baquet*	169
	APPENDIX III—BIBLIOGRAPHY	171
	INDEX	177

Introduction

ALTHOUGH this book conforms largely to the pattern of previous publications on the subject of hypnosis, in other respects it is somewhat different. Apart from the study and practice of hypnotism, the author's principal interest for many years has been the study and experimental examination of what are usually termed psychic, or supernormal phenomena, and this book is written in the light of the results of these researches. That supernormal phenomena do occur there is no real dispute by anyone who has given the subject serious attention. The Society for Psychical Research, a body whose purpose it is to make a scientific examination of alleged cases of such occurrences, has, since it was founded in 1882, published in its *Journal* and *Proceedings* reports of many hundreds of well authenticated cases, some of a spontaneous nature and others observed under exacting laboratory conditions. Similar societies have done likewise on the Continent and in America, and a number of scientists have made independent investigations and testified that these phenomena do, in fact, occur.

The early 'magnetisers' and mesmerists often claimed to have observed startling supernormal behaviour in their entranced subjects, to such an extent that when the Society for Psychical Research was formed one of its first corporate actions was to appoint a committee to investigate these claims. This committee reported that the reality of these phenomena was established beyond all doubt.

That interest in these 'higher phenomena' of hypnotism waned in later years is due in the main to two related but distinct causes: the attitude of the medical profession and the outlook of the majority of leading scientific men at the time.

The medical profession, among whose members were found the majority of the pioneers of mesmerism, or hypnotism as it was later to be termed, had, quite rightly, struggled throughout the years to establish a scientific, rational approach and reputation, and to break completely away from the atmosphere of voodoo and mumbo-jumbo in which it had been cradled. It naturally, therefore, looked askance at claims involving the acceptance of such things as animal magnetism, vital fluids and mysterious, seemingly supernatural forces; and when later on it had perforce to accept the basic facts of hypnosis, it rejected without examination not only the theories of the early workers but the factual evidence as well: another case, it is suggested, of throwing out the baby with the bath water.

INTRODUCTION

The concrete, materialistic science of the nineteenth century, which seemed to be successfully explaining away everything in the universe in mechanistic terms, had made fantastic advances based on its materialistic assumptions, and dismissed as inherently impossible any evidence indicating that mind was more than just a function of the brain. T. H. Huxley had proclaimed that mind was merely the steam given off as the bodily engine worked, and Herbert Spencer had asserted that the notion of a soul was something which primitive man had cooked up out of his dream life.

Although advancing science has now discarded these mechanistic theories as inadequate, the outlook towards psychic phenomena in general, and that associated with hypnosis in particular, has changed but little. This is largely because most scientists have as much as they can do to cope with the ever-expanding volume of research in their own chosen fields, and have neither the time nor the desire to investigate claims which, if established as proven, would demolish many theories hitherto believed to be of cast iron. Another deterrent to the scientist is the lack of any hypothesis which comes anywhere near to providing a comprehensive explanation of these phenomena.

This book is not an attempt to produce anything original in theory or analysis concerning hypnotism or supernormal occurrences. It is an effort to set out certain facts, some in the author's own experience and others from the extensive literature on these subjects, to the records of which the average reader would not have access; or would lack the time, opportunity and special interest needed for carrying out the considerable amount of research involved. Although its paramount concern is with supernormal phenomena as connected with hypnosis, for the sake of completeness and for the benefit of the comparative newcomer to the subject, an historical survey is included, together with chapters on the induction and the general phenomena of hypnosis. It is hoped incidentally, that these chapters will, in some measure, help to dispel the still widely held beliefs, fostered by romantic novels, plays and films, that hypnotism is some form of 'black magic', and that its practitioners are sinister Svengalis who use their evil powers to exploit their innocent victims.

Another source from which much misunderstanding has grown is the stage performance or demonstration, now fortunately rare, in which the hypnotist uses, in addition to his real abilities, many tricks of showmanship to impress the audience with his wonderful 'power'. Such exhibitions have, in addition to spreading a grotesquely distorted impression of hypnotism, resulted in much distress and ill-health in many of those misguided enough to volunteer

INTRODUCTION

as subjects. Fortunately, in England at least, these performances are now strictly controlled by law, and the limited scope now permitted these showmen has made it cease to be worth their while to remain in business. A copy of the Hypnotism Act, 1952, under which these restrictions are made, is appended.

It will be helpful to quote the legal definition at this stage, although more detailed consideration is given to the nature of hypnosis later in the book.

' "Hypnotism" includes hypnotism, mesmerism and any similar act or process which produces or is intended to produce in any person any form of induced sleep or trance in which the susceptibility of the mind of that person to suggestion or direction is increased or intended to be increased but does not include hypnotism, mesmerism or any such similar act or process which is self induced.'

Although the law disregards self induced or *auto*-hypnosis, this is one of the most important aspects of hypnotic phenomena, and one that is treated later at some length, particularly in its relation to the trances of clairvoyants and 'mediums'. A glossary is appended, but it is as well to mention here that *Hypnotism* describes the subject generally and also refers to the technique of inducing the state of *Hypnosis*—from the Greek *hypnos* meaning sleep, although as is shown later, the state bears but little relation to normal sleep. The hypnotist is commonly referred to as the Operator, and the person who is hypnotized as the Subject. Other special or technical terms are explained as they occur in the text.

The medical applications of hypnosis are not dealt with at any length, as these aspects of the subject are already sufficiently covered by well-qualified authorities.

CHAPTER ONE

Historical Survey

That which counts, that which lasts, is the positive truth we bring out; the true affirmation itself displaces the false idea, and without the trouble of refuting anyone, proves to be the best refutation.

HENRI BERGSON

ALTHOUGH the word Hypnotism was not coined until 1843, its practice, in one form or another, is as old as human tradition. Ancient civilizations have left records demonstrating an extensive knowledge of its uses and effects, and the witch-doctors and clevermen of primitive races owe much of their power and influence to its employment. It has played an important part in the ritual and ceremony of many religions and is the principle behind miraculous healing, sacred sleep, soothsaying, prophecy and divination.

The yogis and fakirs of the East, like the Persian magi of thousands of years ago, place themselves in self-induced trances by fixation of the gaze. In parts of India the name of *Jar-phoonk*, from the Hindustani Jarna, to stroke, and Phoonka, to breathe, is used to describe hypnotic methods which have been known to these people from time immemorial. The Egyptian Ebers papyrus, dating from 1500 B.C., describes the 'laying on of hands' in the treatment of disease, and a bas-relief from an ancient tomb at Thebes illustrates a priest in the act of inducing hypnosis. The Hebrew and Christian Scriptures contain many references to phenomena akin to that of hypnotism, and it would seem to have been a common practice in the temples of the ancient Egyptians, Greeks and Hebrews. There is evidence that its therapeutic uses were well known to the Romans, and Esculapius recorded that he could throw patients into a long and refreshing sleep by strokes of the hand and thus subdue the insane and relieve the suffering.

Hippocrates, the 'father' of medicine, is reported by Tacitus to have said: 'It hath oft appeared, while I have been soothing my patient, as if there were some strange property in my hands to pull and draw away from the afflicted parts aches and diverse impurities, by laying my hand upon the place, and by extending my fingers towards it. It is thus known to the learned that health may be impressed on the sick by certain movements and by contact, just as some diseases may be communicated from one to another.'

The accounts of the miracles performed by Christ are more

acceptable if viewed as hypnotic phenomena, and so are the cures and exorcisms, ecstasies and stigmata, and mystical experiences of the saints.

Avicenna, an outstanding physician and thinker of the tenth century, considered that the mind of man could exert an influence not only on his own body, but on the bodies of others, sometimes even at great distances. He also believed that this power could be used to cause illness as well as to cure it.

His ideas were endorsed several hundred years later by the philosopher Pomponatius who said: 'When thou art endowed with this faculty dost operate by employing the force of the imagination and the will, this force affects their blood and their spirits, which produce the intended results by means of an evaporation thrown outwards.' He believed that the so called 'miracle cures' alleged to be brought about by the relics of the saints were, in fact, due to the imaginations of those cured. It was his opinion, which he believed to be secretly shared by the physicians and philosophers of the day, that if the bones of some animal were substituted for those of a saint, so long as the patients were not aware of the change the cures would be just as effective.

In the sixteenth century another physician, Peracelsus, was persecuted by the Church and hounded from place to place because he publicly stated that the power of the mind could be the cause and also the remedy for many different kinds of illness. Although the Christian Church has, throughout its history, known and made use of hypnotic power, it was its policy to condemn and attempt to suppress the use of it for purposes other than its own.

The monarchs of England and France were, for hundreds of years, credited with the power of healing by the laying on of hands, or 'Royal Touch', and special religious ceremonies were performed while such 'healing' was being carried on. It is recorded that Dr Johnson, as a child, was taken to London in the hope that being 'touched' by Queen Anne would effect a cure of scrofula, or King's Evil. The healer Valentine Greatrakes achieved fame largely because of his apparent power to cure this disease.

Greatrakes was born in 1628 in Affane in Ireland, and became famous in England in about 1660. He claimed that all disease was caused through evil spirits and that God had given him the power to cast them out. He employed passes, similar to those used later by Mesmer, and is reputed to have effected many thousands of cures. Some of the most distinguished scientists and theologians of the day, including Robert Boyle, the physicist, examined his claims and testified to the efficacy of his cures.

Around the middle of the eighteenth century a former monk

named Johann Gassner propounded ideas similar to those of Greatrakes and carried out healing by almost identical methods. He claimed that most diseases were caused by demoniacal possession, and his method of exorcism was to command the 'evil spirit', in impeccable Latin, to depart from the afflicted person. He is credited with having cured more than ten thousand sufferers in many European countries. Gassner believed that the power he could exercise over the nervous systems of his patients was of a supernatural nature.

The first serious study of an objective nature seems to have begun at the end of the sixteenth century with the work of the Flemish philosopher and chemist van Helmont, who concluded as the result of his experiments that a fluid of a magnetic nature is radiated by man, and that this fluid, and through it the mind and body, can be influenced by mental effort and the exercise of 'will power'. Of magnetism he wrote: 'It is active everywhere, and has nothing new but the name; it is a paradox only to those who ridicule everything, and attribute to Satan whatever they are themselves unable to explain.'

No further study of an experimental or scientific kind appears to have been made for the next hundred years or so, but in May, 1734, an event occurred that has become a landmark in the history of the subject. This event was the birth, at Iznang on Lake Constance in Germany, of Franz Anton Mesmer, whose destiny it was to become the first to attempt a scientific investigation of these phenomena, and make them familiar to the world by a term derived from his own name.

It was intended that Mesmer should enter the Church, and he was accordingly educated, first in a monastery, and later at a Jesuit college. He showed however, a marked leaning towards the sciences, particularly mathematics, physics and astronomy, and decided that medicine rather than the Church was his metier. He therefore entered the school of medicine at the University of Vienna.

He obtained his medical degree in 1765, on the strength of a thesis entitled 'De Planetarium Influx', in which he postulated a magnetic fluid which pervaded the universe and acted on the mind and body of man. He claimed that illness could be caused by anything upsetting the balance of this fluid. This thesis created much interest, and one who was considerably impressed was a Jesuit priest named Hehl, who, at that time, besides being a professor of astronomy at Vienna University, was Court Astrologer to the Empress Maria Theresa. Hehl believed that magnets could be used to cure disease, and had the strange idea that if a magnet were made in the shape of one of the human organs, it would exercise some curative power over that particular organ. He gave some of these magnets to Mesmer, who achieved such spectacular success with the first patients on whom he employed them that he interpreted this as confirmation of his own theories.

Later however, Mesmer discovered that he could produce equal results without the use of magnets, particularly by the use of manual passes, and was thus led to develop his theories of 'animal magnetism'. He believed he could infuse this animal magnetism into inanimate objects by touching them, and that patients who subsequently came into contact with these objects would receive the benefit of the magnetic force. Out of this idea was conceived his famous *baquet*, a circular wooden tub containing water, to which were added iron filings and a number of glass bottles. The patients, who sat around the tub, were linked together by ropes, and brought into contact with iron rods which protruded from the tub. Mesmer and his assistants then went from one to the other, making passes and stroking each patient until he was seized by a 'crisis' or convulsion, a state of the treatment believed to be indicative of a cure.

Although much of this seems to savour of quackery, it should be borne in mind that at that time all the known physical forces, such as heat, light, electricity and magnetism, were thought to be due to various 'impalpable fluids', and it was not so absurd that Mesmer should believe he had discovered a new such fluid; although, as Sir William Barrett commented, 'Whether such an effluence exists or not, it certainly has nothing to do with magnetism as the latter is known to physical science; nevertheless, the misnomer still widely exists.'

Mesmer's remarkable success created considerable excitement in Vienna. He cured a director of the Munich Academy of Science of paralysis, another professor of his blindness, and many less noted patients of a great variety of complaints. He did not however, receive the recognition from his colleagues that he believed he deserved; in fact, many of them became so strongly antagonistic that the government was persuaded to forbid his experiments, and, disgusted, Mesmer left Vienna and commenced to practise in Paris. In spite of opposition by his profession, which he found almost as strong in Paris as it had been in Vienna, Mesmer and the *baquet* soon attracted hundreds of patients. His popularity became so great that 'magnetic' clubs and societies were soon established throughout the country.

It speaks highly for Mesmer's integrity that throughout his career he constantly strove to interest the medical and other learned societies in his discoveries and to persuade them to examine his methods and pronounce on them. Ironically, when at last this did happen, the examination was by a Commission set up at the instigation of his enemies. As it refused to allow him to demonstrate his methods personally, and contented itself with the reports and experiences of others, it is not surprising that its findings were against Mesmer. It is noteworthy that King Louis XVI, on whose order the Commission was appointed, had attempted at his coronation to cure over two thousand sick people by exercise of the 'Royal Touch'. Of this number only five are reported to have been cured.

Deeply hurt at the findings of the Commission, and conscious of the revolutionary atmosphere in France, Mesmer decided to return to Lake Constance, and remained there for the rest of his life, devoting his time to the free treatment of the poor. He was invited to Berlin by the King of the Prussians, and when he declined, the famous doctor Carl Wolfart was sent to Mesmer to study his methods. Wolfart was later appointed Professor of Mesmerism at Berlin Academy, and given charge of a new 'magnetic' hospital, to which came many of Europe's leading physicians to be taught to practise the new science.

Mesmer died on March 5th, 1815, but the new 'science' to which he had devoted his life and given his name, was kept alive by his pupils and disciples. Notable among them was the Marquis de Puysegur, who took a much more scientific and critical view of the subject than had any previous investigator. De Puysegur found that the 'crisis', or convulsion regarded by Mesmer as essential to successful treatment, was neither necessary nor even desirable, and that a 'sleeping stage' or trance could be produced instead. He formed the opinion that mesmeric cures were brought about by 'belief and will' or 'the action of thought upon the vital principle of the body'. This trance state was first noted by de Puysegur in 1784. He described it as 'artificial somnambulism', and observed that when in this condition a subject's ideas and actions could be controlled and directed. He also noted that many subjects were afterwards unable to remember anything of what took place during the trance.

In the year of Mesmer's death widespread interest centred on the seemingly miraculous cures effected in Paris by the Abbé Faria, a Portuguese monk, who during his travels in India had learned how to send patients into a deep trance by gazing steadily at them and then suddenly giving the command 'Dormez'. He appears to have been the first to appreciate that the trance was caused, not by any 'magnetic fluid' emanating from the operator, but by a subjective process within the patient.

By this time 'animal magnetism', or mesmerism as it was being more widely termed, had made such a firm impression that theological students in Germany, for instance, were being given instruction in physiology, pathology and the healing of the sick by 'vital magnetism'. Unfortunately this wave of interest brought with it a flood of charlatans who, by claiming to cure all and every kind of illness, brought the subject of mesmerism, together with those who seriously studied it, into disrepute. It is only fair to remember this when considering the unscientific and obscurantist attitude taken by the medical profession at the time.

The next step forward was taken by a notable French physician, Dr Alexandre Bertrand, who in 1820 published a treatise on artificial somnambulism in which he rejected the theories of animal magnetism and fluidic forces, and postulated the influence of suggestion as the cause of 'mesmeric' phenomena. He asserted that the patient was made preternaturally alive to the suggestions, expressed or unexpressed, of the operator. Like de Puysegur, he found that in many cases entranced subjects displayed a marked exaltation of intellectual powers, which sometimes even enabled them to make accurate diagnoses of their own cases. They also showed a wonderful appreciation of the passage of time. Bertrand also discovered that full or partial anaesthesia, or insensitivity to pain, could be induced in a considerable proportion of subjects. He asserted too that a community of sensation could sometimes be established between operator and subject, and that a condition of clairvoyance, or seeing at a distance, was occasionally exhibited. He carried out experiments the result of which indicated that telepathic or *willed* instructions were sometimes as effective as verbal ones. If he gave a subject a spoken command and at the same time willed her to do the opposite, she became confused and disturbed until he revoked one of the commands and made both coincide.

At about the same time the Baron du Potet, already famous for his pioneer work in the use of mesmerism for painless surgery, demonstrated to the French Academy of Medicine that it was possible to *mesmerize at a distance* purely by an effort of will.

The Academy published a favourable report on the use of mesmerism for therapeutic purposes, and its use thereafter became extensive throughout Europe. It did not receive any serious attention in England until 1837, when the Baron du Potet visited London. There he met and interested the great British surgeon John Elliotson, who, quick to appreciate the possibilities of mesmerism, carried out some experiments in University College Hospital, and was soon using it both as an anaesthetic and in the treatment of nervous disorders. In spite of his success, he soon aroused the ridicule and antagonism of the medical profession, and under pressure the Council of University College Hospital passed a resolution forbidding the use of mesmerism. Rather than comply, Elliotson resigned, protesting:

'This institution was established for the discovery and dissemination of truth. All other considerations are secondary. We should lead the public, not the public us. The sole question is whether the matter is the truth or not.'

Elliotson continued to use mesmerism and later founded his own 'mesmeric hospital'; also the journal *Zoist*, which in addition to recording the extraordinary cures effected by mesmerism, published many accounts of what had become known as the 'higher phenomena' of mesmerism—clairvoyance, mesmerizing at a distance, thought reading and community of sensation.

In Calcutta another surgeon, James Esdaile, after reading of Elliotson's work, began to use mesmerism as an anaesthetic, and performed some thousands of operations, many of them major ones, with its aid. He was able to reduce the number of operational deaths to a tenth of their previous rate by employing mesmerism. Many of his most remarkable operations were reported in *Zoist*, as were some cases of 'higher phenomena' which he had observed. In spite of confirmation of his achievements by witnesses of the highest integrity, the medical profession as a whole treated Esdaile in the same manner as it had Elliotson, and referring to his work the *Lancet*, leading journal of the profession, commented:

'Mesmerism is too gross a humbug to admit of any further serious notice. We regard its abettors as quacks and imposters. They ought to be hooted out of professional Society. Any practitioner who sends a patient afflicted with any disease to consult a mesmeric quack, ought to be without patients for the rest of his days.'

Much attention at this period was centred on the spectacular demonstrations and remarkable cures performed by a travelling Swiss mesmerist named Lafontaine, who had been arrested in Italy at the instigation of the Church, which declared that his wonderful cures were 'blasphemous imitations of the miracles of Christ'. He was only released on condition that 'he made no more blind people to see nor deaf ones to hear'.

Lafontaine came to England in 1841, and toured the country giving public demonstrations, one of which was witnessed by a celebrated Manchester surgeon, James Braid, who had gone to the performance believing mesmerism a fraud and with the intention of exposing it. He was soon convinced of the reality of the phenomena, but not impressed by the theories put forward to account for them, and began experimenting in the hope of finding the true explanation. As a result he concluded that the action of any force or fluid of a magnetic nature was not involved, and that the phenomena were of a subjective origin. He introduced the word *Hypnotism* (from the Greek *Hypnos*—sleep) as being a more accurate and descriptive term than mesmerism. The word *Hypnosis* describes the hypnotic *state*, Braid having believed that the trance state was a form of sleep. He later changed his opinion on the nature of the hypnotic state, and tried to change the word, which he realized to be a misnomer, but it stuck.

Braid found that he could induce the hypnotic trance by making his subject gaze steadily at a bright object until the eyes became tired, and later that verbal suggestions assisted the process. Tests on a blind person convinced him that the fixed gazing merely assisted the process, and he discontinued the use of it.

In 1842 Braid offered to read a paper on his findings to the Medical Section of the British Association for the Advancement of Science. This offer was scornfully rejected, but such prejudice did not prevent many of its members hearing the paper read at a meeting convened by Braid himself. Like Mesmer, Elliotson and Esdaile, Braid had to contend with violent opposition from his fellow doctors; but opposition came not only from them. Supporters of the old magnetic and mesmeric schools were equally vocal in their condemnation of his theories. Prominent among the adherents to the magnetic hypothesis was the Baron von Reichenbach, who announced the discovery of what he termed an odylic force, which, he claimed, was developed by certain crystals, magnets and the human body. He also claimed that certain sensitive people were able, in darkness, to see a luminance, which he called the *Od Light*, emanating from the poles of a magnet.

In 1848, the use of hypnotism as an anaesthetic received a setback by the discovery of chloroform, which, as even the most ardent champions of hypnotism had to concede, was more certain and positive in its action, and the investigation and use of hypnotism in England came virtually to a standstill. On the Continent however, many serious enquirers continued the work, notably in France, where at Nancy two doctors, Liebeault and Bernheim, did much to demonstrate that the phenomena of hypnosis were of psychological origin. Bernheim, a Professor of Medicine, had at first considered Liébeault a fraud, but later became an ardent convert, subsequently publishing two books, *De la Suggestion* and *La Thérapeutique Suggestive*, works which went far in establishing hypnotism as an important psycho-therapeutic method.

The followers of Bernheim and Liébeault came to be known as the 'Nancy School', to distinguish them from an opposing school of thought led by Jean Charcot, a neurologist at the hospital of the Salpêtrière in Paris, who besides retaining a belief in the power of the magnet, believed the phenomena to be of pathological origin. As his experiments were confined to a few hysterical patients he concluded that only neurotic subjects could be hypnotized, a theory easily demolished by Bernheim, who showed that the more normal and balanced the individual, the greater the ease with which he could be hypnotized.

A renewal of serious interest in England was marked in the year 1882 by the establishment of the Society for Psychical Research, a body of scientific and other learned men, whose object was the scientific investigation of 'that large group of debatable phenomena designated by such terms as mesmeric, psychical and "spiritualistic".'

Outstanding among its founder members were Sir William Barrett, F. W. H. Myers, Edmund Gurney and Frank Podmore, and its first President was Professor Henry Sidgewick, a man much respected in the world of learning and of the highest sobriety of judgment.

Of the six subjects set down for investigation by special committees, the first three were directly concerned with the phenomena associated with hypnotism, and Gurney and Myers in particular made valuable contributions to our experimental and theoretical knowledge; so valuable indeed that T. W. Mitchell has written:

'Gurney's experiments ... were received with incredulity and few realized that he was laying the foundations on which the psychology of abnormal mental states during the next twenty years was to be based ... the theoretical implications of his results was more particularly the task undertaken by Frederic Myers ... Myers put forward a view which was far in advance of the teaching of English clinicians.'[1]

William James described their work as 'an epoch, not only in medical, but in psychological science, because it brings in an entirely new conception of our mental possibilities.'[2]

The work of the Society for Psychical Research and that of kindred associations is considered more fully in a later chapter.

At about this time Sigmund Freud was using hypnosis in his practice in Vienna. He had studied under Charcot, whose works he translated into German, and was strongly influenced by him. Later, when he found that not all patients were susceptible to hypnotic suggestion, he abandoned its use and developed his own method of psycho-analysis. It seems that Freud failed to appreciate that the deep trance was quite unnecessary for many therapeutic purposes. He afterwards admitted however, that hypnosis would be necessary as a short cut if psychotherapy were to become widely used, as his own psycho-analytic methods of treatment could take anything up to five years.

[1] S.P.R. *Proceedings*, Vol. XIV, p. 179. [2] S.P.R. *Proceedings*, Vol. XVII, p.19.

In 1892, a committee appointed by the British Medical Association was unanimous in its acceptance of hypnotism as a genuine and valuable therapeutic method, and in Paris in 1900 an International Congress of Hypnotism made similar pronouncements, in particular endorsing the theories of Liébeault and Bernheim.

As a result of the surer and more scientific footing upon which it was now placed the study and practice of hypnotism grew rapidly, and the names of those who have since added to our knowledge are far too numerous to itemise. Myers, Gurney and Milne Bramwell in Britain; Janet, Richet, Forel, Osty, Moll and Krafft-Ebing on the Continent; and Morton Prince, Boris Sidis and William McDougall in America are but representative, and further reference is made to most of these elsewhere in this book.

During the First World War hypnosis was widely used in the treatment of shell-shock and other forms of battle neurosis and the work of Brown, Thom, and Hadfield was outstanding in this connection. It was Hadfield who coined the term 'hypno-analysis', a method used with conspicuous success in the Second World War, by which time hypnotherapy, as hypnotic treatment had become known, had made great strides. Since then interest has been sustained, and it is now employed in many branches of medicine including dentistry, obstetrics and gynaecology, dermatology and, of course, psychiatry.

Despite the vast amount of study and research carried out since the time of Mesmer, the fact remains that little is still known of the true nature of hypnotism. It is the author's conviction that little further progress will be made in this respect until the results of psychical research, or scientific *parapsychology*, as it is now widely termed, are taken fully into account. Then, and only then, will it be possible to attempt a true understanding, not only of hypnotism, but of the nature of human personality itself.

CHAPTER TWO

The Nature of Hypnosis

We must remain receptive to all theories that seek to explain human nature. Any theory that can replace a vague and unsatisfactory faith with a practical conviction is worthy of the serious consideration of all men.

EILEEN J. GARRETT

THE only acquaintance with hypnotism possessed by the average layman is derived mainly from stage performances, now fortunately rare, from sensational and usually inaccurate press reports in which hypnotism is associated with 'black magic' and other allegedly occult practices, and from the extravagant fantasies of romantic novelists. Occasionally however, the intelligent person is stirred to interest by an authentic account of the use of hypnosis in connection with a major operation or a difficult childbirth, or by its increasing application to the treatment of psychological problems. It will be well therefore, to examine some of the more common hypnotic phenomena and dispose of some misconceptions before proceeding to the consideration of methods of hypnotising, the nature of hypnosis and some of the more complex aspects of the subject.

It is not denied that the stage performances mentioned are genuine demonstrations of hypnotism; on the contrary, their great danger lies in the fact that unsuspecting volunteers who permit themselves to be influenced at these performances may suffer serious mental harm in consequence. Instances of this will be given later. The manner in which such volunteers are 'sent to sleep' by the 'hypnotic gaze' and repeated commands of the music hall hypnotist, and their subsequent obeyance of his every suggestion, are perfectly authentic hypnotic phenomena, although various tricks of showmanship are employed to create as great an impression as possible on both volunteers and audience.

A misconception that needs to be dispelled is the idea that hypnosis is akin to ordinary natural sleep. This belief no doubt arose from the facts that suggestions of sleep are often used in the induction of hypnosis, that normal sleep can sometimes be changed into hypnosis, that a hypnotized person if left undisturbed will drift into natural sleep, and that certain stages of the hypnotic trance bear a superficial resemblance to normal sleep. Braid, who coined the words 'hypnosis' and 'hypnotism', did so in the mistaken belief that hypnosis was a form of sleep. He later discovered his error but by then the terms, which are derived from the Greek word for sleep, had become too firmly established to change.

A moment's reflection will make it obvious that this difference is a wide one. A sleeping person is unconscious of his surroundings and will not respond if addressed, whereas the hypnotic subject will react to every suggestion and carry out highly complicated actions. Medical and scientific tests also show the dissimilarity of the two states. Reflexes are usually the same during hypnosis as in the normal waking state, but are considerably lessened during sleep. The electrical resistance of the body when asleep is up to ten times as high as when awake, but is no higher in hypnosis. The two conditions do however, appear to meet in the case of somnambulism, or sleep-walking, in which the hypnotic state occurs spontaneously.

SUGGESTION AND SUGGESTIBILITY

Hypnosis has been briefly defined as a condition of heightened suggestibility, and this is an accurate, although by no means complete, definition. It is well therefore, to devote some time to the examination of suggestion before considering more fully the nature of hypnotic phenomena.

It should first be understood that suggestion, although frequently confused with hypnotism, sometimes to the point of using the two words as if synonymous, is not the same thing. Suggestibility is an inherent characteristic of all human beings. Hypnotism is a means of heightening and directing that suggestibility, and the hypnotist uses suggestion in order to effect a state of increased suggestibility. This may seem rather Irish, but is in fact correct.

All men, irrespective of race or culture, are susceptible to the influence of suggestion and there appears to be little difference in the degree of susceptibility whatever may distinguish them in other respects. Contrary to popular belief, women are no easier to influence than men, except, for some reason which is not understood, during pregnancy, when they become highly suggestible. Children are invariably susceptible to a higher degree than normal adults, but in most old people suggestibility is somewhat decreased.

Were it not for the effects of suggestion life as we know it would be impossible, for nearly all our actions are the result of suggestions of one kind or another which our subconscious minds have been assimilating throughout our lives. We should think or do but little if all our thoughts and deeds were the result of an appeal to reason. Even when we attempt to formulate reasoned opinions they are influenced to some extent by the power of suggestion. Our emotions —love, hate, fear, awe and the rest, our desires and hopes, religious beliefs and prejudices, gratitude and resentment—rise to cloud the issue whenever we start to think.

If we examine honestly our own opinions and actions we must realize that almost all of them are governed to a large extent by suggestion. Even those trained to resist such influence, men of scientific and logical training, are often governed by suggestion in fields other than those in which they specialize. It is not unknown for a scientist to have seen, in the result of an experiment, that which his theories led him to expect, although the work of others proved that it could not have been so.

We are all aware, particularly since the advent of commercial television, of the complex ways in which suggestion can be employed in advertising, and wherever we go our senses are assaulted by examples of its varying techniques; from the simple exhortation to buy Smith's pink pills or vote for Jones to the more subtle hints that the possession of a certain article is necessary in order to maintain one's social self-respect.

Myers defines suggestion as 'a successful appeal to the subliminal or subconscious self' and says that it is the means by which the operator directs the conditions on which hypnotic phenomena depend, although it does not create them. Hypnosis is the peculiar state which enables certain phenomena to occur, not the means of exciting them. It has been rightly said that suggestion no more explains the phenomena of hypnotism than the crack of the starter's pistol explains a boat-race.

Belief and expectation are factors contributing largely to the acceptance of suggestions, but more important still is the power of imagination. Suggestion is usually considered as divisible into two classes, Auto-suggestion, which is self-explanatory, and Hetero-suggestion or suggestion by another. The latter however, is always resolved into an auto-suggestion before taking effect. The power of suggestion (without hypnosis) is illustrated in a case quoted by Schofield:

'A man was blindfolded, and told that he was going to be executed by having a blood-vessel severed; a slight incision was made in a vein and water allowed to drip in such a way that he could hear it; he believed that an artery had been cut, and he actually died believing that he was bleeding to death.'[1]

Coué asserts, 'When the will and the imagination are at war, the imagination *invariably* gains the day', and this is undoubtedly true. For example, a man who could quite easily walk along a narrow plank lying on the ground might be quite unable to do so if it were raised say, ten feet from the ground, and the more he tried, by an

[1] *The Force of Mind*, London, 1903.

effort of will, to preserve his balance, the more likely he would be to fall. Such victories of imagination over will are illustrations of what is sometimes termed the Law of Reversed Effort. It is evident therefore that susceptibility to suggestion is not, as is commonly believed, an indication of a 'weak will', and that the amount of 'will power' possessed by an individual is no indication of his degree of hypnotizability.

This disposes of the widely held public belief that only weak willed, gullible persons can be hypnotized; in fact, it is now established beyond all doubt that intelligent, well-balanced people are the best hypnotic subjects. Conversely, the mentally deficient and the insane are the most difficult of all to hypnotize. Here it should be emphasized that to be susceptible to suggestion is *not* to be gullible or credulous.

WHO CAN BE HYPNOTIZED?

The statement that hypnotizability is an indication of normality is not meant to imply that all normal persons can be hypnotized to the same degree, nor does it mean that hypnotizability is in any respect a measure of intelligence. Many other factors, about which we still know but little, are involved. Research however, has made it possible to isolate certain traits associated with hypnotizability. Two American psychologists, Sarbin and Madow, carried out a series of experiments using Rorchach, or ink blot, tests. These tests, extensively used by psychiatrists, make use of a series of cards on which are printed blots of various shapes. It is known that persons who judge each blot 'picture' as a whole are generally those whose thinking is of an abstract and generalized kind, while those who pay attention to significant details tend to be shrewd and practical types.

From these experiments Sarbin and Madow concluded that imaginative, abstract thinkers are usually very good hypnotic subjects, whereas shrewd, practical thinkers are less easily hypnotized. In another type of test it was found that persons who failed to complete a puzzle correctly and excused their failure with good-humoured optimism were good hypnotic subjects, but those in whom failure caused excitement or annoyance were not.

Nervous and apprehensive types are often difficult to hypnotize at a first attempt, and need a great deal of reassurance. Surprisingly, the 'you can't hypnotize me' know-all type of customer is usually among the most easily influenced.

Various estimates have been made of the incidence of susceptibility to hypnosis and the more reliable ones are substantially in agreement. Milne Bramwell recorded details of average susceptibility noted by his leading contemporaries at the turn of the century, and in 1933 Hull published this summary of them:

Refractory	10.48 per cent
Light Hypnosis	32.68 ,, ,,
Deep Hypnosis	34.58 ,, ,,
Somnambulism	22.26 ,, ,,

Two later workers, LeCron and Bordeaux, have produced very similar figures:

Uninfluenced	5 per cent
Hypnoidal	10 ,, ,,
Light Trance	25 ,, ,,
Medium Trance	35 ,, ,,
Somnambulistic (Deep) Trance	25 ,, ,,

When considering these figures it is important to realize that by no means all subjects can be hypnotized at the first attempt. In many cases several sittings are necessary before hypnosis can be induced at all, after which deeper trances are aimed for at each subsequent sitting. Milne Bramwell states that in many of his cases which yielded the best therapeutic results, hypnosis was only obtained after repeated failures. In extreme cases the number of these amounted to over a hundred. Vogt, of Berlin, made seven hundred attempts with one subject before inducing a deep hypnosis.

STAGES OF HYPNOSIS

Some explanation of the 'stages' of hypnosis referred to in the tables of susceptibility must now be given. Frequent attempts have been made to divide hypnosis into different stages according to the phenomena exhibited. Most authorities have settled for three, but Liebeault gives six stages and Bernheim as many as nine. These divisions are to a large extent arbitrary and vary greatly from subject to subject. Modern hypnotists generally recognize three degrees, light, medium and deep.

The light stage is typified by feelings of heaviness of the eyes and limbs and sensations of general drowsiness. There is a high degree of relaxation, usually with inhibition of the swallowing reflex and of voluntary movement. Not all of these symptoms need be evident, and the inhibitions will sometimes occur although there is no drowsiness or closing of the eyes. This stage is roughly equivalent to the 'hypnoidal' state.

The medium stage is characterized by increased drowsiness and by the strange phenomenon of *catalepsy* in which one or more limbs or even the whole body can be made completely stiff and rigid by suitable suggestions. Positions which the subject would normally find impossibly tiring and uncomfortable can be maintained for long periods, and the subject feels little or no discomfort after the termination of the hypnosis. *Amnesia*, or loss of memory of what occurred during the hypnosis may sometimes be successfully suggested. Analgesia and apparent anaesthesia can also be obtained, and simple post-hypnotic suggestions will sometimes be effective. (The latter are dealt with at length in a later chapter.)

The Deep Stage, also known as the somnambulistic or trance state, is the one in which the most impressive of all hypnotic phenomena occur, including complete amnesia, often even when no suggestion to that effect is given, and the acceptance of the most complicated post-hypnotic suggestions. The condition of *rapport* appears, in which the subject seems to possess some mental link with the hypnotist and is seemingly indifferent to the presence or the actions of anyone but him. In most cases this *rapport* is more apparent than real, and may be transferred from the hypnotist to someone else, but occasionally it seems to develop a further quality that can only be described as a psychic or telepathic affinity between operator and subject.

THE NATURE OF HYPNOSIS

Despite the vast amount of enquiry and research that has been made and the numerous works on the subject that have been published, the true nature of hypnosis is still very much a mystery. Many theories have been advanced since the time of Mesmer, most of them based on quite erroneous precepts and only made plausible by the (sometimes studied) omission of such facts as fail to fit. Apart from the question of psychic phenomena, with which some later chapters of this book are largely concerned, a notable weakness of many theories in regard to the omission of important facts is pointed out by Milne Bramwell. He says:

'Finally, the subject can be trained to hypnotize himself, and can then evoke phenomena identical with those previously elicited by the operator. In this condition, it is clearly to be seen that it is the subject himself who has gained this new and far-reaching power over his own organism. Thus, every theory which fails to explain the phenomena of *self-hypnosis* must be rejected as unsatisfactory.'[1]

In order to appreciate the manner in which modern theories of hypnosis have evolved it is necessary first to consider the beliefs of the early mesmerists and 'magnetizers'. They believed the phenomena to be due to odylic forces and magnetic fluids emanating not only from the operator, but from various objects such as magnets,

[1] *Hypnotism, its History, Practice and Theory*, London, 1903.

crystals, and suitably 'charged' glasses of water. Different substances were alleged to produce different effects on the subject. From time to time claims were made that the existence of these fluidic forces had been experimentally demonstrated, but later attempts to confirm them have produced no positive results, and Braid eventually demonstrated that hypnosis was largely of a subjective nature. The 'magnetic' theories were summarized by Esdaile thus:

'There is good reason to believe that the vital fluid of one person can be poured into the system of another. A merciful God has engrafted a communicable, life-giving, curative power in the human body, in order that when two individuals are found together, deprived of the aids of art, the one in health may often be able to relieve his sick companion, by imparting to him a portion of his vitality.'

Before passing to more modern theories mention must be made of the pathological one advanced by Charcot, who, great neurologist though he was, made the most unscientific experiments using as subjects hysterical patients from his clinic at the Salpêtrière hospital. In consequence he came to the absurd conclusion that hypnosis was a symptom of morbid hysteria, and was therefore possible only with neurotic subjects. When Esdaile, who at the time was performing the most amazing feats of surgery with the aid of hypnosis in India, heard of Charcot's theories he said:

'I cannot possibly see how hysteria has got into my hospitals, where I never saw it before—coolies and felons not being at all nervous subjects. As natural hysteria may be supposed to be more powerful than imitation, I shall look with impatience for the announcement in the *Morning Post* that Mrs Freake has been cured of her nervous headaches by the skilful application of hysteria, and that Lady Tantrums has had her arm cut off while in a fit of hysterics without knowing it. These should be easy feats for our fashionable physicians and surgeons, as they have the disease and the antidote ready made to hand, whereas it costs me and my assistants great trouble to make the coolies and prisoners of Bengal hysterical to the degree necessary to render them insensible to the loss of their members.'[1]

Braid originally held the view that hypnosis was due to mental concentration producing a state of 'monoideism' in which the mind was so occupied with one idea that it was oblivious to all others. Braid's theory was a physiological one; he claimed that hypnosis depended on a definite physical change in the brain of the subject, resulting from the methods employed to induce it. Bennett elaborated this theory, holding that suggested ideas took effect because the

[1] Quoted by Bramwell in *Hypnotism, its History, Theory and Practice*, London, 1903.

check action or inhibitory power of certain higher centres of the brain were temporarily suspended.

The purely psychological aspect of this view of hypnosis is closely similar to the theories of most of the followers of the Nancy school, in particular Bennett and Bernheim. The latter claimed that in hypnosis a single idea received the whole nervous force of the subject's concentration, and that this concentration was shifted from one idea to another by the suggestions of the hypnotist. He held that in the normal state we are subject to errors, illusions and hallucinations which we sometimes accept without challenge; and we also tend to accept and act upon ideas suggested by others, but we do question before we decide whether to accept or reject them. In hypnosis, however, the suggested idea is acted upon before the intellectual inhibition has time to prevent it. Hypnosis, he asserted, was absolutely identical with normal sleep, and the apparent differences between the two states was entirely due to suggestion. Everyone was influenced by suggestion, and if it were suggested to someone that he became more suggestible, he would be hypnotized. In other words, suggestion was not only the means of producing hypnosis, but the explanation of it.

Milne Bramwell effectively demolishes these theories, according to which, he says, 'suggestion not only starts the race, but also creates the rowers and builds the boat!' He continues:

'Although Braid and Bernheim differ on many points, they are in complete agreement as to the main factor in the problem. According to both, the essential condition is one of *monoideism*. The mind of the subject is concentrated on a single idea. Only one function is active at any one time; and intensely so, because all the attention is given to it. Other functions are inactive, other sensations unperceived, because the subject has no attention left to give to them. Bernheim, as we have seen, stated that, while the attention might be directed from one point to another, concentration remained. This was regarded as essential and characteristic; the existence and explanation of hypnotic phenomena depended on it. Impressions, which under ordinary circumstances would reach consciousness, now ceased to do so, not only because they did not happen to be attended to, but also because the subject had nothing left wherewith to attend to them. Thus, this is not only a 'concentration of attention' theory, but a 'concentration and limited quantity of attention' theory.

'... The fact that numerous and varied hypnotic phenomena can be simultaneously evoked in the same subject has been repeatedly observed and recorded by others, and, strange to say, even by those who attempt to explain hypnosis by the concentration of the attention upon a single point. It is solely the importance of these facts with regard to this particular theory, which has hitherto been so largely overlooked.

'Granting that hypnotic phenomena are the result of changes in the attention, one is forced to conclude that these are the exact reverse of those stated by Bernheim as explanatory of the hypnotic state. The simultaneous presence of many phenomena clearly shows that hypnosis cannot be explained by the concentration of the attention on any one given point. Again, the fact that the multiple phenomena are sometimes similar to the isolated ones, indicates that the explanation of hypnotic phenomena by means of the amount of attention concentrated is also fallacious. If all the attention is still requisite for the production of one phenomenon, and, while it lasts, many other hypnotic phenomena are simultaneously induced, whence do the secondary ones derive that excessive amount of attention which is said to be necessary for the induction of the primary one? The hypnotic condition differs then from the normal, not only because one phenomenon can be manifested in it at once, but because it may present simultaneously many and more varied phenomena than can be evoked in the normal state at any one time. In one word, hypnosis is a state of *polyideism*, not of *mono-ideism*'.[1]

Pavlov, famous for his discoveries in connection with conditioned reflexes, was another who believed that hypnosis was a form of normal sleep. He maintained that the various hypnotic phenomena were further examples of conditioned reflexes, and this view found much support among followers of the Behaviourist school, although not all of them agree that hypnosis is merely natural sleep. Of all the modern theories this is undoubtedly the least credible.

A theory more, though by no means entirely, in accord with modern knowledge is that of Janet, who regarded hypnosis as a condition of mental dissociation in which part of the field of consciousness could break away, forming a secondary personality. Disciples of Freud have claimed that he exploded Janet's theory by demonstrating that although an hysterical person may have a 'split consciousness' he is still able to revive and remember 'blacked-out' experiences. In view of the strange and easily disproved theories put forward by certain Freudians, however, the author feels that little reliance can be placed on their views concerning the theories of others. R. White, for instance, has defined hypnosis as 'a goal-directed striving in which the individual attempts to behave like a hypnotized person, as this has been continually defined by the operator and understood by the subject.'

This claim is, of course, easily refuted. The author, in common with many other hypnotists, has experienced cases in which the

[1] 'What is Hypnotism?' S.P.R. *Proceedings*, Vol. XII, pp. 241-3.

subjects had not the slightest idea of what was expected of them, and some in which they did not even realize they were being hypnotized.

Another Freudian, Sandor Ferenczi, who is a noted European psycho-analyst, holds that hypnosis is the result of the subject's desire to return to infancy, the hypnotist taking the place of one of his parents. The subject responds because he finds in the hypnotist a generalized image reminding him of the emotional security found in parental protection during early childhood. McDougall 'debunked' this theory by pointing out that if this were true those for whom the hypnotist took the place of a mother could only be hypnotized by a woman, while conversely those who saw in the hypnotist a father image would only be hypnotized by a man. In actual fact, the relative sexes of hypnotist and subject are sometimes a factor in the successful induction of hypnosis, but certainly not for the reason advanced by Ferenczi. The requirement laid down by Milne Bramwell, that any theory worthy of consideration must explain the phenomena of self-hypnosis, is obviously not met in either of these psycho-analytic theories.

The last theory to be considered, and in the author's opinion, the one coming nearer than any other to a true explanation of hypnosis, and indeed to many other aspects of human personality, is the *subliminal consciousness* theory of F. W. H. Myers. This concept, which in its entirety embraces many of the hitherto completely unexplained qualities manifested in humanity, can only be appreciated by a study of Myers' monumental work, *Human Personality*, but a lucid and concise summary of the section directly relevant to hypnosis has been made by Milne Bramwell:

'Within recent times another theory has arisen. This, instead of attempting to explain hypnotism by the arrested action of some of the brain centres which subserve normal life, would do so through the arousing of certain powers over which we normally have little or no control. This theory appears under various names—"Double Consciousness", "Das Doppel Ich", etc.—and the principle on which it depends is largely admitted by science. William James, for example, says, "In certain persons, at least, the total possible consciousness may be split into parts which co-exist, but mutually ignore each other." The clearest statement of this view is given by Mr Myers; he suggests that the stream of consciousness in which we habitually live is not our only one. Possibly our habitual consciousness may be a mere selection from a multitude of thoughts and sensations—some at least equally conscious with those we empirically know. No primacy is granted by this theory to the ordinary waking self, except that among potential selves it appears the fittest to meet the needs of common life. As a rule the waking life is remembered in hypnosis, and the hypnotic life is forgotten in the waking state—this destroys any claim of the primary memory to be the sole memory. The self below the threshold of ordinary consciousness, Mr Myers terms the "subliminal consciousness", and the empirical self of common experience the "supraliminal". He holds that to the subliminal consciousness and memory a far wider range of both physiological and of psychical activity is open than to the supraliminal. The latter is inevitably limited by the need of concentration upon recollections useful in the struggle for existence, while the former includes much that is too rudimentary to be retained in the supraliminal memory of an organism so advanced as man. The recollection of processes now performed automatically and needing no supervision passes out of the supraliminal memory, but may be retained in the subliminal. The subliminal or hypnotic self can exercise over the nervous, vasomotor, and circulatory systems a degree of control unparalleled in waking life.

'He suggests that the spectrum of consciousness, as he calls it, is indefinitely extended at both ends in the subliminal self. Below its supraliminal physiological limit lie a vast number of complex processes belonging to the body's nutrition and well-being. These our remote ancestors may possibly have been able to modify at will, but to us they seem entirely withdrawn from our sphere of volition. If we wish to alter them we must do so by drugs and medicaments, whether the body to be treated is our own or another's.

'At the superior or psychical end the subliminal memory includes an unknown category of impressions which the supraliminal consciousness is incapable of receiving in any direct fashion, and which it must cognize, if at all, in the shape of messages from the subliminal consciousness.

'Mr Myers arranges hypnotic phenomena into three divisions.

'(1) The great dissociative triumph of hypnotism, namely, the inhibition of pain under conditions of nerve and tissue with which it is usually inevitably connected.

'Here, psychologically, the whole interest lies in the question whether pain is suppressed together with sensations of every kind, or whether other sensations persist, pain alone being inhibited. ...

'... The insensitiveness to pain which runs wild in hysteria is now being directed into useful channels by "hypnotic suggestion". Some intelligence is involved in a suppression thus achieved; for this is obtained, not as with narcotics by a general loss of consciousness, but by the selection and inhibition, from among all the percipient's possible sensations, of disagreeable ones alone. This is not a mere anaesthetization of some particular group of nerve-endings—such as cocaine produces; it involves the removal also of a number of concomitant feelings of nausea, exhaustion, anxiety, not always directly dependent on the principal pain, but needing, as it were, to be first subjectively distinguished as disagreeable before they are picked out for inhibition. This freedom from pain is obtained without either deadening or dislocating the general nervous system; with no approach either to coma or to hysteria. The so-called hypnotic trance is not always necessary: sometimes the pain can be prevented by post-hypnotic suggestion destined to fulfil itself after the awakening. And if there be trance, this is often no mere lethargy, but a state fully as alert and vivid as ordinary waking life.

'Mr Myers argues from this that it is plain that hypnotic analgesia thus induced is by no means a mere ordinary narcotic—a fresh specimen of such methods as are already familiar for checking pain by arresting all conscious cerebration. It is a new departure; the first successful attempt at dissociating forms of sensation which throughout the known history of the human organism have almost invariably been found to exist together.

'(2) The associative or synthetic triumph of hypnotism, namely, the production and control of organic processes which no effort of the ordinary man can set going, or in any way influence.

'Hypnotic analgesia, Mr Myers says, may be classed with equal justice as a dissociative, or as an associative act. The sensations are severed from the main supraliminal current and thus far the act is dissociative. The group itself, however, has to be formed and the more complex it is, the more this involves some associative act. Inhibition of all the pain consequent on an operation is in reality a complicated associative process. It involves (1) the singling out and fitting together of a great number of sensations which have only the subjective bond of being disagreeable, and (2) the inhibition of all of them, which thus leaves the supraliminal consciousness in perfect ease.

'In further illustration of the associative powers of hypnotism, Mr Myers refers to alterations in the pulse, the secretions, excretions, etc. He also cites Delboeuf's case of two symmetrical burns on the same subject, one running the ordinary course of inflammation, the other in which morbid action was arrested by suggestion.

'(3) The intellectual or moral achievements of hypnotism. These, like the others, are based upon physiological changes, but present problems still more profound. The removal of the craving for alcohol and morphia, the cure of kleptomania, bad temper, excessive indolence, etc., are cited as illustrating the moral and psychological changes which suggestion can effect.

'According to Mr Myers, the hypnotic subject is not a maimed or stunted normal individual, but one who, while he has gained increased power over his own organism, has not at the same time lost his volition, or the mental and moral qualities which formerly distinguished him. He admits that there is some difficulty in explaining hypnotic obedience, but holds that this will be refused when the act suggested is contrary to the subject's moral nature. He believes that a complete comprehension of the suggested act exists in the subliminal strata; and that, when grave need arises, the subliminal self will generally avoid compliance—not by awakening the organism into ordinary life, but by plunging it into a hysterical access, or into a trance so deep that the unwelcome order loses its agitating power. The moral tone of the somnambule is, in Mr Myers' opinion, the precise opposite of the drunken condition. Alcohol, apparently by paralysing first the higher inhibitory centres, makes men boastful, impure, and quarrelsome. Hypnotization, apparently by a tendency to paralyse lower appetitive centres, produces the contrary effect. The increased refinement and cheerfulness of the developed somnambule is constantly noticed.'[1]

This theory is partially restated in simpler terms by Eric Cuddon:
'The mind has two aspects—The Inner and the Outer. The Inner is the true controlling and driving force, the Outer is a small conscious part of the Inner and in ordinary waking life acts the part of general supervisor, and directs intelligently the forces at its disposal. But it is a part which at times, as in sleep, temporarily may cease to direct and control the organism leaving the larger and normally unconscious Inner to carry on the work alone.

The Outer directs and controls the organism in response to messages received from the Inner which the Outer recognizes as emotions, or desires, or perhaps simply as conclusions the result of reasoning.

In every case it is the Inner which accepts suggestions, whether in Hypnosis or in the normal state. It communicates these to the Outer, when the suggestions are given in the normal state, or are to take effect as the result of a post-hypnotic suggestion. In the normal state the Outer may hinder the suggestions from reaching the Inner to a varying extent, thus giving rise to different degrees of suggestibility.

'Hypnosis is a state in which all active opposition of the Outer to allow suggestions to reach the Inner is temporarily arrested with the result that any suggestions given by the Hypnotist have direct access to the Inner, which, subject to certain limitations, accepts and acts upon them. In its extreme form the condition of Hypnosis bears a superficial resemblance to ordinary sleep, though, in fact, as we have seen, it differs from it in many important particulars.'[2]

[1] 'What is Hypnotism?' S.P.R. *Proceedings*, Vol. XII, p. 243.
[2] *Hypnosis, its Meaning and Practice*, London, 1955.

CHAPTER THREE

The Technique of Hypnotism

In all social reactions it is the emotional factor that counts, not the ideas that are expressed. It is not possible to make a man do what he does not wish to do; but it is quite possible to create an atmosphere in which he does wish to do it, and therefore does it.

HUGH ELLIOT

TRUE as Elliot's words are of everyday life, they are even more applicable to hypnotism, and particularly to the induction of hypnosis, when the personality and skill of the hypnotist, the environment and the chosen methods are all directed towards the creation of a condition in which the subject has no desire to do anything but act on the suggestions made to him. Let us consider the factors mentioned in this order; the hypnotist, the environment and the various hypnotic techniques.

THE HYPNOTIST

Whilst the subjective nature of hypnosis is now generally accepted, there is no questioning the fact that the personality of the hypnotist is a factor of the highest importance. In all walks of life the man who can inspire confidence, command respect and impress his will upon others will attain success where the rest may fail, and as such qualities seem to be the endowment of but a fortunate few, the hypnotist who possesses them has a marked natural advantage over those who do not. It is true to say therefore, that whilst no magical thaumaturgy or 'magnetic power' is involved, it is not possible for more than a gifted few, comparatively speaking, to become really outstanding hypnotists.

Other necessary qualities which can, however, be cultivated are patience, a sympathetic understanding of human problems and above all, confidence. The successful hypnotist must be able to judge with some accuracy the psychological make-up of his subjects, and know how to be authoritative without being authoritarian. He must know how to allay any fears and apprehensions, and when to change or modify his methods.

Moll has said that calmness, tact and patience are vital qualities, and that it is easier for the average doctor to write a prescription than to spend hours trying to induce hypnosis. In other words, being a hypnotist is a specialist's job.

Krafft-Ebing states that a hypnotist who is a good psychologist can always succeed, and that the personality of the hypnotist is far more important than any artificial or mechanical aids.

There is also an intangible something, a vital psychic factor that defies definition, without which no aspiring hypnotist can really succeed. It is comparable to an ear for music; if one has it then it can be trained and cultivated, but without it all the training in the world will achieve nothing. No less an authority than Robert E. Laidlow, Chief of the Psychiatric Clinic at the Roosevelt Hospital, New York, and one of the most distinguished of present day hypnotic practitioners, has said, 'I have no way of proving this, but I have a definite feeling that there is some extra-sensory or para-psychological factor in hypnosis.'

ENVIRONMENT

The aim of the hypnotist is to produce in the subject a state of concentration and abstraction, in which his attention is focused entirely upon the hypnotist, and an environment which assists this process is most desirable. Quiet, warmth and freedom from all kinds of distraction are almost essential, and a comfortable chair or couch is, of course, necessary. Draughts, bright lights and colourful furnishings are things to be avoided, and the surroundings should be as restful and soothing as possible.

In this connection much interesting and useful information has recently been contributed by Dr J. Bordeaux.[1] During the last war he observed marked reactions in hospital patients when they were moved from room to room, and concluded that these were caused by the different colour schemes with which the rooms were decorated. After the war he continued his observations with a number of hypnotic subjects and, as the result of his experiments, reached the following conclusions:

RED surroundings excited or irritated most subjects.

YELLOW stimulated imagination and usually caused the suggestions to be carried out in an exaggerated manner.

GREEN created a 'sick' atmosphere.

PINK was liked by women but not by men.

SOFT BLUE was liked by both sexes, but in the case of abnormal patients as many were upset as were soothed by it.

BROWN was liked least of all.

DEEP VIOLET increased the ease of hypnotic induction.

The author has found that a pale blue-grey colour scheme is in

[1] 'Hypnotic Experiments with Colour and Light', *British Journal of Medical Hypnotism*, Vol. I, part 4, p. 7.

general most effective. This can easily be modified or augmented when desired by the use of slightly tinted sources of light. Some of his patients have expressed a dislike for deep violet, which they seem to find depressing.

METHODS OF HYPNOTIZING

Whatever method of inducing hypnosis is chosen, and there are probably as many different methods as there are hypnotists, the operator's vital first step must invariably be to create the right emotional atmosphere, and then to ensure that his suggestions harmonize with the emotional state of his subject. The more feeling there is behind his words and actions the more conviction will his suggestions carry. Deference must be paid to the subject's idiosyncrasies; to his disposition, constitution, and mood at the time. The ability to judge human character and to act on this judgment is a prerequisite of the successful hypnotist.

To gain the subject's confidence and at the same time, if the subject is a patient seeking treatment, to reach enlightenment on various aspects of his trouble, it is always desirable to encourage the subject to tell his story in his own way. Besides giving useful information concerning his problems the subject will become much more *en rapport* with the hypnotist if he has unburdened his mind and found a sympathetic and understanding listener.

As already stated, the methods of inducing hypnosis are innumerable, and the selection of the one best adapted to the individual is a matter of experience. So also is the knowledge of how best to vary one's technique to suit the personality of a particular subject. There are however, a number of simple tests that can be applied to determine the extent to which a subject is likely to be susceptible to hypnotic suggestion, and these often give an indication of the most suitable method to adopt. Those most commonly used and easily applied will now be described.

The degree of susceptibility can usually be judged with some accuracy from the *postural sway test*. The subject stands with his back to the hypnotist and is told to fix his attention on a point straight in front of him and a little above eye level, at the same time concentrating on holding himself completely stiff and rigid 'like a board balancing on end'. The hypnotist places his hands on the subject's shoulders and rocks him slightly backwards and forward, repeating the instruction to concentrate on becoming absolutely rigid, and then saying that when he withdraws his hands the subject will feel himself being drawn backwards. In many cases the subject will then fall back into the hypnotist's arms still holding his body straight and stiff, and astonished to find that he has done so. The extent to which this test succeeds is nearly always a reliable indicator of the subject's suggestibility.

In the *hand clasping test* the subject is told to interlock the fingers of each hand and to press them together, at the same time keeping his eyes fixed on the hypnotist's. The suggestion is repeated that the subject's fingers are becoming locked tightly together, and then he is told that he will not be able to unclasp them. Many subjects, despite much straining and pulling, find themselves quite unable to take their hands apart until the hypnotist gives his consent. This test is a favourite with stage hypnotists, who are thus able to select 'easy' subjects from the audience.

In the *hand levitation test* the subject is seated with hands on knees and is told to concentrate his gaze on the tip of one finger. The suggestion is repeated that the hand is becoming lighter and lighter, and the degree of response noted. As an alternative, or to supplement this test, suggestions that the hand is becoming heavier will often make it impossible for the subject to raise his arm.

Many people, if told to close their eyes tightly, are unable to open them when challenged to do so, and such a test is of help in selecting subjects from a group for experimental purposes. Others can be 'rooted to the spot' by telling them that their feet are stuck firmly and that the more they try to move, the more firmly they will become fixed. Once the degree of susceptibility has been ascertained and the method of induction decided upon, the attempt to hypnotize should commence with the minimum of delay, before the subject recovers from the state of receptivity following the results of the tests.

Before passing to the description of modern hypnotic methods it is instructive to look briefly at the way in which these have evolved from the 'passes' used by the early mesmerists and 'magnetisers'. Mesmer used to place his hands on the patient's shoulder's, bring them down the arms, and then hold the thumbs firmly for several minutes. These 'passes with contact' were repeated and made over the parts of the body affected by pain, following, where possible, the direction of the nerves. Mesmer's method is reminiscent of the description of the use of the hand which occurs in Solon, translated by Stanley (History of Philosophy 1666) thus,

> 'The smallest hurts sometimes increase and rage
> More than all art of physic can assuage;
> Sometime the fury of the worst disease
> The hand, by gentle stroking, will appease.'

Esdaile used to send his patient to bed in a darkened room, instructing him to close his eyes and concentrate on sleep. He then breathed gently upon the patient's eyes, at the same time making 'passes without contact' over him. In this way he succeeded in influencing many patients to such an extent that they were able to undergo major operations without pain.

Braid's original method, still widely employed to-day, was to hold some bright object about a foot from the subject's eyes and instruct him to gaze steadily at it and keep his thoughts fixed on it. After a time the subject's eyes would flicker and close through fatigue, and Braid would then give suggestions that they remained so. Later he found that in some cases discomfort and slight conjunctivitis were brought on by prolonged fixed gazing, and he therefore modified his method and directed the subject to close his eyes at an early stage of the induction. Later still he formed the opinion that verbal suggestions were far more effective than any other means, and used these almost exclusively.

Liébeault used to seat his subject in an armchair, tell him to think of nothing and gaze steadily into his eyes. If the subject did not close his eyes spontaneously after a short time, he was instructed to do so. Suggestions were then given that he was becoming drowsy and that his limbs were becoming numb, and these were repeated until hypnosis was effected. These methods were developed by Bernheim, who made it clear that the hypnotic influence was effective even if a sleeping state were not reached by the subject.

Beaunis favoured the fixed gazing method for a first induction but claimed that for subsequent hypnoses any method would succeed.

Wetterstrand, who ran a famous hypnotic clinic in Stockholm, used three darkened rooms. While previously hypnotized patients were resting, treatment was given to new cases. Wetterstrand made use of 'passes with contact' and pressure of the hand on the heart, and also employed the fixed gazing method. When a number of patients were hypnotized he would pass from one to the other, whispering individual suggestions to each subject.

Richet found that if he held the subject's thumbs firmly for a few minutes he could cause him to experience sensations of heaviness in the arms and wrists. He then made downward passes in front of the eyes, keeping his arms outstretched but not making contact with the subject.

Luys, another Frenchman, made his subjects gaze at a revolving mirror, modified from the bird catching device known as the lark mirror, and rotated by clockwork.

Moll used various methods, but found that some subjects only became hypnotized when he placed his hand on their foreheads.

Milne Bramwell's methods were, in the main, based on those of

Liébeault and Bernheim; he also succeeded in hypnotizing several patients who were completely deaf by giving suggestions in writing. He considered that although passes, which he sometimes employed, were successful, this was purely because the subject associated them with the idea of being hypnotized.

Gurney and Myers held that the effect of passes must be more than mere suggestion, as blindfolded subjects could sometimes be influenced by their use.

Most modern hypnotists use methods based on those of Braid, as developed and elaborated by the leading figures of the Nancy school. The method advocated by the author, which he normally employs in his own practice, is as follows.

At the first consultation the patient is put at ease and encouraged to give his own account of his problems, with as little interruption or guidance as possible, and any fears or misconceptions he may have concerning hypnotic treatment are allayed. He is given an outline of the manner in which such treatment is carried out and encouraged to ask questions. No attempt to induce hypnosis is made until the patient is completely satisfied and has expressed his willingness for this to be done, and the first consultation is usually devoted entirely to these preliminaries, except possibly for some simple tests of susceptibility.

Before deciding on the method to be adopted, the patient is asked whether he has ever been hypnotized or has seen anyone else so influenced. If he has, and was impressed by the experience, the probability is that the method he saw employed, or some recognizably similar one, will be the most effective in his case. Not only will the degree of expectation be higher, but the risk of failure through the subject becoming analytical and losing concentration through making a comparison between the new method and the one with which he is familiar, is obviated. Conversely, if he has watched a demonstration of hypnotism in the past but was not favourably impressed with it, it would be courting failure to make use of the methods employed on that occasion.

The preliminaries completed, in the case of a patient with no previous knowledge of hypnotism the process of induction is commenced. The patient is told that he will first be given an exercise in relaxation, and is asked to make himself quite comfortable in an armchair or on a couch, whichever he prefers. He is told that the relaxation is to be progressive, starting from the feet and working upwards, and that all he need do is concentrate on the hypnotist's words and follow his instructions which are then given in a firm, but soft, droning voice. The following quotation is of the author's actual words recorded during a hypnotic session with a subject who had never previously been hypnotized. He was seated in an armchair and the author stood just behind and to one side of him.

'... that's right—let yourself go limp—head back—eyes closed tightly—limp and *relaxed*—now, start with your toes, let every bit of tension go out of them—now your feet as well—let them *relax*—just as if they were two lumps of lead on the floor—all the tension gone from them—completely *relaxed*—now your legs, knee joints—let them go limp—limp and *relaxed*—toes, feet, legs, knees—all limp and *relaxed*—no tension in them at all—completely *relaxed*.—Now your hands—wrists—arms—let them flop—let them hang—all limp and *relaxed*—all *relaxed*—toes, feet, legs, knees,—hands, wrists, arms —all com*pletely relaxed*.—Now let your head sink back—and back— sinking back—all of you com*pletely relaxed*, limp and *relaxed*—no tension anywhere—re-l-a-x-e-d. Breathe slowly and deeply—slowly and deeply—s-l-o-w-l-y and d-e-e-p-l-y—s-l-o-w—d-e-e-p and re-l-a-x—r-e-l-a-x—r-e-l——a——x.'

In this case, long before the last 're-l-a-x' was spoken, the subject was away, deeply hypnotized, *and he had been hypnotized without knowing it*. The monotonous repetition, with the reiterated emphasis on the word 'relax', had been sufficient, and it had not even been necessary to mention sleep at all. This was by no means an exceptional case, and similar results have been obtained on many occasions with subjects of both sexes.

In most instances however, the 'relaxation exercise' does not in itself bring about hypnosis, and indeed, that is not its basic purpose. It is really part of a conditioning process designed to accustom the subject to acting on the hypnotist's suggestions and associating his voice with relaxation and drowsiness. The subject is afterwards asked to describe his feelings and sensations, and the very act of talking about them increases their impression on him.

After a short break, and a cigarette if he wants one, the subject is told that the next step is a little more advanced, but that all he has to do is relax and do just as he is asked. He is then told to close his eyes and relax again, just as he did before, 'completely relaxed' etc., and to imagine that he is sinking back, back—back, that now a feeling of drowsiness—sleepiness is coming over him, and so on, and in most cases this second attempt, or rather first attempt proper, is successful.

If the subject does not appear to be going into hypnosis the suggestions are discontinued by saying, 'Right, that's enough for now. I want you to sit up, wide awake, and tell me how you felt'. By the subject's description of his sensations a good idea can be formed of the effect of the suggestions, and the process is repeated with appropriate alterations. So the hypnosis is deepened, step by step, until the trance is sufficiently deep to serve the purpose for which it has been induced. A light trance is often sufficient for suggestive therapeutics, but for certain kinds of hypno-analysis, for instance, deeper hypnosis may be desirable.

This method of repeatedly hypnotizing and terminating, deepening the hypnosis at each repetition, is sometimes referred to nowadays as 'fractionation', and tests are made at each step to determine the depth of hypnosis. Some of the phenomena associated with each of the hypnotic stages were described in the last chapter, and more will be dealt with in the next. Any of these can be used as an indication of the stage so far attained.

The method just described, although the author's favourite one, is not, of course, the only technique he uses, and no subject is considered to be unhypnotizable until several different methods have been tried without success. It is not claimed that this method is necessarily superior to others, and the fact that it is most effective in the author's case may well be because it happens to be suited to his manner and personality. A summary of various other methods is now given, and the student is advised to evolve a technique of his own after experimenting with some of them.

Most modern hypnotic methods have one thing in common, the direction of the subject's attention to a change of some kind in the function of certain muscles. Although it is usual to begin with the eyes this is by no means necessary and is sometimes even undesirable. We have seen that a limb will, on occasion, appear to lose its power when the attention of the subject is directed to it, and whatever inhibition is most easily brought about may well be the best starting point. It should be remembered that it is almost invariably easier to inhibit a movement than to cause one. The methods most commonly used, however, conform roughly to the following patterns.

The subject is made comfortable and then asked to gaze steadily at some bright object. This is usually held by the hypnotist about a foot in front of the subject and slightly above eye level, so that it cannot be seen without some strain. The subject is told to concentrate his whole attention upon it, and suggestions are repeated thus: 'Your eyes are becoming tired and heavy—tired and heavy, your eyelids are beginning to quiver, your eyes are becoming hot and tired, they want to close,—heavy now, heavier and heavier,—heavy and drowsy, drowsy and sleepy,—your eyes are so tired,—tired and heavy, heavy and sleepy,—you cannot keep them open, tired—heavy,—sleepy (the eyes will probably have closed by now), —heavy, drowsy s-l-e-e-p-y. Sinking down,—down—down into a deep sleep,—deep, restful sleep,—' and so on.

Variations of this method are the use of a pinpoint light source as the focus of concentration, or a small bright object fixed on the wall or ceiling or given to the subject to hold. Some hypnotists tell the subject to gaze steadily into their eyes, and this certainly has the advantage of making the process a more personal one and establishing a closer *rapport* in many cases. The establishment of *rapport* is also assisted by suitable suggestions: 'Always sleep when *I* tell you'. 'You will not hear any sound except *my* voice'. etc.

A method used with great success by Erskine was to count slowly, telling the subject to open and close his eyes as he did so, closing the eyes as each number was spoken and opening them when the word 'and' was said between them. Erskine found that as the counting continued the subject's eyes opened less wide and for briefer periods, until they ceased to open at all, by which time the subject was deeply hypnotized. A similar method makes use of a metronome or a clock with a visible pendulum.

A more recently developed method, known as the confusional technique, has proved of great value in the case of subjects who for one reason or another will not respond to straightforward suggestions, in particular those who are unable to refrain from attempting to analyse the process of induction or who have a highly critical attitude. This method depends for its success on the giving of a number of different suggestions in such quick succession that the subject is unable to maintain his resistance. A typical sequence of suggestions is the following by Ambrose and Newbold:

'Your right arm is becoming heavier. At the same time your left arm feels lighter and the right foot feels numb. Now your right arm feels lighter still while the left is becoming heavier and heavier and begins to fall. The left hand is also feeling numb and cold. At the same time you notice how warm your left foot is getting; while your right arm is becoming so heavy that you cannot lift it without considerable effort. All this while your left hand continues to feel warmer and warmer and, as it does so, it gets lighter and lighter ...'[1]

Constant suggestions of this kind are too much for the subject to analyse, and he will often give up trying and accept them instead.

It is possible to induce hypnosis without any allusion to sleep or similar conditions, and in this case the subject will sometimes exhibit all the normal hypnotic phenomena while remaining completely conscious. This method was developed by an American, Professor W. R. Wells, who terms it 'waking hypnosis'. It is usually induced by a modified form of the fixed gazing technique already described. No suggestions of tiredness are given, the hypnotist concentrating on rendering the subject unable to open his eyes.

From time to time various mechanical devices have been used as

[1] *A Handbook of Medical Hypnosis*, London, 1956.

an aid to the induction of hypnosis, and some have claimed that the hypnotic state can be brought about by their use alone. Patients at the Salpêtrière were alleged to have become hypnotized through watching the flashing of the Drummond light, and Luys advocated the use of a clockwork apparatus rotating a drum to which were fixed a number of small mirrors. An American 'mail order' hypnotist markets various accessories including a revolving spiral disc, a glass 'hypnotic eye' and an electric metronome to which a flashing light is connected. Most authorities seem to be in agreement that such so-called aids are of little real value.

Also of American origin is the hypnotic gramophone record, and there is no doubt that hypnosis could sometimes be induced by a suitably worded one, but as no two subjects are alike, and suggestions need to be varied considerably from one to another, such inflexible methods must have a very limited application. An interesting sidelight on suggestibility is shown in a report by Estabrooks concerning the use of a gramophone record. A group of people who knew very little of hypnotism had expressed a wish to hear such a record and Estabrooks said he would play it to them. On reaching for the record, however, he found that it was missing, so for a joke he put on the first record that came to hand. To his astonishment he noticed that after a few minutes one of the group became deeply hypnotized. Estabrook's astonishment is not surprising, for the record in question was a Swiss yodelling song.

Before leaving the subject of hypnotic methods and Estabrooks, it is noteworthy that such an authority has made the following 'flat statement', as he terms it. '... everyone could be thrown into the deepest stage of hypnotism by the use of the Russian method—no holds barred, deliberate disintegration of the personality by psychic torture, and hypnotism only at this point. The subject might easily be left a mental wreck but war is a grim business.'[1] Estabrooks, it should be noted, makes it quite clear that he has not tried this method.

Many experiments have been carried out in an effort to establish whether drugs can be an effective aid to the induction of hypnosis. Among the early hypnotists Schrenck-Notzing employed alcohol with some success, Bernheim sometimes gave injections of morphia, and both used chloral occasionally. Herrero claimed that chloroform enabled otherwise unresponsive persons to become hypnotized, and described several experiments in support of his claim at the first International Congress of Hypnotism held in Paris in 1899. The barbiturate drugs, notably nembutal and sodium amytal, have been found especially helpful in assisting relaxation in difficult cases. A

[1] *Hypnotism*, London, 1959.

British hypnotist and psychiatrist, Dr J. Stephan Horsley, who has earned an international reputation for his work in 'narco-analysis', has made an intensive study of the use of drugs for hypnotic purposes, and considers sodium pentothal to be the most effective. Much is hoped for from the new tranquilizing drugs such as Thorazine and Promazine, with which experiments are now being made in America. One well-known doctor in England frequently gives his patients a 'whiff' of gas at the beginning of a hypnotic session.

The author has had no personal experience of the use of any of these drugs except alcohol, which he finds is sometimes helpful when given to a patient, and always enjoyable when he consumes it himself.

Many authorities have claimed that it is possible to change normal sleep into hypnosis. The method advocated by Wetterstrand, who appears to have used it successfully on many occasions, particularly with children, is as follows:

A hand is placed upon the sleeping person's forehead and the body is gently stroked with the other, while the subject is addressed in a soft, gentle voice. When he replies it indicates that *rapport* has been established. Moll, Bernheim and Forel claimed equal success using similar methods, but Milne Bramwell and many later workers have reported failure at every attempt. The author has been able to change the sleep of a natural somnambule into hypnosis, and has also been successful with persons who talk in their sleep, but only at times when the sleep talking or walking was actually occurring. Attempts at other times have invariably failed.

Changing natural sleep into hypnosis is, of course, one method of hypnotizing a person without his knowledge or consent, and the 'relaxation exercise' described earlier in this chapter is another. It is also sometimes possible to hypnotize a person who is susceptible but unwilling, by inviting him to watch someone else being hypnotized. It is not unlikely that he will then become hypnotized more quickly than the actual 'subject'. The author has certain knowledge of one case in which a woman was hypnotized against her will by telling her, quite untruthfully, that a powerful hypnotic drug had been added to her tea. She was told it would soon take effect and that symptoms were already becoming evident. After five minutes of such suggestions she was in a deep trance.

There is no doubt whatever that many imaginative persons could be hypnotized by this, or a similar subterfuge, in the same manner as the cure of a variety of ills is effected by the administration of bread-pills, or placebos. A hypnotist with a sufficiently strong personality can often hypnotize a subject despite his objection and opposition, by the sheer force of that personality. The following news item from the *Daily Express* of 13th November, 1959, may assist in dispelling the widely held and highly dangerous misbelief that no person can be hypnotized against his will.

'TYPIST IN TRANCE AGAINST HER WILL
A doctor warns on hypnotism
By Chapman Pincher

'The first medical proof that a woman can be hypnotized against her will—as Svengali hypnotized Trilby—is put on record to-day by Dr Ian Oswald, an Oxford University psychiatrist.

'Until now doctors have denied that hypnotism without the co-operation of the patient could ever be achieved.

'Dr Oswald claims to have hypnotized a 21-year-old typist against her will and induced her to accept treatment she would otherwise have refused.

'Dr Oswald was treating the typist by hypnotism for a nervous difficulty. She did not realize that she was being hypnotized and went into a deep trance.

'To help hypnosis later, Dr Oswald said: "Whenever you sit in a chair and look at me and I clap my hands you will immediately return to the state you are in now."

'When she recovered consciousness the typist realized she had been hypnotized. She was so distressed to find she could not remember what had happened that she refused any further treatment. She told Dr Oswald she was frightened of him.

'Later Dr Oswald made an excuse to enter the room while the girl was being interviewed by another doctor. He attracted her attention and clapped his hands.

'Almost immediately she became glassy-eyed and said her mind was "going queer", Dr Oswald reports. After two more hand-claps she went into a trance. While hypnotized she agreed to continue the treatment, which was eventually successful.

' "This case supports the view that if such a person can once be hypnotized, then subsequent rehypnosis can be achieved despite strongly motivated refusal by the subject," Dr Oswald writes.

'This would probably be true with an unscrupulous hypnotist.'

TERMINATION OF HYPNOSIS

Before discussing the methods used to awaken a subject from the hypnotic trance, it is necessary to dispose of the popular misconception that danger lies in the possibility of a hypnotist being unable to bring his subject out of the trance. In fact, this cannot occur, for a hypnotized subject if left to himself will either awaken spontaneously or drift into a natural sleep from which he will eventually awaken in the normal manner. The hypothetical problem of what would happen should a hypnotist drop dead or go off and forget his entranced subject, is explained in the same way. As Hull has stated, the real problem in hypnosis is always not how to waken the subject, but how to keep him in the trance.

Before actually terminating the hypnosis it is essential to ensure that any experimental suggestions given during the trance are adequately cancelled, and that post-hypnotic ones to be carried out afterwards are clear and unambiguous. General suggestions of well-being and of benefit from the hypnosis should always be given as a matter of course. If it is intended to re-hypnotize the subject at a later date he should be told that a certain 'key' word, such as 'relax' or 'sleep', when spoken by, but only by, the hypnotist will bring about hypnosis immediately. Subsequent hypnoses, however, are almost invariably much easier to induce than the first one, even when no such suggestion is given.

The actual method of termination is not important so long as the subject clearly understands what is expected from him. The early mesmerists used to blow in the subject's face or make certain passes, but the simple command, 'Wake up now' is far more effective. With subjects who are accustomed to being hypnotized, the author uses a clap of the hands as the waking signal, the subject having previously been told, of course, of its meaning. After the first hypnosis, however, it is always desirable to terminate gradually, and the well tried method of counting slowly up to ten, telling the subject that he will become wide awake at the end of the count, cannot, in the author's opinion, be bettered.

CHAPTER FOUR

Hypnotic Phenomena

Miracles do not happen in contradiction to nature, but only in contradiction to that which is known to us of nature.

ST AUGUSTINE

SOME of the more usual phenomena associated with hypnosis were mentioned in the two previous chapters. Of those about to be described, by no means all can be elicited in every subject, and whilst many are typical of what may be produced by almost any good deep trance subject, some, on the other hand, are extremely rare and only acceptable to belief by virtue of the integrity of those who have reported them. No special significance should be attached to the order in which they are mentioned, although so far as possible, the more general classes of phenomena are dealt with first.

CHANGES IN THE VOLUNTARY MUSCULAR SYSTEM

The first muscular changes observed are usually those associated with the induction of hypnosis, in most cases the flickering and closing of the eyes. Sometimes they are held closed more tightly than is normal by pronounced muscular spasm, but at others they remain slightly open. There is occasionally a slight quivering of the eyelids which may be maintained throughout the hypnosis, and if an eyelid is lifted by the hypnotist the eyeball may be seen to be turned upwards. The extent to which these changes occur depends largely, of course, upon the method of induction.

The condition of muscular contraction known as catalepsy can normally be induced in all but the lightest stages of hypnosis, varying from just sufficient contraction to keep an upraised arm in that position, to a complete stiffening of the whole body. In the latter case it is sometimes possible, even with a comparatively frail subject, to place his head on one chair and his feet on another and then to sit on his middle, without causing the body to bend at all. These cataleptic positions can be maintained for long periods without movement, periods far exceeding those possible in the normal waking state. There is also a marked difference from normal in the movements of limbs after catalepsy; thus, an arm held up rigidly by hypnotic suggestion would eventually drop slowly and gently, whereas one held up for as long as possible in the normal state would begin to tremble and then fall in a much more jerky manner.

Apparent increases in strength during hypnosis are frequently noted. Braid, for instance, had a subject who, although normally so weak and feeble that he could not lift a weight of twenty pounds, was able when hypnotized to lift a quarter of a hundredweight with his little finger and swing it round his head with ease. Many authorities deny that any actual increase in muscular power is involved, pointing out that the full strength of the human body is far greater than is generally realized, and that hypnosis merely removes the inhibiting ideas normally present, thus enabling the full strength to be used.

In some subjects it is possible to cause the muscular tone to relax to such an extent that the limbs can be bent at the joints into the most unusual and uncomfortable positions, which will then be maintained. This condition, known loosely as 'waxy plasticity', is termed *flexibilitas cerea*.

Any or all of the voluntary muscles may be paralysed by suggestion, the way in which the paralysis occurs varying with different subjects. In some the muscles necessary for the performance of a movement fail to contract, whilst in others these muscles act but are counteracted by the contraction of antagonistic ones. A hypnotically induced paralysis does not conform to the anatomical distribution of the nerves, but takes the form imagined by the subject to be appropriate.

Automatic movements of a complicated and strenuous nature can frequently be induced, and will be maintained for quite long periods. For example, a subject could be made to 'mark time', thump his chest and open and close his mouth rhythmically, and would have to continue carrying out these movements despite all his efforts to stop. An absence of muscular tedium after such violent exertions is another notable phenomenon of hypnosis.

Recent work by Professor H. J. Eysenck, of London University, demonstrates that although physical strength may not actually be increased by hypnosis, endurance certainly is. Using apparatus which measured the pulling strength of the little finger, he found that although the first pull of a hypnotized subject was no greater than that achieved in the normal state, the ability to continue repeating the pulls was heightened and the amount of fatigue reduced.

HALLUCINATIONS, ILLUSIONS AND DELUSIONS

Among the more spectacular kinds of hypnotic phenomena the most outstanding are, without doubt, those produced by hallucination of the senses. These striking illustrations of the stimulating effect of hypnosis upon the imagination may be caused to occur either during the trance or, by means of post-hypnotic suggestions, at some time after its termination. The stage hypnotist, of course, owes much of his success to their use, as, for example, when he tells a group of female volunteers that there are mice running about the stage and they immediately climb screaming on to their chairs; or when he makes an entranced victim play a tune, with much feeling, on a purely imaginary musical instrument.

To the hypnotized person these hallucinations seem absolutely real, and his reactions to them are as they would be if he were faced with similar circumstances in reality. If told, for instance, that a large bull-terrier was walking up to him, the dog lover would address the imaginary animal in a friendly way, pat it, and if handed a hallucinatory biscuit, feed it; whereas someone afraid of dogs would give evidence of fear, retreating or calling for the creature to be removed. Similarly, the suggested approach of a policeman would be received with equanimity by a law-abiding citizen, but with apprehension by a criminal or a harassed motorist.

The examples just given are of visual hallucinations, but any of the senses may be hallucinated in the same way. A favourite trick of the stage hypnotist, and incidentally, a very useful test of the depth of hypnosis, is to give the subject a bottle of ammonia with the instructions to 'smell this lovely perfume'. If the reaction is one of pleasure it is certain that the subject is in a quite deep state of hypnosis. The test can be reversed, and a bottle of scent made to produce the same effect on the subject as would normally be caused by some obnoxious smelling liquid.

It is possible to make a subject beautifully 'tight' by suggesting that a glass really containing water is filled with something more potent, and the effect will be the same as is normally produced by alcohol on that particular individual. If, however, the same suggestion is made to a staunch teetotaler, he will, in almost every case, refuse to drink the water. Conversely, it is possible to make the latter take real alcohol by suggesting to him that a glass of say, whisky, is only a harmless soft drink. In these cases there is illusion as well as hallucination. While on this subject, it is interesting to note that a Russian psychologist, Platanof, has claimed to have given several subjects large quantities of alcohol and, by suitable suggestions, kept them perfectly sober, both during the hypnosis and afterwards. (The author has never attempted this last experiment himself, and regards it as a deplorable waste of a valuable commodity.)

If told that he is standing on an iceberg at the North Pole the subject will shiver with cold, whilst the suggestion that he is working in the stokehold of a ship will make him sweat profusely as he performs the actions of shovelling. Given the hallucination that he is taking part in a boat-race, he will not only go through the motions of frantic rowing, but, so real is the scene to him, when told that it is over he may well collapse breathlessly with his heart pounding away at a highly accelerated rate.

Negative hallucinations can be produced in the same manner as the positive ones just instanced: the subject will apparently become unaware of the presence of an object or person, be unable to hear certain noises, or detect specified odours and tastes. In many cases of negative hallucination the subject will automatically add a positive one on his own account. For instance, if it is suggested to him that a certain person is no longer in the room he will not only become apparently unaware of that person, but will have a visual positive hallucination of what he thinks is behind that person.

If the person who has 'disappeared' is handed some object, it will then appear to the subject to be suspended in mid-air. If the suggestion is given that an observer's clothes have vanished, the subject will declare that the observer is naked. Told that lumps of salt and sugar are both tasteless substances he will not be able to differentiate (orally, at least) between them. By telling him that a gun is a 'noiseless' one, it is possible to fire it close to his ear without producing any discernible reaction.

In the case of a negative hallucination the subject must first see the object or person to be obliterated in order that this can occur. If, for example, one card out of a pack of otherwise identical ones is marked in some way, and the subject is told that when they are dealt out he will not see the marked one, before the negative hallucination can take effect it will be necessary for him to see and recognize that card.

Liégeois classified hallucinations thus:

1. Positive, where the subject sees hallucinatory objects, which act as though they were real in preventing the view of other objects.

2. Negative, where the object disappears in response to suggestion and then apparently ceases to obscure other objects.

3. Retroactive, where it is suggested to the subject that he has heard or seen imaginary things and on awakening he remembers them and believes in their reality.

4. Deferred, where the appearance of the hallucination is delayed by suggestion and appears at a suggested time afterwards. (Post-hypnotic suggestion is given in this case.)

5. Hallucinations of memory, where the subject later remembers as real something he believes he saw during hypnosis.

6. Personality changes, where the subject assumes a suggested role and speaks and acts in accordance with his conception of the part. Liégeois considered this to be a veritable hallucination.

An important seventh class, not mentioned by Liégeois, is that of motor hallucinations, where if the subject, though at rest, is told that he is making certain movements, the physical phenomena usually associated with these movements appear. The subject believes that the act is really being performed because the idea is aroused in the ideomotor centres of the brain.

Liégeois's sixth class of hallucinations, changes of personality, are actually delusions rather than hallucinations, although the latter term is commonly used loosely to describe them. A simple example, also widely used by the stage hypnotist, is that in which the subject, when told that he is a wild animal of some kind, walks around on all fours making what he imagines are suitably ferocious noises. At the other extreme, some subjects when told they are famous historical or fictional characters, will act out the parts with a quite incredible degree of histrionic ability. These delusions, together with the other hallucinatory phenomena described, can, by suitable suggestions, be made to persist after the termination of hypnosis, and this aspect is considered in the chapter on post-hypnotic phenomena.

Several different kinds of hallucination can be made to occur simultaneously, and a highly complicated 'dream' may thus be suggested to the subject, in which imaginary scenes change and events follow one another in whatever sequence the hypnotist chooses to determine. In a similar manner it is possible to cause the subject to 'relive' certain experiences from his past, although in the normal waking state these events may have been completely forgotten. This latter phenomenon is often of great value in the treatment of psychological disorders, where it enables repressed memories to be brought to the surface. Sometimes, in certain forms of psychosomatic illness, for instance, the patient can be made to relive, and so 'work off' the experience from which his trouble arose. This process, called *abreaction*, a term coined by Freud, is almost invariably a highly dramatic one, and can often be most distressing.

This method of recalling hidden memories by suggesting that the subject is reliving some long forgotten incident in his past, is known as *age regression*, for the many experiments carried out seem to demonstrate that the process is something far more complicated than a straightforward heightening of memory. Told, for example, that he is back in time to his fifth birthday, the subject will not only remember in great detail the events of that birthday, but the day of the week on which it fell, the state of the weather at the time, and the names and style of dress of those who attended his birthday party. Further, he will react to intelligence tests as would a child of that age, and his physiological reflexes will also be appropriate.

Boris Sidis[1] has recorded that an adult subject, regressed to the age of ten, became unable to write in English, but signed his name in a script used by certain Eastern Jews. The subject's brother confirmed that he (the subject) knew no other language when he was ten, and did not learn English until much later. He also stated that the subject's actual writing at that age was very similar to the specimen produced while hypnotized. It should be remembered however, that throughout the test the subject, although unable to write English, must have been able to understand it, for the instructions of the hypnotist were all given in that language.

A case has been reported in which a subject who had worn spectacles for many years complained during an age regression that she could not see properly. Removal of her glasses improved vision, and when she was regressed step by step to early childhood her eyesight became progressively better.[2]

A subject who has suffered an illness in the past can be made to reproduce the symptoms if regressed to the period at which it occurred. One middle-aged man who was regressed to the time of his third birthday evinced all the symptoms of a severe attack of asthma, including a high pulse rate and bubbling noises in the bronchi. His parents confirmed that he had suffered from asthma in his childhood and that his third birthday had been marred by a particularly severe attack.[3]

Wolberg[4] once regressed a somnambulistic subject to the first year of his life, when he became unable to speak and exhibited definite sucking and grasping movements. Several reliable authorities claim to have made subjects recall the actual experience of being born, and Nandor Fodor[5] asserts that 'organismic consciousness' may even carry the memory of the violence of pre-natal intercourse.

Of the genuineness of age regression Wolberg has said: 'The consensus at the present time is that regression actually does produce early behaviour in a way that obviates all possibility of simulation. This is the opinion of such authorities as Erickson, Estabrooks, Lindner, and Spiegel, Shor, and Fishman. My own studies have convinced me of this fact, although the regression is never station-

---

[1] *The Psychology of Suggestion*, New York, 1898.
[2] *Experimental Hypnosis*, New York, 1952.
[3] *Experimental Hypnosis*, New York, 1952.
[4] *Medical Hypnosis*, New York, 1948.
[5] *The Search for the Beloved*, New York, 1947.

ary, constantly being altered by the intrusion of mental functioning at other levels.'[1]

From time to time claims have been made that the technique of hypnotic age regression has enabled a subject to evoke memories of a previous life, and that such experiments afford proof of the theory of reincarnation. An analysis of these claims and the conclusions to be drawn from them is made elsewhere in this book.

HYPERÆSTHESIA

The acuteness of the senses can undoubtedly be heightened by suggestion in certain subjects, even in cases where they are normally well up to the average level. A classical experiment to demonstrate heightened visual sense is that in which the subject is shown a number of blank cards and told that on one of them is a certain picture. The subject hallucinates the picture and the operator then marks the back of it so that it can be identified later. The cards are shuffled, and as they are dealt out the subject will correctly indicate the one on which the imaginary picture was formed. Apparently the subject notes some very slight difference, a tiny mark, smudge or other *point de repère* which, although indistinguishable to the observer, enables him to pick out the 'picture' card.

Bergson, the celebrated French philosopher, once carried out some experiments in 'thought transference' in which the subject seemed able to identify telepathically the words being silently read by Bergson from a book which he was careful to keep behind the subject's head. It was noted, however, that the experiment was only successful when the subject was able to see Bergson's face, and subsequent tests proved that the subject was actually reading the reflections of the print in Bergson's eyes. It was estimated that the size of the reflections could not have been more than a two hundred and fiftieth of an inch high. This subject was afterwards found able to describe photographs in detail from similar microscopic reflections.

The sense of hearing can be rendered more acute and also more discriminating in the same way. Forel's warders, when on night guard over suicidal and homicidal patients, were hypnotized and trained to sleep beside their charges, ignoring all sounds not concerning their duties, but awakening instantly if the patients attempted to leave their beds. By this means the warders were enabled to perform night duties, sometimes for up to six months at a stretch, in addition to their arduous daytime tasks.

[1] *Medical Hypnosis*, New York, 1948.

Milne Bramwell carried out some tests using a stop-watch, and demonstrated that the range of hearing in hypnosis was frequently double that found in the normal waking state. Beaunis recorded similar observations, and also noted an acceleration in reaction time to auditory sensations.

Bramwell also reported that one subject, who could normally only play a few simple tunes on the piano with the music in front of her, and who was so nervous that she could not play in the presence of strangers, could, when hypnotized and blindfolded, play the same tunes much more brilliantly, and in a room full of people.

Braid demonstrated that hyperæsthesia of the sense of smell could also be induced in a hypnotic subject. One of his subjects, although blindfolded, could identify any person known to him in this way. Given a glove, he would recognize its owner purely by the sense of smell. If his nostrils were plugged, however, his ability to perform these feats disappeared completely.

A favourite trick of the early stage hypnotists was to take the handkerchiefs of a number of people, mix them together, and instruct the subject to return them to their respective owners. This the subject would do, even when precautions were taken to ensure that no other sensory clues were obtainable. Carpenter repeated Braid's experiment, and his subject found the owner of a glove from among sixty other persons. Moll reported that a subject of his could do the same thing with such articles as keys and coins as well as gloves. The same subject could identify the pieces of a torn-up visiting card purely by the sense of smell; pieces torn from a similar card were rejected.

That the sense of touch is accentuated by hypnosis was demonstrated by Milne Bramwell, Berger and Moll, who showed that a hypnotized subject could distinguish two skin pricks when they were so close together that in the normal waking state they would be taken for one. Delboeuf claimed that one of his subjects, after simply posing on his finger tips a blank card taken from a pack of similar ones, could pick it out from the pack again by its 'weight'.

Braid observed that some subjects could recognize objects placed half an inch from the skin, and that others could walk about in an absolutely dark room without bumping into anything recognizing the position of various obstacles by changes in the resistance of the air and in the temperature. Milne Bramwell and Alcock filled two test-tubes with tepid water and added a few drops of cold to one of them. When given the test-tubes to hold, a subject was in this way able to discriminate between minute differences of temperature which neither of the experimenters was able to detect and which the subject could not appreciate in the normal state.

ANÆSTHESIA AND ANALGESIA

Hypnotic phenomena with rather more practical applications than those of hyperæsthesia, and at the same time easier to produce, are anæsthesia, or loss of sensation, and analgesia, or inhibition of pain. A simple example is the stage hypnotist's trick of pushing a needle through the flesh of the forearm of an entranced subject, who obviously feels no pain and who is unaware afterwards that such a thing has been done. It is not uncommon nowadays to read a newspaper report of the painless delivery of a child during hypnosis, and the lay press usually makes much of such an occurrence. It is in fact nothing new, and in the time of Elliotson and Esdaile an announcement of a birth in the newspapers was sometimes followed by the statement: 'painlessly during mesmeric trance'.

The most fantastic painless operations every carried out with the aid of hypnosis were, without doubt, those performed by Esdaile in India. As mentioned earlier, these numbered several thousands, many of them major ones. Here are Esdaile's own descriptions of two representative ones:

Case 1. 'S., aged 27, came to the Native Hospital with an immense scrotal tumour as heavy as his whole body. He was mesmerized for the first time on October 10th, 1846, then on the 11th and 13th, on which latter day he was ready for operation. The operation was performed on the 14th. The tumour was tied up in a sheet to which a rope was attached, and passed through a pulley in the rafter. The colis was dissected out, and the mattress then hauled down to the end of the bed; his legs were held asunder, and the pulley put in motion to support the mass and develop its neck. It was transfixed with the longest two-edged knife, which was found to be too short, as I had to dig the haft in the mass to make the point appear below it, and it was removed by two semicircular incisions right and left. The flow of venous blood was prodigious, but soon moderated under pressure of the hand; the vessels being picked up as fast as possible. The tumour, after half an hour, weighed 103 pounds, and was as heavy as the man's body. During the whole operation, I was not sensible of a quiver of his flesh. The patient made a good recovery.

Case 2. 'Two years before, the patient, a peasant, aged 40, began to suffer from a tumour in the antrum maxillare; the tumour had pushed up the orbit of the eye, filled up the nose, passed into the throat, and caused an enlargement of the glands of the neck. ... In half an hour he was cataleptic, and a quarter of an hour later I performed one of the most severe and protracted operations in surgery; the man was totally unconscious. I put a long knife in at the corner of his mouth, and brought the point out over the cheek-bone, dividing the parts between; from this I pushed it through the skin at the inner corner of the eye, and dissected the cheek-bone to the nose. The pressure of the tumour had caused absorption of the anterior wall of the antrum, and on pressing my fingers between it and the bone it burst, and a shocking gush of blood and matter followed. The tumour extended as far as my fingers could reach under the orbit and the cheek-bone, and passed into the gullet—having destroyed the bones and partition of the nose. No one touched the man, and I turned his head in any position I desired, without resistance, and there it remained until I wished to move it again; when the blood accumulated, I bent his head forward, and it ran from his mouth as if from a spout. The man never moved, nor showed any signs of life, except an occasional indistinct moan; but when I threw back his head, and passed my fingers into his throat to detach the mass in that direction, the stream of blood was directed into his windpipe, and some instinctive effort became necessary for existence; he therefore coughed, and leaned forward to get rid of the blood, and I suppose that he then awoke. The operation was finished, and he was laid on the floor to have his face sewed up, and while this was being done, he for the first time opened his eyes.'[1]

Esdaile was afterwards informed by the patient that he was unaware of having coughed, and had remained completely unconscious throughout the operation. The patient made a satisfactory recovery.

Further comment on the anæsthetic and analgesic value of hypnosis would surely be superfluous, and yet not only Esdaile and his contemporaries, but hypnotic practitioners right up to the present day, have constantly been accused of being frauds and charlatans, and these accusations have come in the main, be it noted, from members of the medical profession.

MISCELLANEOUS PHENOMENA

It is possible not only to inhibit pain by hypnosis but, by means of suggestion, to cause it. Thus, if a hypnotized subject were touched on the arm by a lighted cigarette, if told that it was not alight he would feel no pain, but if told that an unlighted one was alight and would burn him he would react exactly as if he were being burnt by it. Many authorities claim that in this way it is possible for an imaginary burn to produce a severe blistering, whilst a real one leaves practically no mark.

[1] Quoted by Bramwell in *Hypnotism, its History, Theory and Practice*, London, 1903.

Liébeault had one subject who could be made to bleed from the skin by suggestion. If letters were traced on his arm with a blunt pencil they would appear later as letters of blood. Stringent precautions are necessary in making this sort of test, for so strongly does the subject feel impelled to produce the suggested phenomenon that he will sometimes cut or scratch himself in order to ensure the desired result.

Krafft-Ebing reported success in causing a subject's body temperature to change, sometimes to the exact degree suggested. Other workers have noted that certain subjects were able to produce opposite changes in the temperature of each hand, one becoming warmer at the same time as the other grew colder.

Forel and Milne Bramwell succeeded in exciting or arresting menstruation by suggestion, and in regulating its duration and intensity. Alex Erskine, a later hypnotic practitioner, claims that hypnosis can be used for birth control. He says: 'The general question of sterility, so far, at least, as the female is concerned, presents no difficulties to hypnosis. Conception is functional. It can be prohibited just as surely as and as easily as drink or drugs can be prohibited. It can be excluded from possibility, permanently or for a specified period, and the ban on it can be removed at any time without ill effects.' Erskine states that hypnotic methods of birth control cause no interference with normal sex life, desires remaining normal and with no interruption in functions. He also asserts that the production of abortion by hypnosis is as simple as the achievement of sterility, that it has been performed abroad, and that he has produced sterility in England.

Many cases have been recorded where the action of the bowels has been controlled by hypnotic suggestion, even to the extent of checking the action of aperients. Micturition and the secretion of urine has, according to Wetterstrand, been regulated in a similar manner.

The lachrymal secretion can also be affected by hypnosis, and Beaunis claimed that he was able to produce tears from one of a subject's eyes while the other remained normal.

Esdaile reported that he once stopped the secretion of milk by hypnosis for his sister-in-law, who was suffering pain from an accumulation of milk when weaning her child. Braid did the reverse. A woman whose child was fourteen months old was caused to secrete milk again, and she continued to suckle her baby for another six months afterwards. Others have stated that in cases where the secretion of milk has ceased owing to emotional causes, it can rapidly be restored by suggestion.

CHAPTER FIVE

Post-Hypnotic Phenomena

Nature is always consistent, though she feigns to contravene her own laws. She keeps her laws, and seems to transcend them.

R. W. EMERSON

AMONG the many fascinating phenomena associated with hypnosis, some of the most interesting and useful are those produced by what is commonly referred to as 'post-hypnotic suggestion'. The term is an unfortunate misnomer, in that it appears to denote a suggestion given after hypnosis, whereas it actually describes a suggestion given to a hypnotized subject which is to be fulfilled after the termination of the hypnosis. Generally speaking, it is true to say that in this manner any of the phenomena which occur during hypnosis can be caused to occur afterwards, provided always that the trance has been of sufficient depth.

There are two ways in which post-hypnotic phenomena may be produced; (a) by suggesting to the subject during hypnosis that any of the phenomena then occurring will persist after he has awakened, or (b) by suggesting to the subject during hypnosis that at a given time or in response to a given signal certain phenomena will occur. In the case of (a) for example, a hypnotized subject might be told that his arm was locked in a certain position and that it would remain so after he awoke until the hypnotist gave him permission to move it, or until some 'trigger' signal was given. In the case of (b) the subject might be told that at a given time after waking, or when some signal was given, he would carry out a certain action.

Simple suggestions will be acted upon after a light trance, but complex or unusual ones are generally effective only if made during a deep state of hypnosis. The subject always feels a strong compulsion to take the suggested action and is rarely able to resist. If he does resist, it invariably causes him considerable uneasiness and often very real distress. Should the suggestion be one that cannot be carried out without attracting attention, the subject will rationalize, and concoct some reason which to him seems quite plausible for his unusual behaviour.

A subject will sometimes evince a rather dazed, 'not with us' attitude while carrying out a suggestion, but not if he has also been given the suggestion that he will remain perfectly wide awake and act quite normally while doing so. Some hypnotists claim that post-hypnotic suggestions are never executed in the normal waking state, and that there is, in effect, a new hypnosis existing for the time it takes to carry out the act. This view, first advanced by Milne Bramwell, is supported by Erickson, one of America's greatest present day authorities. Others, including Estabrooks, an equally eminent contemporary of Erickson, deny this. Moll considered that there were four distinct conditions under which post-hypnotic suggestions were carried out:

1. A state in which a new hypnosis, characterized by suggestibility, appears during the execution of the act, with loss of memory afterwards and no spontaneous waking.
2. A state in which no symptoms of a fresh hypnosis are discoverable, although the act is carried out.
3. A state with or without fresh suggestibility due to suggestion, with complete forgetfulness of the act and spontaneous waking.
4. A state of susceptibility to suggestion with subsequent loss of memory.

It was agreed by Moll that these differences in post-hypnotic states and the phenomena associated with them were largely a matter of training.

Moll's summary introduces one of the most important of all post-hypnotic phenomena, namely *amnesia*, or the loss of memory of what takes place during the hypnosis. In the case of a deep trance subject or *somnambule*, this amnesia is usually complete and spontaneous, but in lighter degrees of hypnosis it is not present to any appreciable extent except as the result of a suggestion to that effect. It is always possible successfully to suggest to a somnambule that all or part of what occurred during hypnosis will be remembered. A hypnotized subject can always be made to remember anything which took place during a previous hypnosis.

Some authorities, in particular Beaunis, have claimed that post-hypnotic amnesia is fundamentally different from any other kind in that it cannot be broken by any chance association of ideas, but this view is not shared by Moll and Bernheim, who assert that the lost memories of hypnosis can be recalled by direct association of ideas; that if told something of what had occurred the subject would begin to recall the rest, and by chance associations acting in the same way as in everyday life. Others claim that the amnesia is not real, as subjects when in the normal waking state will react to conditioned reflexes previously set up during hypnosis. As the reaction to such a reflex is at an unconscious level however, this seems to the author to be an invalid argument.

What probably happens in a case of spontaneous amnesia is that the subject associates hypnosis with normal sleep, possibly through the word having been used during the induction of the trance, and subconsciously acts in a manner typical of normal sleep.

A good subject can also be made to forget events in his past waking life. By suitable suggestions it is not usually difficult for instance, to prevent him from remembering his own name or address, or even to make him believe he has quite different ones. In the same way a false memory of fictitious events can be implanted, and the subject will swear that such events did, in fact, take place. If told that complete strangers are his close friends he will treat them accordingly, and conversely, he can be made to ignore intimate acquaintances and insist that he has never met them.

Post-hypnotic suggestions can also cause a subject to become deaf, blind, or incapable of any specified action. If, for example, a suggestion were given that ten minutes after he awoke he would become deaf and dumb, and would remain so for five minutes, the subject would, after the lapse of the stated period, suddenly lose completely all sense of hearing and all power of speech, and would not recover them until the five minutes had passed.

Any of the hallucinatory phenomena described in a previous chapter can be caused to occur post-hypnotically, and when so produced are even more spectacular than those effected during hypnosis. If it is suggested that a person known to the subject will be sitting in the room when he awakens, the subject will act as if this person is indeed present, carrying on a one-sided conversation and behaving in every way as he would if the person were real. If the actual person should then enter the room, the subject will ignore him and continue his conversation with the hallucination. If the real person speaks the subject will hear and reply, but will imagine that the voice emanates from the hallucinatory person. If the real person then goes to the part of the room where he is imagined to be, the subject will 'blend' the two together and the hallucination will no longer seem to exist.

Should a negative hallucination be suggested, i.e. that certain objects or persons actually in the room are not there at all, the subject will appear not to see them. If he comes accidentally into contact with, to him, an invisible object, he will register surprise, but still seem to be unaware of its presence.

The author once told a subject that when she awoke from hypnosis she would not be aware of his dog, a large boxer, who was at the time asleep in an armchair facing that in which the subject was seated. After the hypnosis was terminated the author asked her if she would move into the other chair. Without hesitation she went to comply, and attempted to sit down on top of the sleeping dog. Despite the ensuing pandemonium as the dog, howling protest and indignation, leapt to the floor, sending her flying as he did so, the subject remained completely unaware of having attempted to sit on the animal and, apologizing for having 'tripped over', took her seat as requested.

When, at a pre-suggested signal (the offer of a cigarette), the hallucination was removed and she became aware of the dog, she merely said, 'Hallo, there's "Butch",' and expressed no surprise at all that he should have suddenly appeared from nowhere, eyeing her with a decidedly baleful expression.

While on the subject of dogs it seems appropriate to mention a case recorded by Estabrooks.[1] A doctor friend of his was once consulted by a very unhappy patient who complained that a large, black dog had been following him around for several days. He knew quite well that it was a delusion, but was unable to throw it off. It was eventually elicited that he had volunteered as a subject at a performance by a stage hypnotist, had been put into a deep trance and had remembered nothing of what had taken place during the show.

The doctor, on making enquiries among the patient's friends, discovered that he had caused much amusement at this performance by running around the stage pursued by an imaginary black dog. It was necessary for the patient to be hypnotized several times before the post-hypnotic suggestion, which presumably had been accidental and unintended by the stage hypnotist, could be removed.

This case is a good illustration not only of the absolute necessity for removing every suggestion at the end of a demonstration of hypnotism, but of the very real dangers attending all stage performances. One well-known stage hypnotist, at an early part of his act, used to tell a group of subjects that every time they heard a certain tune, the name of which, aptly, was 'So Tired', they would fall asleep immediately. At intervals during the show this tune would be played by the orchestra, and to the delight of the audience, the subjects invariably reacted by going into trance.

The story goes that a man who had been a subject at such a performance was driving his car several days afterwards when the same tune came over on the radio. He immediately fell asleep over the steering wheel, and it was only the prompt action of his passenger that averted an accident.

The undesirability of these stage demonstrations of hypnotism is referred to in greater detail elsewhere in this book.

Post-hypnotic suggestions are known to have been executed many weeks, months and even years after the hypnosis at which they were given took place. Beaunis and Liégeois caused hallucinations to

[1] *Hypnotism*, London, 1959.

appear after periods of up to a year, and Liébeault once gave a highly complicated suggestion which was accurately carried out by the subject over a year later. The most amazing case of all however, is one reported by Estabrooks.[1] During the first World War he had a subject to whom he suggested that whenever he (Estabrooks) said, 'Watch the front', the subject would reply 'Call out the guard. Here comes Paul Revere'. This 'stunt' as Estabrooks called it, was quite succesful. *Twenty years afterwards* he met this subject again and during a conversation suddenly said, 'Watch the front'. The former subject hesitated and then replied, 'Call out the guard. Paul Revere is coming'. He did not realize why he had said this, but remarked that for some reason he was recalling various memories of the war.

Most somnambules have an almost uncanny appreciation of the passage of time and without the aid of any watch or clock will carry out post-hypnotic suggestions at a given number of minutes, hours or days after the suggestion is made. Delboeuf carried out a number of experiments with two illiterate servant girls, in which they executed certain commands at the correct times when the instructions were given in numbers of minutes. Told, for instance, that she would perform various acts after 1500 minutes, one of them carried out the suggestion with absolute accuracy, although both were quite incapable of the simplest calculations, and even had difficulty in telling the time by the clock.

Milne Bramwell was also successful with similar experiments. His subject, a nineteen-year-old girl whose only education had been at board school, required a pencil and paper in order to work out the simplest sum, and normally possessed no special aptitude for appreciating the passage of time. When given a post-hypnotic suggestion that after 21,400 minutes she would write a cross on a piece of paper, she executed the suggestion within two minutes of the stated period. She was equally accurate when the suggested intervals were 21,428 minutes and 21,434 minutes. Bramwell states that of fifty-five experiments made, forty-five were completely successful and eight partially so.

In addition to making a cross, this subject wrote down the time at which the suggestion fell due for execution, and on many occasions, when the time occurred during the night, she was found to have written it in her sleep. Commenting, Bramwell states, 'The primary consciousness has no recollection of the hypnotic suggestions; it does not know that the secondary consciousness, after the hypnotic state had been terminated, first solved the problems and then directed the motor acts which recorded the solutions: it is also unconscious of the motor acts themselves.'

[1] *Hypnotism*, London, 1959.

Some experiments made by Edmund Gurney seem to confirm Bramwell's hypothesis. A hypnotized subject was asked a mathematical question or one concerning his past life, and before he could reply was quickly awakened. To engross his conscious attention he was told to count backwards from a hundred. It was found that while doing this he was able to write down the answer to the question without realizing that he had done so. Similar cases of 'automatic writing' will be considered in a later chapter.

Further experiments on time appreciation by somnambules were carried out by T. W. Mitchell, who made a detailed and thorough analysis of his results. Here is an extract from his observations on the nature of these phenomena:

One very curious result to be noted in these experiments is the apparent limitation of the amount of error, no matter what the time-interval may be. An error of one minute seems as likely to be made when the suggestion is for fifteen minutes as when it is for three minutes. We might have supposed that a Subject who has just performed at the end of two minutes an act suggested to be performed in three minutes, would be likely to perform in ten minutes an act suggested to be performed in fifteen minutes. But it is not so. The most likely time for the fifteen minute suggestion to be fulfilled is in fourteen, fifteen or sixteen minutes. The maximum error met with was one of six minutes in a time estimation of eighteen minutes; but this occurred in one of a complicated series in which four suggestions were running concurrently. In the great majority of cases, in the estimation of periods up to half an hour, the maximum error was not more than one or two minutes. In thirty per cent of the trials on all subjects, the time-interval was accurately determined.

'In experiments of this description it would seem that there is an actual watching of the minutes as they pass. ... But since minutes are purely artificial divisions of time and have not for us the concrete character which days have, the way in which this watching is done needs some explanation. It is comparatively easy to understand how a subconscious intelligence may watch the passage of days and count them as they pass; but it is by no means easy to understand how this same intelligence, unaided by any artificial mechanism such as a clock, can accurately subdivide "time's continuous flow" into periods which correspond to a given number of minutes. ...

'In seeking an explanation of the time-appreciation of somnambules we seem bound to look to the methods used when similar judgments are made by the ordinary waking consciousness. If in the waking state we are denied all ordinary means of marking the passage of time we can still make judgments, less or more accurate, as to the length of any given interval. If we sit with our eyes closed and try to determine when five minutes have elapsed, we may arrive at a very close approximation to the proper interval if we set ourselves deliberately to count. We have ingrained within us a sense of rhythm, based upon memories of certain sensory experiences, which enables us to revive fairly accurately the time-intervals in the swing of a second pendulum. By summing up three hundred such imaginary pendulum beats we may, if we keep the rhythm true, judge very accurately when five minutes have elapsed. Even if our minds are occupied in some other way and we do not attempt to count, we may still make a guess as to when the time is up. Such guesses, however, are very liable to gross error, and it seems evident that the accurate appreciation of time-intervals by somnambules cannot be accounted for on any hypothesis of mere guessing.

'Apart from rhythmic counting, when cut off from all changing sensory impressions derived from the outer world, we seem to have no faculty for judging accurately of the passage of time. Yet a somnambule in the hypnotic trance, deprived of all such sens-impressions, and, so far as his hypnotic consciousness is aware, not deliberately counting or making an effort to note the passage of time, makes such judgments with an accuracy which precludes the possibility that they are the results of mere guessing. If we believe that the accurate time-estimates of somnambules during the trance are the result of some form of conscious counting, the want of knowledge during hypnosis as to how it is done forces us to suppose that the process must be carried on below the threshold of hypnotic consciousness, or by some fragmentary portion of this consciousness temporarily dissociated from the hypnotic stratum as a whole; and a similar supposition must be made with reference to the equally accurate time-appreciation which takes place subconsciously, in response to suggestion, during the waking state. Further, if such a form of subconscious counting takes place, it is not necessary to suppose that it is a counting of some imaginary rhythm. For it seems probable that the lower strata of consciousness can take cognizance of various organic processes which are, or may be, unperceived or generally unattended to by the waking self. And if a correlation has been subconsciously established between such phases of organic life and our artificial divisions of time, the subconscious watcher is provided with an objective time-measure which is liable to only slight variations of regularity. Such variations as normally take place in the rate of the heart-beat or of respiratory movement, are just such as would account for the inaccuracies exhibited by somnambules in their estimates of short periods. In longer periods of true time-watching the organic rhythm will usually average its normal rate, and consequently the amount of error in time-estimates of the subject is not likely to be greater for half an hour than for five minutes.

'While some such explanation seems necessary to account for the accurate appreciation of short time-intervals, there is another possibility which must be taken into consideration in regard to the fulfilment of post-hypnotic acts at a particular moment which has been previously determined by subconscious calculation. That possibility is that these somnambules may have the power, exhibited sometimes by individuals who have never been hypnotized, of knowing the time of day, intuitively as it were, without any conscious or subconscious perception of such sensory impressions as normally give us this information.'[1]

In the author's opinion the explanation set out in the last paragraph of the above quotation is the most probable, and experiments he has made appear to support it.

[1] 'The Appreciation of Time by Somnambules', S.P.R. *Proceedings*, Vol. XXI, pp. 2-59.

CHAPTER SIX

Auto-Suggestion and Self-Hypnosis

In my youth I regarded the universe as an open book, printed in the language of physical equations and social determinants, whereas now it appears to me as a text written in invisible ink, of which, in our rare moments of grace, we are able to decipher a small fraction.

ARTHUR KOESTLER

WHEN considering the nature of hypnosis, mention was made of the statement by Milne Bramwell that any satisfactory theory must take into account the fact of self-hypnosis, in which phenomena identical to that elicited by a hypnotist can be produced by the subject himself. The process by which self-hypnosis is accomplished is that usually known as auto-suggestion, a term made famous by Emile Coué, whose teachings, particularly as expounded by Baudouin in his book *Suggestion and Autosuggestion*, at one time induced thousands of people to make a daily habit of repeating the formula, 'Every day and in every way I am getting better and better'. Coué and Baudouin maintained that if, when relaxed, self-suggestions were repeated and the desired result imagined, the subconscious mind would accept and act on those suggestions. Although the theories of Coué have been largely discredited, there is no doubt that his work was of value in that it stimulated interest in this aspect of hypnotic suggestion.

Self-hypnosis may be initiated in any good subject by the use of post-hypnotic suggestion. For instance, a person who suffered from insomnia could be hypnotized and given the suggestion that whenever he wished to sleep he need only repeat the word 'sleep' say, five times, to place himself in a deep refreshing sleep from which he would awaken at any desired time. A subject who found difficulty in concentrating on his work could, in a similar way, be given the suggestion that by repeating a certain formula he could render himself deaf to all distracting noises for as long as he wished.

It is possible for a person to teach himself the technique of self-hypnosis without the aid of a hypnotist. To accomplish this he should make himself comfortable, relax, and talk to himself, either aloud or 'mentally', making appropriate suggestions of drowsiness etc. After some practice, the onset of hypnosis will be recognized by feelings of lethargy, frequently accompanied by a general heaviness and numbness of the limbs. With the arrival of this stage suggestions may be commenced. The chief difficulty is in achieving a condition of balance in which, on the one hand, active suggestions can be given without awakening, and on the other, deep sleep does not intervene before the suggestions can be made. Test suggestions can be given, such as the loss of some sensation or the production of an hallucination. Post-hypnotic suggestions may also be attempted. The technique of self-hypnosis is by no means an easy one to master, but once acquired, the command it gives the subject over his own personality makes the effort well worth while.

A warning here is necessary however. The use of self-hypnosis can, in some circumstances, be attended with certain dangers. This is particularly true in the case of its use for the relief of pain and the removal of bad habits, for whereas in hetero-hypnosis the hypnotist is, or should be, a person who fully understands what he is doing, self treatment by auto-hypnosis is, in some respects, very much as if a patient had free access to a chemist's shop and attempted to dispense his own medicine. Such self treatment without the aid or advice of a competent person is strongly to be deprecated.

Self-hypnosis often occurs without being recognized as such, as when the enthusiasm and concentration of the creative worker brings about a state in which time and the external world seem no longer to exist, and the depths of the subconscious, with its vast store of knowledge and experience, become accessible, thus producing inspiration, or what Myers termed 'subliminal uprush'. Throughout history we find repeated examples of self-hypnosis producing a wonderful ascendancy of intellectual and artistic activity over such handicaps as poverty, ill health and suffering. It typifies the meditations and exaltations of the Saints, and explains the fantastic feats of concentration of the Indian Mahatmas.

The stigmata of the wounds of Christ produced on the bodies of certain highly religious persons, as for instance, St Catherine of Siena, need no longer be regarded as either fraudulent or miraculous when viewed as the result of self-hypnosis produced by intense concentration and spiritual exaltation, for many famous hypnotists, including Liébeault, Forel and Krafft-Ebing, were able to bring about similar results in subjects upon whom they experimented.

A case which was the subject of a critical and intensive investigation was that of Louise Lateau, who could bleed at will from the parts of her body corresponding to the wounds of Christ merely by concentrating her attention upon them. A Commission appointed by the Royal Academy of Medicine of Belgium to enquire into her case came to the unanimous conclusion that the stigmata and 'ecstasies' were real and that they could be explained physiologically. A more recent case, that of the German 'wonder girl' Therese Neumann, has received even more extensive investigation by many noted doctors and psychologists. When in an auto-hypnotic trance she has hallucinations of the crucifixion of Christ, claims to feel his suffering, sheds tears of blood and bleeds from the hands and feet.

Many of the powers attributed in the past to witches and wizards were undoubtedly the result of self-hypnosis, both in the witches and wizards themselves and in those who believed in them. When a witch claimed that she had been visited by the Devil and carried off to take part in the rites of the Witches' Sabbath, she may well have honestly believed this to be true, having hallucinated the whole business during self-hypnosis. The same process, no doubt, was at work in cases where people believed that they were transmogrified, and walked about on all fours in the belief that they had been changed into wild animals. Magical practices, 'black' and otherwise, and also the *voodoo* and *ju-ju* of primitive races, exert their power, to a large extent at least, by the aid of auto-suggestion and self-hypnosis.

At the other extreme, the same process lies at the root of genius and the inspirations of the great writers, artists and composers. Paul Richter wrote, 'The man of genius is in many respects a real somnambulist. In his lucid dream he sees farther than when awake, and reaches the heights of truth.' Many poets and musicians have produced their greatest works in a state of self induced hypnosis. Goethe has said that many of his best poems were written in a condition bordering on somnambulism, and Seckendorf and Klopstock both declared that their inspirations came as in dreams. Coleridge is said to have written *Kubla Khan* in his sleep, and Ovideo observed that Tasso, when composing, was like a man possessed, and that 'when the inspiration was over, he lost his way in his own creations, and could no longer appreciate their beauty or be conscious of it.'

Mozart described his musical inspirations as being aroused in him independently of his will, like dreams, and Hoffman used to sit at his piano, close his eyes, and play what he seemed to hear. Lamartine declared that he did not think; his ideas thought for him, while Newton worked out the most complicated mathematical problems in his dreams.

That auto-suggestion is the process behind the working of the 'evil eye' and the curses of native witch-doctors, is nowadays widely accepted, but it is not so generally realized that it is also the underlying cause of many illnesses which, at first sight, appear to have quite different origins. The most common cases are those of hypochondria, in which 'feelings of uneasiness or even pain originate in the mind a suspicion of disease existing in particular parts of the body, it may be the lungs, stomach, heart, brain, liver, or kidneys. Slight irregularities and functional disturbances in the action of these organs being noticed are at once suggestive, to those hypochondriacally disposed, of serious and fatal disease progressing in the part to which the attention is conveyed. This deviation from a natural state of certain functions frequently lapses into actual structural disease, as the effect of the attention being for a lengthened period morbidly concentrated on their action.'[1]

Two excellent examples of auto-suggestion acting in this way were given by McComb:

'A youth is struck by the fact that the majority of the members of his family die of heart disease at a given period of life, and he is forced to believe that a like fate awaits him. But the day is as yet distant: he is young, and the idea does not unduly worry him. Still it exists in the subconscious region of his mind; and occasionally it reappears as the years pass by. But the time approaches when his family weakness is accustomed to disclose itself: the auto-suggestion gathers strength unless the healthy elements in consciousness can suppress it. Often the imagination creates nervous cardiac pain, and the sufferer feels palpitations and flutterings and these will give a basis, a point of support for the auto-suggestion, and at once a conviction that the disease is real, and the fatal hour has struck, seizes the mind with overpowering force. And this conviction reacts on the physical organ, giving rise to all kinds of nervous complications. The man sinks into chronic invalidism—the victim of an auto-suggestion.

'The other illustration is afforded by a sufferer whose trouble is to be traced to the reading of a medical work—a practice which the non-medical person would do well to avoid. Nowhere is the adage so much to the point as here: "A little knowledge (*sic*) is a dangerous thing." Our lady friend, while feeling, from some accidental and temporary cause, depressed and melancholy, happened to read that slow and difficult speech is a sign of approaching paresis or paralysis. She at once felt that such a fate would be hers, and sure enough, soon afterwards she developed a slow, drawling utterance which of course tended to confirm the original self-suggestion. The experts were agreed that there was no organic disease present and convinced the patient of that fact: nevertheless, the self-suggestion had done its work and the speech defect persisted. The remedy was found in reversing the psychical process that brought about the mischief, in substituting a true for a false auto-suggestion.'[2]

Illustrations of this order may be found among all sufferers from

[1] *On the Obscure Diseases of the Brain and Disorders of the Mind*, New York, 1900.
[2] *Religion and Medicine*, New York, 1908.

nervous disorders; indeed, hysteria has been defined as a form of unconscious auto-hypnotism.

Fortunately the same processes can be as effective in the cure of illness as in its induction, and the direction of auto-suggestion and self-hypnosis to this end can be traced from primitive beliefs in the curative power of the charm and the fetish to the efficacy of prayer and faith healing, covering, as Myers puts it, 'a range as wide as all the superstition and all the religion of men'.

The comment of Pomponatius, that if the bones of an animal were substituted for the relics of a saint, the cures attributed to them would be just as effective so long as the patient was unaware of the change, has already been noted, and this principle undoubtedly lies behind the 'miracles' of Lourdes, and the cures effected by the Christian 'Scientists' and so-called 'spiritual' healers.

The circumstances of a pilgrimage to a shrine such as Lourdes, and the tense religious atmosphere and 'build-up' preceding the actual ceremony are all calculated to increase the suggestibility of the patient to a high degree, and the illnesses actually cured at these places are of the type known to be curable by hypnotic suggestion. The official pronouncements of the Catholic Church, that certain organic diseases were miraculously cured at Lourdes, were investigated with commendable care and objectivity by Donald West, a qualified medical man and a former research officer of the Society for Psychical Research. His report[1] shows quite clearly that there is no real evidence to warrant the term 'miracle' in any of the eleven most famous cases which were the object of his investigation and analysis.

A further indication that suggestion rather than faith is the principal factor involved in such cures as are effected, is found in the many cases where sufferers with little or no faith have nevertheless been cured by visits to Lourdes and similar shrines, whereas some deeply religious pilgrims have received no relief whatsoever. This is to be expected, for in the same way, the disbelieving sceptic is often easily hypnotized, whereas the person who has faith in the power of hypnosis to alleviate his suffering is not necessarily a good subject. F. W. H. Myers summarizes thus:

'Self-suggestion, whatever this may really mean, is thus in most cases, whether avowedly or not, at the bottom of the effect produced ... where patients in large masses are supplied with effective conceptions, which they thus impress repeatedly upon themselves without the need of a hypnotist's attendance on each occasion. The "Miracles of Lourdes" and the cures effected by "Christian Science" fall, in my view, under this category. We have here suggestions given to a quantity of more or less suitable people *en masse*, much as a plat-

[1] *Eleven Lourdes Miracles*, London, 1957.

form hypnotizer gives suggestions to a mixed audience, some of whom may then be affected without individual attention from himself. The suggestion of the curative power of the Lourdes water, for instance, is thus thrown out, partly in books, partly by oral addresses; and a certain percentage of persons succeed in so persuading themselves of that curative efficacy that when they bathe in the water they are actually cured.'[1]

The cult of Christian 'Science' merits consideration at some length, not only on account of its dubious beginnings and inherently absurd tenets, but for the loud condemnation of hypnotism voiced by all its followers. They never speak of hypnotism by any name other than 'magnetism', and refuse to admit that it has any connection with their own unorthodox healing methods.

The founder of Christian Science, which certainly began as a money-making 'racket', was an extraordinary and unscrupulous woman named Mary Baker Eddy, born in 1821. The youngest child of simple and deeply religious New England farming parents, Mary was subject to hysterical fits and hallucinations. Her first husband died not long after their marriage, whereupon she began to conceive strange ideas, including the belief that she would not sleep unless rocked like a baby in an oversized cradle.

She remarried, this time to a travelling dentist named Patterson, whom she divorced after he was taken prisoner during the Civil War. She went to live with a sister, at whose house she claimed to hear spirit rappings on the walls, and later persuaded an old lady to give her accommodation on the pretext that the spirits had insisted that she should live with her. After a fall she became paralysed, and spent several years in bed until a 'magnetic healer' named Quimby,[2] recognizing that her illness was of an hysterical nature, cured her by suggestion.

After recovering, Mary practised as a spiritualist medium, claiming that the spirit of her dead brother acted as her 'guide' and also attempted, with but little success, to set up as a healer, using the methods advocated by Quimby, who had by that time died. She gained possession of some manuscripts he had left, which, with the addition of some biblical extracts and a few ideas of her own, were rehashed by one of her pupils, Spofford, and published as her own work under the title *Science and Health*.

She married again, this time to a friend of Spofford named Eddy, and then, jealous of Spofford's growing popularity, accused him of transferring his patients' illnesses, by a process of 'magnetism', to

---

[1] *Human Personality*, London, 1903.
[2] Quimby, incidentally was the anæsthetist at the first 'mesmeric' operation performed in America.

herself. She is said to have unsuccessfully sued Spofford, alleging that he practised witchcraft. It is also said that she even attempted to procure his murder, but with no greater success.

Soon afterwards, her third husband died, and Mary moved to Boston where she began publication of the *Christian Science Journal*. She also founded a 'School', at which students paid high fees for instruction in her methods, with such success that branches were soon opened in a number of other cities, including Chicago and New York. Not content with the handsome income derived from these sources, she then conceived the idea of 'absent healing', in which, on payment of a fee, 'healing thoughts' were sent from healer to patient, the efficacy of the treatment being, it was claimed, quite independent of the distance separating the two.

In 1895 the so-called First Church of Christ, Scientist, was opened in Boston, since when this strange and illogical cult has spread throughout the western world. Mary Baker Eddy died in 1910, aged eighty-nine.

Many fantastic cures are claimed to have been effected by Christian Science practitioners, always, unfortunately, without any attempt at real substantiation, and many unnecessary deaths have certainly occurred as the result of husbands, wives and parents refusing, as Christian Scientists, to allow their near and dear ones to receive urgent medical attention.

Equally loath to submit to scientific or medical investigation are those spiritualists who practise or claim to have benefited from so-called 'spiritual healing'. Here the claim is usually made that the 'healer', who is also a medium, is controlled by 'spirit doctors' on 'the other side'. As the diagnoses as well as the alleged cures are more often than not effected by the same 'spirit doctor', many of the far-fetched claims made for 'spiritual healing' may be dismissed on this score alone. Of the remaining cases few, if any, stand up to serious, objective examination, as was ably demonstrated by Dr Louis Rose in a paper recently published in the *British Medical Journal*.[1] He analysed ninety-five claimed cures by the best known British 'spiritual healer', and reached the following conclusions.

In fifty-eight cases no medical or other records were available, so that the claims could not be confirmed.

In twenty-two cases the claims were so much at variance with the records that further investigation was hopeless.

In two cases the 'healer' *may* have contributed to the amelioration of an organic condition.

In one case organic disease was relieved after, but not necessarily as the result of, intervention by the 'healer'.

[1] 'Some Aspects of Paranormal Healing', B.M.A. *Journal*, 4th December, 1954.

In four cases there was improvement at first but relapses followed.

Four cases showed improvement in function but no improvement in the organic state.

Four cases showed improvement when healing was being given, but orthodox medical treatment was being given at the same time.

In one case the patient's condition, which was deteriorating before 'healing' was given, continued to deteriorate afterwards.

The author of this book does not, by any means, wish to imply that there can be nothing whatsoever in the various forms of 'psychic' healing; indeed, he has himself effected cures by hypnotism which seem quite beyond medical understanding; but the fact remains that the indiscriminate practice of these various forms of 'faith' and 'spiritual' healing, has a great potential for very real harm as well as possible good. It must also be remembered that even if any such cures can be proved to be genuine, this by no means indicates that the theories advanced by their supporters are correct explanations of how and why they occur. That many rogues and charlatans have jumped on the healing 'band-wagon', battening on the credulity of the masses and the eternal hope by the sick for some way by which their suffering may be relieved, is illustrated by the advertisements appearing in issue after issue of the spiritualist newspapers and occult magazines.

Most 'healers' however, are, without doubt, completely honest and sincere and they take up the work in a genuine desire to be of service to humanity. Even those who make the wildest claims, such as the performance of 'psychic' operations during trance or sleep, usually believe implicitly in the truth of their illusions.

A Committee appointed by the British Medical Association to investigate the claims of spiritual healers included in its Report, published in 1956, the following statement:

'As far then as our observation and investigation have gone, *we have seen no evidence that there is any special type of illness cured solely by spiritual healing which cannot be cured by medical methods which do not involve such claims*. The cases claimed as cures of a miraculous nature present no features of a unique and unexpected character outside the knowledge of any experienced physician or psychiatrist. ... We find that, whilst patients suffering from psychogenic disorders may be 'cured' by various methods of spiritual healing, just as they are by methods of suggestion and other forms of psychological treatment employed by doctors, we can find no evidence that organic diseases are cured solely by such means. The evidence suggests that many cases claimed to be cured are likely to be either instances of wrong diagnosis, wrong prognosis, remission, or possibility of spontaneous cure.'

Although the claims of the spiritual 'healers', Christian 'Scientists' and the like are not actually disproved, there is virtually no evidence indicating that such cures as are effected constitute anything more than examples of the power of auto-suggestion and self-hypnosis. Psychic methods of diagnosis are quite a different matter, and are referred to in a later chapter.

CHAPTER SEVEN

Dissociation and Multiple Personality

Every fact is a solemn thing; it is the voice of Truth in Nature.
R. W. EMERSON

MUCH of the phenomena already described, whether induced by a hypnotist or brought about by auto-hypnosis, involves the process known as *dissociation*, in which certain mental activities become separated from normal consciousness. The case of 'automatic writing' described on page 53 is an example. The subject was completely unaware of what he was writing, also of the events that had occurred during hypnosis which were the cause of his actions. Here are two more examples, both from eminent authorities.

Dr Boris Sidis gave a hypnotized subject a negative hallucination that she was unable to see his hands or a newspaper which he held before her. Tests proved his suggestions to be effective, yet when his finger pointed to any word in the newspaper she was able to pronounce it. Immediately afterwards she would forget the word, but recalled it when the finger indicated it again. When the newspaper was removed she did not remember any of the words she had read out. 'On awakening at the end of this long series of experiments, the subject had no recollection of what had passed. She was then asked to shut her eyes and a pen was given her. She was told to try to recollect what occurred when asleep, but she could not remember anything. The pen meanwhile wrote without the subject's knowledge an account of what had occurred.'[1]

George Estabrooks, one of the best known present day hypnotists, had an ex-army friend who was able to read a book and do automatic writing simultaneously, without being at all conscious of what he wrote. When Estabrooks pricked the writing hand with a needle, his friend showed no reaction, but the hand 'burst into a stream of cuss words that would have made any top sergeant blush with shame', and told Estabrooks 'where he could go and how to get there.' All this time, says Estabrooks, 'The subject was reading *Oil for the Lamps of China* without the slightest idea that his good right arm was fighting a private war."[2]

Little is known of the real nature and mechanism of dissociation, which can vary in degree from the comparatively simple actions of

---
[1] *Borderland of Psychical Research*, London, 1906.   [2] *Hypnotism*, London, 1959.

an absent-minded person to the highly complex form shown in the case of certain psychological disorders, as when an attempt is made to escape from some mental conflict. States of great concentration such as reverie and abstraction are conducive to, if not the cause of dissociation. Marini, for instance, when writing his *Adone*, is said not to have felt a severe burn of the foot, and Sir Walter Scott wrote one of his novels while recovering from an illness, forgetting it completely when his health became normal again. According to G. H. Lewes, Dickens, 'amid silence and darkness heard voices and saw objects, of which the revived impressions to him had the vividness of sensations, and the images his mind created in explanation of them had the coercive of realities. Every word said by his characters was distinctly heard by him.'

Sometimes, however, these subconscious mental actions can assume a systematic or organized form, and develop into 'secondary personalities' acquiring distinct chains of memories of their own which appear quite independent of, and alternate with, the primary, or 'normal' chain. One of the most common modes of origin of such dissociated personalities is natural somnambulism or 'sleep-waking', the events and memories of which sometimes repeat and consolidate themselves until they form a memory chain of their own. In other cases illness or some emotional shock or crisis may bring about a state of auto-hypnosis from which the secondary personality emerges. Repeated suggestions by a hypnotist can be directed successfully towards the same result.

A notable case of dual personality, in which no less an authority than Professor William James was concerned, was that of the Rev. Ansel Bourne, a sixty-year-old Baptist clergyman, of Providence, Rhode Island, U.S.A. A detailed report[1] of the case was made by Dr Richard Hodgson, who played an important part in its investigation.

Earlier in his life Ansel Bourne had had some unusual mental experiences which were attributed to a form of epilepsy. He had also once been hypnotized by a stage performer. On January 17th, 1887, he suddenly disappeared from his home, and despite the extensive publicity his disappearance received, nothing was heard of him for nearly two months, by which time his family had given up all hope of tracing him. On March 14th, however, they received a telegram from a doctor in Norristown, Pa., saying that Bourne had been found in that town, suffering from a loss of memory of all his actions in the last eight weeks.

Early on the morning of March 14th, Bourne awakened after seeming to hear an explosion like the report of a gun, and was

[1] 'A Case of Double Consciousness', S.P.R. *Proceedings*, Vol. VII, pp. 221-58.

astonished to find himself in a completely strange room. He felt very weak, and thought that he might have been drugged. For about two hours he remained in the room, fearing that he might be mistaken for a burglar, but eventually, hearing someone in the next room, he went and asked where he was. His informant, the owner of the house, addressed him as Mr Brown and assured him that he was all right. When Bourne denied that his name was Brown and insisted that he did not know where he was, the man called a doctor, to whom Bourne said that his last recollection was of walking along a street in his home town.

It transpired that about a fortnight after he had disappeared, Bourne arrived at Norristown, where he rented a shop in the name of A. J. Brown and commenced business as a retailer of sweets and toys. From then until the morning of March 14th, he had conducted his business in a perfectly proper and honest manner, making occasional trips to Philadelphia to purchase stock. He was regular and normal in his habits, attended church on Sundays, and no one suspected there was anything unusual about him.

The report of his doctor read as follows: 'Bourne said he was a preacher and a farmer, and could not conceive why he should have engaged in a business he knew nothing about, and never had any desire to engage in. When asked about purchasing and paying for goods, and paying freight bills, he said he had no recollection of any such transactions. There are a number of circumstances connected with and preceding the peculiar dual condition that have satisfied me that he is a sincere man, and not an impostor.'

Professor James suggested that Bourne should be hypnotized in the hope that he might, while in the trance, be able to recall what had occurred and give some explanation of his strange behaviour, and also that he might be given post-hypnotic suggestions to prevent a recurrence of the condition.

When hypnotized, Bourne stated that his name was A. J. Brown, and gave a detailed account of his activities from the time he disappeared until the 'explosion' woke him up. He also made a number of statements about his early life, not all of which were correct. He had gone to New York and thence to Philadelphia before arriving at Norristown. He remembered the date of his first marriage, but not his wife's name, and was very hazy concerning his children and other members of his family. While hypnotized he claimed to have been born at Newton, N.J., and gave his correct date of birth, although he was actually born in New York, and had never even visited Newton. While hypnotized he denied having ever heard of Ansel Bourne, and in the normal waking state knew nothing of A. J. Brown. All attempts at fusing the two personalities into one were unsuccessful, and it was not possible to ascertain any clear association between them. This seems to have been an isolated incident in the subject's life, which reverted to normality and remained so afterwards.

Janet had a subject in whose case two distinct personalities additional to her normal one appeared. She was the remarkable 'Mme B', whose fantastic telepathic accomplishments are described in another chapter. F. W. H. Myers, who made an intensive study of this case, wrote the following report:

'In these researches Mme B. in her every-day condition is known by the name of Leonie. In the hypnotic trance she has chosen for herself the name of Leontine, which thus represents her secondary personality. Behind these two, this triple personality is completed by a mysterious Leonore, who may for the present be taken as non-existent. A post-hypnotic suggestion was given to Leontine, that is to say, Leonie was hypnotized and straightway became Leontine, and Leontine was told by Professor Janet that after the trance was over, and Leonie had resumed her ordinary life, she, Leontine, was to take off her apron—the joint apron of Leonie and Leontine—and then to tie it on again. The trance was stopped, Leonie was awakened, and conducted Professor Janet to the door, talking with her usual respectful gravity on ordinary topics. Meantime, her hands—the joint hands of Leonie and Leontine—untied her apron, the joint apron, and took it off. Professor Janet called Leonie's attention to the loose apron. "Why, my apron is coming off!" Leonie exclaimed, and, with full consciousness and intention, she tied it on again. She then continued to talk, and for her—Leonie—the incident was over. The apron, she supposed, had somehow come untied, and she had retied it. This, however, was not enough for Leontine. At Leontine's prompting, the joint hands again began their work, and the apron was taken off again and again replaced, this time without Leonie's attention having been directed to the matter at all.

'Next day Professor Janet hypnotized Leonie again, and presently Leontine, as usual, assumed control of the joint personality. "Well," she said, "I did what you told me yesterday! How stupid the other one looked"—Leontine always calls Leonie 'the other one'—"while I took her apron off! Why did you tell her that her apron was falling off? I was obliged to begin the job all over again."

'Thus far we have dealt with a secondary personality summoned into being, so to say, by our own experiments, and taking its orders entirely from us. It seems, however, that, when once set up, this new personality can occasionally assume the initiative, and can say what it wants to say without any prompting. This is curiously illustrated by what may be termed a conjoint epistle addressed to Professor Janet by Mme B. and her secondary personality, Leontine. She had left Havre more than two months when I received from her a very curious letter. On the first page was a curious note, written in a serious and respectful style. She was unwell, she said, worse on some days than on others, and she signed her true name, Mme B. But over the page began another letter in a quite different style, and which I may quote as a curiosity. "My dear good sir, I must tell you that B. really, really makes me suffer very much; she cannot sleep, she spits blood, she hurts me; I am going to demolish her, she bores me, I am ill also, this is from your devoted Leontine." When Mme B. returned to Havre I naturally questioned her about this singular missive. She remembered the *first* letter very distinctly, but had not the slightest recollection of the *second*. I at first thought that there must have been an attack of spontaneous somnambulism between the moment when she finished the first letter and the moment when she closed the envelope. But afterwards these unconscious, spontaneous letters became common, and I was better able to study their mode of production. I was fortunately able to watch Mme B. on one occasion while she went through this curious performance. She was seated at a table, and held in her left hand the piece of knitting at which she had been working. Her face was calm, but her eyes looked into space with a certain fixity, but she was not cataleptic, for she was humming a rustic air; her right hand wrote quickly, and, as it were, surreptitiously. I removed the paper without her noticing me, and then spoke to her; she looked around, wide awake, but surprised to see me, for in her state of distraction she had not noticed me approach. Of the letter which she was writing she knew nothing whatever.

'Leontine's independent action is not entirely confined to writing letters. She observed (apparently) that when her primary self, Leonie, discovered these letters, she (Leonie) tore them up. So Leontine hit on the plan of placing them in a photographic album into which Leonie could not look without falling into catalepsy (on account of an association of ideas with Dr Gibert, whose portrait had been in the album). In order to accomplish an act like this Leontine has to wait for a moment when Leonie is distracted, or, as we may say, absent-minded. If she can catch her in this state Leontine can direct Leonie's walks, for instance, or make her start on a railway journey without luggage, in order to get to Havre as quickly as possible.

'We now come to consider the third personality, Leonore. Although Leonie's unconscious acts are sometimes (not always) coincident with Leontine's conscious ones, Leontine's conscious acts are never included in Leonie's memory, any more than in Leontine's own. They belong to some other, to some profounder manifestation of personality, to which M. Janet has given the name of Leonore.

And observe that just as Leontine can sometimes by her own motion and without suggestion write a letter during Leonie's waking state and give advice which Leonie might do well to follow, so also Leonore can occasionally intervene of her own motion during Leontine's dominance, and give advice which Leontine might well obey.

' "The spontaneous acts of the unconscious self," says M. Janet, here meaning by *l'inconscient* the entity to which he has given the name of Leonore, "may also assume a very reasonable form, a form which, were it better understood, might perhaps serve to explain certain cases of insanity. Mme B. during her somnambulism (i.e. Leontine) had had a sort of hysterical crisis; she was restless and noisy, and I could not calm her. Suddenly she stopped and said to me with terror, 'Oh, who is talking to me like that? It frightens me.' 'No one is talking to you.' 'Yes! there on the left.' And she got up and tried to open a wardrobe on her left hand, to see if some one was hidden there, 'What is it that you hear?' I asked. 'I hear on the left a voice which repeats, "Enough! enough! be quiet; you are a nuisance".' Assuredly the voice which thus spoke was a reasonable one, for Leontine was insupportable; but I had suggested nothing of the kind and had had no idea of inspiring a hallucination of hearing. Another day Leontine was quite calm, but obstinately refused to answer a question which I asked. Again she heard with terror the same voice to her left, saying: 'Come, be sensible, you must answer.' Thus the unconscious sometimes gave her excellent advice."

'And in effect, so soon as Leonore, in her turn, was summoned into communication, she accepted the responsibility of this counsel. "What was it that happened," asked M. Janet, "when Leontine was so frightened?" "Oh, nothing; it was I who told her to keep quiet; I saw she was annoying you; I don't know why she was so frightened."

'Just as Mme B. was sent by passes into a state of lethargy from which she emerged as Leontine, so also Leontine in her turn was reduced by renewed passes to a state of lethargy from which she emerged no longer as Leontine, but as Leonore. This second awakening is slow and gradual, but the personality which emerges is in one most important point superior to either Leonie or Leontine. Alone among the subject's phases this phase possesses the memory of *every* phase. Leonore, like Leontine, knows the normal life of Leonie, but distinguishes herself from Leonie, in whom, it must be said, these subjacent personalities appear to take little interest. But Leonore also remembers the life of Leontine, condemns her as noisy and frivolous, and is anxious not to be confounded with either.

'Yet one further variation, and I end my brief *résumé* of this complex history. Leonore is liable to pass into a state which does not, indeed, interrupt her chain of memory, but which removes her for a time from the possibility of communicating with other minds. She grows pale, she ceases to speak or hear, her eyes, though still shut, are turned heavenwards, her mouth smiles, and her face takes an expression of beatitude.

'This is plainly a state of so-called ecstasy; but it differs from the ecstasy common in hysterical attacks in one capital point. Not only is it remembered—indistinctly, perhaps—by Leonore, who describes herself as having been dazzled by a light on the left side, but also brings with it the most complex of all the chains of memory, supplementing even Leonore's recollection on certain acts which have been accomplished by Leonore herself.'[1]

This case is of immense psychological interest because of the apparently independent way in which the three states are held apart from each other and the highly organized nature of each personality. In fact the only reason for terming any one of them the primary personality is that 'Leonie' is the one best adjusted to normal life.

The most extraordinary and complex of all recorded cases of multiple personality however, is undoubtedly that of Professor Morton Prince's famous patient, Miss Beauchamp.

This young lady, a student nurse in a hospital at Boston, first came under observation as a result of her peculiar behaviour, attributed at the time to severe neurasthenia. After the usual methods of treatment had proved unsuccessful, Prince decided to try the effect of hypnotism, and was able to induce a state of deep somnambulism without difficulty.

After long and intensive study, Prince came to the conclusion that the body of Miss Beauchamp was controlled at various times by no less than four quite distinct personalities. The personality evident when she first came to his attention he termed B.1, and later, because of her demure, highly religious and somewhat morbid outlook, 'The Angel'.

During hypnosis a quite different personality, subsequently termed B.2, made its appearance, and it was observed that, for no apparent reason, this personality frequently rubbed her eyes. B.2, who only appeared during hypnosis, could usually remember the events which had taken place during a previous trance, but on one occasion she became unable to do so and denied all knowledge of these events. It was discovered that the state she failed to recall was actually a second stage of hypnosis in which a third distinct personality had appeared. This third personality Prince termed B.3.

Thus, at this period there were these separate personalities: B.1, of

[1] *Human Personality*, London, 1903.

Miss Beauchamp's 'normal' state, B.2, of the first hypnotic condition, and B.3, of the second hypnotic condition. B.1 was unaware of the existence of B.2 or B.3, B.2 knew B.1 but not B.3, and B.3 knew both B.1 and B.2.

It was noticed that B.3, like B.2, continually rubbed her eyes, and when asked why she did so replied that she was 'trying to get them opened'. It appeared that it had been B.3 who had previously rubbed B.2's eyes.

Shortly afterwards, while at home, an emotional upset resulted in a trance, in which B.3 took control, rubbing her eyes this time until she succeeded in getting them open. From that time onwards B.3 always dated events as having occurred before or after 'I got my eyes opened'. Often she would take control spontaneously, but at other times remained in the background, 'squeezed', as she put it, by B.1 but always aware of all that went on.

B.3 dubbed herself 'Sally Beauchamp' after reading the name in a book, and Prince later adopted the surname Beauchamp in his report for all the personalities. A rather childlike personality, she was utterly irresponsible, devoid, apparently, of all conscience and lacking any moral scruples. She seemed to take a violent dislike to B.1, and would go to any extreme to upset her. For instance, knowing B.1's great antipathy to insects, in particular, spiders, B.3 placed some in a box which she posted, first ensuring that it would be collected by B.1. On a number of occasions she took the last bus at night to some remote spot in the country, where she 'withdrew' into the background, leaving B.1 to make the long walk home. If B.1 went to church, a thing B.3 loathed, the latter would revenge herself by going out drinking and having associations with men, leaving B.1 to return to the hospital afterwards filled with remorse and shame.

B.1 was once making a baby's blanket for a friend, and she worked on it for nearly a year. Every time it came near completion B.3 would unravel it all, and in the end B.1 regained consciousness one day to find herself standing in the middle of the room completely entangled in the strands of yarn, and having to cut them up in order to extricate herself. B.1 took a great pride in her clothes and other personal property, so B.3 made a practice of throwing them all into a pile on the floor, delighting in B.1's distress at finding the mess and having to sort it out.

A curious feature of the B.3 personality was that she could never assert herself while her eyes were closed. Prince's report says, 'With her eyes closed she can feel nothing. The tactile, pain, thermic, and muscular senses are involved. You may stroke, prick, or burn any part of her skin and she does not feel it. You may place a limb in any posture without her being able to recognize the position which has been assumed. But let her open her eyes and look at what you are doing, let her join the visual with the tactile or other senses, and the lost senses return.'

Prince realized that he would have to eliminate B.3 altogether in order to restore B.1 to normality, and knowing this, B.3 resorted to all sorts of devices in an attempt to foil his efforts. She wrote letters making appointments which B.1 hated keeping, others to Prince himself asking him to discontinue his treatment of B.1, and more to B.1 threatening dire consequences if she did not take certain courses agreeable to B.3. She tried to deceive Prince by attempting to simulate B.1 or B.2, but was always easily detected, and she then began tormenting B.1 by such methods as hiding her money, putting her on an allowance of a few cents a day, making her lie awake all night and threatening to cut off all her hair. B.1 was thus kept in absolute terror, only hearing of these things through Prince or her friends, as she was completely unconscious at the times when B.3 was in control.

B.3's objective was the complete control of B.1's body, which she resented ever having to relinquish, and at times she became frightened at the thought of the possibility that B.1 might die, wondering what would then become of herself, i.e. B.3.

Later, yet another personality began to appear. Known as B.4, she was unaware of the activities of B.1, B.2 and B.3, and there were gaps in her memory corresponding to the times at which they appeared. This however, B.4 was never willing to admit, and although anxious to know, would never ask about their activities. She was a very different personality from the other three, showing far more strength of character, albeit irritable, headstrong and quick-tempered. B.3, sensing in the newcomer a threat to her own chances of gaining full control, conceived an even greater hatred of her than of B.1, for B.4 made it quite clear that she intended to get rid of B.3.

Prince then made the important discovery that if he hypnotized B.4, B.2 appeared, and that B.2 retained all the memories of both B.1 and B.4. B.2 appeared to be a far more mature and well balanced personality than the others, and Prince concluded that B.2 was, in fact, the real Miss Beauchamp. By hypnotic suggestion he was able to obtain this real self for several hours at a time.

Next he suggested to B.2 that when awake as B.1 she would remember all about B.4, and when awake as B.4, she would remember all about B.1, thinking and feeling in the manner of B.1 also. By repeatedly hypnotizing and awakening her alternately as B.1 and B.4, a synthesis of the two personalities was at last achieved, and the real Miss Beauchamp was thus re-created. B.3, by the use of hypnosis, was pushed back into the unconscious of the reintegrated person.

Before finally disposing of 'Sally', or B.3, Prince was able to obtain a wealth of information from her, including an account of her 'life'. Although the other personalities knew nothing of her, she proved that she was aware of their every thought and action. For instance, she could describe B.1's dreams accurately and in detail. She claimed to have hypnotized B.4, copying the methods she had seen Prince use when he first hypnotized B.1. She attempted, at Prince's request, to write an autobiography of herself, but B.4 discovered the manuscript and destroyed it several times. An account of her life was finally obtained however, in which she claimed to remember events from Miss Beauchamp's earliest childhood. She always insisted that she possessed a consciousness quite distinct from that of Miss Beauchamp. Here is an extract from her autobiography:

'She (Miss Beauchamp) was a little girl just learning to walk, and kept taking hold of chairs and wanting to go ahead. She didn't go ahead, but was all shaking in her feet. I remember her thoughts distinctly as separate from mine. Now they are long thoughts that go round and round, but then they were little dashes. Our thoughts then went along the same lines because we had the same experiences. Now they are different; our interests are different. Then she was interested in walking, and I was too, only I was very much more interested, more excited, wildly enthusiastic. I remember thinking distinctly differently from her; that is, when she tried to walk she would be distracted by a chair or a person or a picture or anything, but I wanted only to walk. This happened lots of times.

'Learning to walk was the first experience of separate thoughts. I remember before this there wasn't anything but myself, only one person. I don't know which came first. I remember when I was there further back than *she* can, and therefore why wasn't I the person?

'I remember lots of little things. When she was a little bit of a thing (so small that she couldn't walk very well) she had visions very often. I didn't, but I was conscious of her having them. Her visions didn't represent real things as they do now. I thought they were interesting and enjoyed her having them. During all her childhood I remember enjoying many of the things she did. She was awfully fond of out-of-door things—climbing, running, etc. I enjoyed them and wanted to go farther than she did. Some people she liked and I didn't. Some people she went to see and walked with I didn't want to see, but couldn't help it.

'I suggested things to her sometimes by thinking hard. I didn't really do them; she did them, but I enjoyed it. I don't know that I made her; I thought about them very hard. I didn't deliberately try to make her, but I wanted to do the things, and occasionally she carried out my thoughts. Most times she didn't when my thoughts were entirely different from her own. Sometimes she was punished for doing what I wanted; for example, I didn't like going to school; I wanted to play "hookey". I thought it would be awfully exciting, because the boys did it and were always telling about it. She liked going to school. One day she stayed away all day after I had been thinking about it for a long time. She didn't want to, but she did. She was punished and put to bed in a dark room, and scolded in school and made to sit on one end of the platform; she was shy and felt conspicuous.

I always knew her thoughts; I knew what she was thinking about on the platform. She was thinking partly of being penitent and partly of fairy-tales, so as not to be conscious of the scholars and teacher, and she was hungry. I was chuckling, and thought it amusing. I did not think of anything else except that her fairy-tales were silly. She believed in fairies, that they were very real. I didn't and don't. At this time she was a little girl.'[1]

It seemed that B.3 never slept, and that she had but little idea of time, being quite unable to distinguish between ten seconds and five minutes. Prince considered that she represented Miss Beauchamp's subliminal consciousness, and wrote, 'I was able to get an actual autobiography of a subliminal consciousness, in which are described the contemporaneous and contrasted mental lives of two consciousnesses, the subliminal and the dominant, from early infancy to adult life.'

A contemporary of Morton Prince, with whom he is often confused, was another American psychologist, Dr Walter Franklin Prince, a former Research Officer of the American Society for Psychical Research, who also made important contributions to our knowledge of multiple personality and its close connection with hypnosis. At the time when Morton Prince's report on the Beauchamp case was arousing great interest in psychological circles, Walter Franklin Prince was investigating an alleged 'spirit medium', a young lady named Doris Fischer, and comparison of her behaviour with that of Miss Beauchamp led him to the conclusion that Miss Fischer's was a similar case.

Adopting the technique so successfully employed by his namesake, he hypnotized his subject, and by this means caused two separate and distinct personalities, quite unlike the normal Miss Fischer, to emerge. By the use of hypnosis, two of these personalities were

[1] *The Dissociation of a Personality*, New York, 1906.

eventually fused together to form the 'real' Miss Fischer, while the other, like Sally Beachamp, was pushed back into the unconscious. Walter Franklin Prince later adopted the young lady, who matured, as his daughter, into a perfectly well balanced woman.

A recent case, showing a remarkable resemblance to those just described, has received wide publicity and provoked much interest and speculation through the publication of a popular book, *The Three Faces of Eve*, and the world-wide screening of a film bearing the same title. A second book, *Strangers in My Body, or The Final Face of Eve*, describes the case in autobiographical form from the point of view of the subject, who is one of the joint authors. Eve White, as the first personality was labelled, was born of unsophisticated country parents, and led an unhappy and repressed childhood, chiefly because of the strong personality and strict Baptist outlook of her mother. An abnormal fear of death was instilled by two unfortunate incidents, which her mother used as instruments to secure good behaviour. The birth of twin sisters and ensuing feelings of insecurity aggravated her trouble, and five months later, when after the death of her grandmother she was forced against her will to kiss the corpse, causing near hysterical terror, she began sleep-walking. Shortly afterwards she started having 'black-outs', during which a second personality, Eve 'Black', emerged for brief periods, creating mischief and havoc for which the unknowing Eve White received punishment, which naturally increased her sense of insecurity and unwantedness.

Eve Black remained more or less quiescent during schooldays, but began to emerge more frequently when Eve White, who had to leave college before graduating, became a wage earner. Marriage, to a Catholic husband, was not a particularly happy union, and disharmony was made worse by Eve White's Baptist conscience objecting to the Catholic upbringing of their child.

Violent headaches and loss of memory led her to seek medical advice and eventually, psychiatric treatment. By the use of hypnosis Eve Black was enabled to emerge as a distinct and separate personality. The difference between the two Eves was fantastic, for whereas Eve White was timid, over-conscientious and highly religious, Eve Black was completely uninhibited, irresponsible and amoral, with an irresistible *joie de vivre* and a racy but pungent vocabulary.

As therapy continued the marriage situation deteriorated, largely through Eve Black's exploits, until a divorce seemed inevitable. At this stage the psychiatrist revealed the existence of Eve Black to the husband and parents and soon afterwards the former left and Eve returned to work, her parents taking charge of the child. From then onwards Eve Black became more and more dominant, wrecking job after job and spending money extravagantly. She undermined physical health by such tricks as going out drinking all night and leaving Eve White to face the next day with a hangover.

Then, during a consultation with the psychiatrist, Eve White suddenly fell into a state of hypnosis, and a third personality, quite different from and with no memory of the others, emerged. Jane, as she called herself, seemed to be a much better integrated personality than the other two and was eventually made aware through hypnosis of the past actions of Eve Black and Eve White. The psychiatrist was able to cause any one of the three personalities to 'come out' at his request, until abreaction of the corpse kissing incident resulted in the disappearance of both Eve White and Eve Black, leaving Jane in complete control.

By this time a divorce had taken place, and shortly afterwards Jane met a man, Earl Lancaster, whom she married, telling him first of her position. This marriage was not in the beginning any more successful than the first, Jane proving frigid (as, indeed, the two 'Eves' had both been), egocentric and generally by no means as well balanced a personality as she had at first seemed. Domestic troubles grew worse until, realizing that she had lost her husband's affection and feeling unable to go on without it, Jane attempted suicide by taking an overdose of sleeping pills.

Before the poison could take effect however, she awoke, this time as yet another personality, completely unlike the other three but with a full knowledge of their memories. Eve Lancaster, as this personality became known, proved a far more balanced individual; she combined the best characteristics of the others, and settled down happily with her husband and child.[1]

[1] *The Three Faces of Eve* and *Strangers in My Body* are written in a racy journalese which the author of this book, concerned only with the extraction of factual information, found extremely tiresome. Much more scholarly is the report of this case, written by Drs Thigpen and Cleckley in 1954 for the *Journal of Abnormal and Social Psychology*, and so also is the paper published in the *Psychiatric Bulletin*, Vol. III, No. 4.

CHAPTER EIGHT

Psychic Phenomena

The importance of a new contribution to human knowledge can often be estimated by a consideration of the attacks made upon it by the learned world. The scientific mind is, unfortunately, only too often divided into watertight compartments, and presents the strange spectacle of the true and the false, the sublime and the ridiculous, all flourishing under the same mask of a united personality.

E. J. DINGWALL

FROM the simplest primitive tribes to the greatest civilized nations, from the equator to the poles, from the darkest childhood of the human race to present day sophisticated society; wherever and whenever man has lived there has existed a belief in what is commonly termed the supernatural—the ju-ju of witch-doctors, the prophecies of oracles, 'second sight', apparitions, hauntings, miraculous healing of the sick, omens and portents—and although such things are nowadays usually dismissed by all but the credulous as superstitious nonsense, the fact that they have persisted throughout human history lends weight to the probability that beneath the dross of mumbo-jumbo a little of the gold of truth may be found.

Until the advent in the nineteenth century of the 'age of honest doubt', belief in the actuality of most, if not all of these things was largely a matter of irrational faith, often fostered by religious leaders for their own purposes, and it was only when advancing science had made clear the value of rational and objective thinking that any serious investigation was attempted or even considered worth while. Even so, it was but a small enlightened minority who deemed these matters worthy of study, most scientists of the period disdaining to consider anything not in accordance with their tidy theories of mechanistic materialism.

Interest in the supernormal was stimulated in the early part of the nineteenth century by two things, the rise of 'spiritualism' and the great hold it took on public interest, and the frequent claims by the early mesmerists that transcendal powers were sometimes demonstrated by their entranced subjects. An increasing number of scholars and scientists then began to enquire into what Sir William Barrett has called 'that debatable borderland between the territory already conquered by science and the dark realms of superstition and ignorance ... the importance of which it is impossible to exaggerate if the alleged facts be incontestably established.'[1]

[1] *Psychical Research*, London, 1911.

The first organized investigation began with the appointment in 1869 of a Committee by members of the London Dialectical Society, the report of which declared the phenomena to be worthy of more serious attention and study. In 1882 Sir William (then Professor) Barrett convened a conference of interested enquirers, the outcome of which was the formation in the same year of the Society for Psychical Research, with the declared object of investigating 'that large group of debatable phenomena designated by such terms as mesmeric, psychical and spiritualistic'. The stated aim of the Society was 'to approach these various problems without prejudice or prepossession of any kind, and in the same spirit of exact and unimpassioned enquiry which has enabled science to solve so many problems, once not less obscure nor less hotly debated.' On the reasons for its formation Sir William Barrett was later to write,

'Those of us who took part in the foundation of the Society were convinced that amidst much illusion and deception there exists an important body of facts, hitherto unrecognized by science, which, if uncontestably established, would be of supreme importance and interest. By supplying scientific methods to their investigation these obscure phenomena are being gradually rescued from the disorderly mystery of ignorance: but this is a work not of one, but of many generations.'[1]

From its inception until the present day the S.P.R. and its American counterpart the A.S.P.R. have numbered among their members many of the world's greatest thinkers, and it has been truly said that nowhere else can there be found such a collection of the names of our most eminent men of letters and science as in the membership lists, past and present, of these societies. The records of their Past Presidents are even more imposing, and none but the wildest sceptic could, after studying them, honestly or reasonably maintain that all these distinguished people were either credulous or deluded. And yet, in the *Journals*, *Proceedings* and other publications issued over many years by them, appear many hundreds of well-attested reports of a wide variety of supernormal occurrences.

Neither are these reports to be dismissed as merely accounts from a less critical past. The work of these societies is still actively continued and similar bodies are now established in many other countries. Equally important and valuable is the research being carried out in America at the Parapsychology Laboratory of Duke University under Dr J. B. Rhine and by the Parapsychology Foundation, whose President is Eileen J. Garrett, a famous sensitive and the author of many scholarly works on the subject. In England

[1] *Psychical Research*, London, 1911.

notable work has also been accomplished by the College of Psychic Science, London.

Although there are widely differing opinions concerning much of the material investigated, in particular that which purports to be communication from the spirits of the dead, there are two important classes of phenomena, the existence of which have been proved beyond any shadow of doubt. These are telepathy or thought transference, and clairvoyance or 'second sight'.

Telepathy, a term introduced by F. W. H. Myers, describes the extra-sensory perception of the mental activities of another person.

Clairvoyance is the extra-sensory perception of *objective events* as distinguished from telepathic cognition of the mental activities of another person.

Both telepathy and clairvoyance come under the general title designated E.S.P., as does *Precognition* or cognition of a future event which could not be known through rational inference. The evidence for precognition is almost as incontrovertible as that for telepathy and clairvoyance, and there is also quite strong laboratory evidence of *Psychokinesis*, the direct influence of mind upon matter without the aid of any known physical energy or instrumentation.

Such then, is the factual background against which the 'higher phenomena' of hypnotism must be considered. To ignore, or to dismiss as baseless superstition, or to reject *a priori* as antecedently improbable to the extent of being impossible, is surely to be guilty of obscurantism of the worst kind.

CHAPTER NINE

Clairvoyance

Occurrences which, according to received theories ought not to happen, are the facts which serve as clues to new discoveries.

SIR JOHN HERSCHEL

RIGHT from the time of Mesmer, claims have constantly been made that some hypnotized subjects are able to produce what is usually termed 'the higher phenomena', and much of the early literature of psychical research is devoted to detailed, substantiated reports of experiments in which hypnotic subjects became highly psychic, such faculties as clairvoyance, telepathic perception and precognition being demonstrated on many occasions, although the subjects often revealed no such abilities when in a normal state of consciousness.

The most frequently reported type of phenomena, and that for which there is strongest evidence, is clairvoyance, variously known as 'second sight', 'open vision', 'seeing without eyes' and, by the Zulus, 'opening the gates of distance'.

It is not claimed or even suggested that hypnosis is the cause of these or similar phenomena; indeed, to many people these powers seem to be a natural endowment, unsought and sometimes even unwelcome. It is certain however that such powers, latent or otherwise, are sometimes heightened to a remarkable degree. In short, whilst hypnosis assists these faculties, it does not create them.

There is no doubt that Mesmer, although he made no public claims during his lifetime, had observed clairvoyance in a number of his patients. In his writings we find, 'At times somnambulism can perceive the past and the future by means of the inner sense', and elsewhere, 'Man, by his inner sense, is in touch with the whole of nature and is always capable of feeling the concatenation of cause and effect. Everything in the universe is present, past and future are only different relations of the separate parts.'

In his memoirs he wrote of man being 'gifted with a sensitivity by which he can be *en rapport* with the beings who surround him, even at a great distance.'

'We possess,' he wrote, 'an interior sense which is in connection with the whole of the universe, and which might be considered as an extension of sight. ... We possess the faculty of sensing in the universal harmony the connection between *events* and beings with our own *conservation*. This faculty we have in common with the other animals, though we make less use of it—it is called *instinct*.'

That Mesmer should make little known in his lifetime of his observations of these 'higher phenomena' is easily understood. He already had more than enough opposition to face without bringing down the wrath of the Catholic Church upon himself for engaging in 'occult' practices.

Some of his followers were not so reticent however, and probably the earliest record of the use of hypnosis to increase psychic powers is that of the Marquis de Puysegur, a pupil of Mesmer, who discovered that a stupid peasant lad when in a deep trance showed not only considerable intelligence but also marked clairvoyant powers.

This discovery, and that of the somnambulistic trance, de Puysegur made by accident, but he found by subsequent experiments with other somnambulant subjects that sometimes another personality would seem to emerge evincing higher faculties and clearer vision. He noted also that after the trance was terminated, no memory of what had passed during the trance seemed to remain.

Dr William Brown, Wylde Reader in Philosophy at Oxford University, famous for his hypnotic treatment of shell-shock cases during the first World War, has stated that numbers of his patients became clairvoyant while under hypnosis.

A more complex type of phenomena is that usually known as 'travelling clairvoyance', in which the subject recounts what he or she seems to see occuring at some distant place. A celebrated case is that in which Pierre Janet, the famous French psychologist, sent a hypnotic subject on what he called a 'psychic excursion' from his home at Le Havre to Paris, to see Professor Charles Richet and a Dr Gibert. The entranced subject suddenly became very agitated and cried 'It is burning!—it is burning!' It was subsequently confirmed that Richet's laboratory was in fact burnt out on that day.

A famous English hypnotist, Alexander Erskine, records that he once hypnotized the young son of a well-known diplomat and caused him to describe the actions of his father at the time. The father, who had apparently been in a rather compromising situation, was so embarrassed when told about it that he extracted a promise from Erskine never to repeat such an experiment involving him.

Dr Eugene Osty, a celebrated hypnotist and pioneer of psychical research, carried out a large number of experiments with clairvoyant subjects and advanced convincing theories to account for the phenomena he observed. One of his best known cases is the following.

At Cours-les-Barres in March 1914, an old man named Lerasle went out for a walk and failed to return. When, after a fortnight's search no trace of him had been found, a neckerchief belonging to the missing man was sent to Dr Osty to see if one of his clairvoyant somnambulists could provide any information. Dr Osty gave it to one of his hypnotic subjects, a Madame Morel, without telling her anything about it. Under hypnosis she described minutely the appearance of the old man, how he was dressed, the place where he lived, and the walk he had taken on the day of his disappearance; stating finally that his body was lying in a wood, near a stream, among thick bushes; lying on its right side, with one leg bent. She said that he had felt ill, lain down to rest, and died.

On the strength of this information a fresh search was organized, and Lerasle's body was found in exactly the spot and position described by the somnambulist. Every detail was correct except for one thing: the body was not on its side with one leg bent, but lying flat with the legs out straight.

It has been suggested as a possible explanation of the error that the neckerchief enabled the clairvoyant to establish a condition of *rapport* with the spirit of the dead man, making it possible for him to describe the events leading up to his death right until the moment when he laid down to rest; lying, as is natural, on his side. If the movements of the death agony caused the body to assume a supine position (the position of stable equilibrium in which a body agitated by convulsive movements finally stiffens) the presumption is that the dying man was in a comatose state, and as a 'spirit', did not remember it. The information he gave to the clairvoyant was therefore a true picture of his last earthly memory. This of course is not the only possible explanation.

Madame Morel became one of the best known of all hypnotic clairvoyants and Osty gave many demonstrations of her astonishing ability. A typical one was that given in response to a request by Dr Boirac, Rector of the Academy at Dijon. When asked for some article with the history of which he was familiar, Dr Boirac gave Osty a pocket manual of Esperanto. Later, after Boirac had left, Osty put Madame Morel into a hypnotic trance and placed the book in her hands, asking her what information she could give concerning its owner. The clairvoyant then described a tall, slightly built young man, saying that there was nothing very characteristic in his appearance except his eyes, which were unlike other people's. She said there was nothing wrong with them, but their form was unusual.

Then, with much circumstantial detail, she described a battle scene, the young man being wounded, his capture and subsequent death.

Osty sent an account of this seance to Dr Boirac, who replied that the book belonged to a young army officer who had recently been killed in action, the circumstances of his death being almost exactly as Madame Morel had described.

It is noteworthy that the manual of Esperanto was found in a pocket of the young officer's civilian clothes, which he last wore several months before his death. Madame Morel's description of him was confirmed as being very accurate. He was, as she said, tall and slight, and his eyelids had an unusual fold, giving him a markedly oriental appearance.

F. W. H. Myers reported a case in which a doctor arranged with a patient in a nearby village that the latter should be in a certain room at home at an agreed time. This patient was recovering from a severe illness and was very thin and emaciated.

At the appointed time the doctor placed a subject, who did not know the patient, in trance and told her to describe the occupant of the room at the patient's house. To his surprise, after describing the inside of the house correctly she said 'Is that a man?' 'Yes,' replied the doctor; 'Is he thin or fat?' 'Very fat,' she answered, 'but has he got a cork leg?'

The doctor thereupon gave up the experiment as unsuccessful.

The following morning his patient informed him that feeling too tired to stay up late, but wishing to test the clairvoyant fairly, he had stuffed his clothes tightly into the form of a corpulent human figure, and placed the resulting effigy in the room where he had agreed to sit.

One of the early American psychical researchers, Dr Osgood Mason, made a study of hypnosis in what he termed its psychical aspect, and recorded a number of cases where paranormal phenomena were apparent, in some of which he was personally concerned.

In one of these a subject whom he had first hypnotized for medical purposes later showed psychic perception and clairvoyance to a remarkable degree. Once, while she was in a state of hypnosis, he asked her if she could 'go away' and see what was happening in other places, as, for instance, her own home. She replied that she would try. He then told her to 'go to her home', which was in a small town some three hundred miles away, and of which he knew nothing, and describe the occupants of the house and what they were doing. After a minute had passed she announced that she was at the house. On being instructed, 'go in', she said, 'There is no one at home but my mother. She is sitting in the dining room by the window: there is a screen by the window which was not there when I left home. My mother is sewing.—She is making a waist (blouse) for my little brother.'

The doctor wrote down the details of her account and then terminated the hypnosis. He told the subject, who remembered nothing of what had occurred, to write to her mother asking who was in her house at the time of the experiment, where she was, and what she was doing. The mother's reply confirmed that what her daughter had described was perfectly correct.

A strange case was that of a young girl who when hypnotized and completely blindfolded, could sight read and play on the piano any piece of music put before her; even if the piece were newly composed and could not possibly be known to her. This subject, a Mlle Nydia, gave public demonstrations throughout Europe. A typical demonstration, which took place at the Théâtre de la Monnaie in Brussels, was described by a correspondent of the journal *Russie*.

'Mlle Nydia was led up to the director of music, M. Dupuys, who gave her a piece of music, of his own composition, to play; this piece had never been published. To the surprise of the audience, after holding the manuscript in her hands for one minute (her eyes always securely bandaged), Mlle Nydia sat down to the piano, and played the piece perfectly.'

In reply to a request by *Le Messager*, a psychic journal in Liége, for confirmation of the truth of this report, M. Sylvain Dupuys, the musical director, wrote stating that the facts were perfectly correct and that several doctors had witnessed the demonstration. Reporting this, *Le Messager* observed, 'It was not probable that a person in M. Dupuys's position should amuse himself in mystifying the public.'

A report of a demonstration under test conditions given at the Hotel Cecil in London reads as follows.

'... Two doctors examined her under the state of hypnosis, and declared that she was thoroughly insensible to the exterior world; alternate series of black and white bandages were placed over her eyes, and she then sat down before a grand piano. Mr Moss, the hypnotizer, then declared that she would be able to play any piece of music presented to her, however difficult it might be; he added that it would be better to hand her new, unpublished music.

'One of the persons present placed before her the score of a new opera; the hypnotist looked at his subject, and at once the latter began to play, very delicately, the music in front of her.

'Another gentleman, recently arrived from New Zealand, presented a piece which had never been played in England. Mlle Nydia played it immediately; with some dexterity she also played a piece of manuscript music composed that morning by E. German.

'Finally, a lady wrote the title of a piece of music on a scrap of paper which she enclosed in an envelope (sealed). The envelope was held to Mlle Nydia's forehead: prolonged silence. The hypnotizer drew nearer to the sensitive: at once she began to play, with much beauty of expression, the Moonlight Sonata of Beethoven.

'A few rapid passes by the hypnotizer sufficed to awaken her immediately.'[1]

No suggestion is made anywhere in this report that Mlle Nydia was not an accomplished pianist when in her normal waking state, or that hypnosis, in this case, improved her ability as a musician. The feat would have been a remarkable one however, if she had done no more than pick out the pieces of music on the piano with one finger.

More recently a Swedish psychologist, Dr John Bjorkhem of Stockholm, has carried out a vast number of hypnotic experiments involving over three thousand subjects, of which the following two examples are typical.

The hypnotized subject, a young woman, was told to 'go in her thoughts' from the flat in which the experiments were being conducted to another flat in the same building, the interior of which she had never seen. She described accurately the layout of the rooms, gave the measurements of a mirror mounted in one of the doors and correctly stated the colour, shape and position of the main items of furniture. She said there was an album on the table containing photographs (it was actually a family Bible with a section for photographs), and gave detailed descriptions of the pictures.

Another subject, a Lapp girl, once described a scene in her home which was several hundred miles away. She reported the actions of her parents, even mentioning an item in the newspaper which her father was reading. Soon afterwards the parents telephoned to enquire whether anything was amiss. *Her apparition had appeared before them*, and they had assumed that it meant bad news.

Clairvoyance in the form of *psychometry*, or object reading, is another little understood phenomenon sometimes manifested by an entranced subject. The best authenticated example is to be found in the report of the work of Dr Pagenstecher of Mexico, and his hypnotic subject Senora Reyes de Z.[2] When, during a deep trance, this subject was given an object to hold, the *rapport* seemed to be transferred from the hypnotist to the object, and she was able to obtain clear impressions of places and events connected with the object. Given a piece of Roman marble, for instance, she gave a detailed and accurate description of the Forum and its temples, and supported her description with a number of drawings. A note written by a man on the verge of apoplexy elicited a perfect description of

---

[1] *The Annals of Psychical Science*, Vol. I, pp. 191-2.
[2] 'Past Events Seership' (a Study in Psychometry), edited by Walter Franklin Prince. A.S.P.R. *Proceedings*, Vol. XVI, Part 6.

his case, whereas a blank sheet of paper enabled her to give an account of the factory where it was manufactured and the processes involved. A dead soldier's belt, articles from a church and various objects of historical significance were also psychometrized with striking success.

Senora Reyes de Z. did not merely seem to see the events taking place: she felt as if she were actually taking part in them. She stated that all her senses were alert; she heard, felt, saw and tasted, and lived in the scenes like one virtually present.

A scientific committee which investigated this case made a large number of tests which eliminated all possibility of conscious or unconscious cheating. The most striking was that in which four pieces cut from the same block of pumice stone were subjected to different treatments and then given to the subject at random. The four pieces were treated thus:

1. Soaked in tincture of gentian and asafœtida.
2. Shut up for three weeks beside a clock.
3. Rolled in sugar and saccharine.
4. Heated by burning sulphur.

The first resulted in sensations of taste, the second in an impression of rhythmic sounds, the third sweetness and the fourth a feeling of heat and the odour of sulphur dioxide.

Dr Walter Franklin Prince, who took a leading part in these investigations, devised an equally impressive experiment. In each of two identical boxes he placed a piece of silk, one piece from a church altar and the other newly obtained from the manufacturer. When he touched the first box against the sensitive's fingers she gave a vivid description of a Mexican church. In the case of the second she recounted her impressions of a French ribbon factory. On another occasion Prince handed her a garment which a farmer had been wearing when he was murdered. In spite of repeated attempts, her only impression was of a cloth factory. When, however, Prince placed her finger on a part of the garment that was stained with the dead man's boood, she gave a detailed account of the murder. Prince knew little then of the manner in which the crime was committed, and Pagenstecher even less, but subsequent enquiries proved the description to be perfectly correct.

The word psychometry was first used to describe object reading by an American doctor named Buchanan, who discovered that certain subjects were able to identify the contents of sealed envelopes by holding them to their foreheads. He also found that by doing the same with letters they were able to describe the lives and characters of the writers. The choice of this word is unfortunate, as besides being absurdly inaccurate when used in this sense, it is employed quite differently, and with more regard for its literal meaning, in experimental psychology.

A Russian doctor, Chowrin, had a subject who could not only describe the contents of sealed envelopes, but was able to recognize by touch the colours of different objects, even when they were wrapped in tissue paper. He seldom made a mistake, and when he did the error lay in the confusion of the true colour with the complementary one related to it. This subject could also experience the sense of taste through any part of his skin. For example, when pads soaked in odourless liquids were placed under his armpits he was able to identify the various tastes associated with them.

The author has experimented with a large number of subjects himself and has on occasion observed a high degree of psychic perception. He has always found however, that a given subject will produce widely varying results on different occasions, and that the information received in this manner is by no means all true. The examples following are representative of the best results so far attained.

Miss B., a young Portsmouth woman, rather excitable but with a well-balanced personality, was first hypnotized by the author for therapeutic reasons. Casual tests were made for evidence of any psychic faculty over a period of three years and were in the main negative. On the rare occasions, however, when she did demonstrate clairvoyance, it was of a high order indeed.

The author once collected a sealed parcel, the contents of which were quite unknown to him, from a friend at Brighton. He put it into his suitcase, placed the case in the boot of his car which he locked, and drove to Portsmouth where he called on Miss B., leaving the case locked in his car outside her home.

Later that day, while Miss B. was hypnotized, it occurred to the author to ask her if she could describe the contents of the parcel, about which she could have known nothing in the normal way and which had not been mentioned to her. When asked she was unable to do so, and the matter was apparently forgotten, but half an hour afterwards, just at the termination of the hypnosis, she suddenly exclaimed, 'There's a book in that packet—a big red book.'

The author was under a promise not to open the parcel, which contained a present, until the following day, his birthday. When he did so he found that it did contain a large book—the Definitive Edition of Kipling's Verse (Hodder & Stoughton, 1948). The dust jacket was grey, but on its removal the book was seen to be bright red in colour.

Planned attempts to repeat this achievement with the same subject were never successful; in fact, the only outstanding results she has produced have been of a more or less spontaneous character. She did, however, on several occasions give detailed and accurate descriptions of events taking place at the author's home in the Isle of Wight, over four sea miles away.

A rare but well authenticated form of clairvoyance demonstrated by certain somnambulists is the accurate diagnosis of disease. Sometimes termed 'autoscopy', it was the subject of an intensive study by the famous Nobel prizewinner Charles Richet, who, in addition to being a Professor of Physiology at the Faculty of Medicine of the University of Paris, was one of the greatest of all psychical researchers.

Richet experimented with a large number of subjects and patients, and his method was to give the subject an object such as a letter or a lock of hair belonging to the patient, and to note the impressions the subject received from it. In no case was the patient known to the subject or present at the time of the experiment. He summarizes some of the best results thus:

'In a case of strong diarrhoea Eugenie said, "Inflammation of the intestine". On a child with measles, Helena said, "It is measles, I saw his face all red." The best of the experiments ... Helena said, "Severe pain, choking, pain here (pointing to the epigastric region). There seems to be a sac that ought to be emptied; that sac under my heart gives me great pain." The case was one of tuberculosis, with an abcess full of pus, at the base of the left lung, accompanied by suffocation, dyspnea, and esophagitis.'[1]

Dr Herbert Mayo, F.R.S., an eminent English physiologist, once sent a lock of hair from one of his patients to an American friend in Paris. This friend gave it to a hypnotized subject, who stated that the patient was suffering from a partial paralysis of the hips and legs, also that he habitually used a surgical instrument in connection with another ailment. These statements were confirmed as perfectly correct.

Dufay, another French doctor, has recorded that he once received a letter from a friend, an army officer serving in Africa, which stated that he was ill with dysentery. Dufay enclosed the letter in two plain envelopes and took it to a somnambulist. Holding the sealed letter, she stated that it concerned a soldier who was suffering from dysentery. She said she saw him in a tent, lying on a rough bed made from boards fixed on stumps driven into the sand. He was very thin and pale. She also saw some 'women in white with beards', presumably Arabs.

On another occasion Dufay handed the same subject a packet

[1] *Thirty Years of Psychical Research*, London, 1923.

containing a piece of a necktie with which a prisoner in the local gaol had hanged himself. She affirmed that the packet contained something with which a man had killed himself, a cord or a cravat, and that he was a prisoner who had done so because he had assassinated a man with a hatchet. He had thrown the hatchet away, she said, and described the place where it was lying. In a subsequent search the hatchet was found in the location she had indicated.

The most extraordinary, but nevertheless well-attested illustration of this type of clairvoyance is undoubtedly the career of the American 'sleeping doctor', Edgar Cayce. Born in 1876 on a farm in Kentucky, U.S.A., he received but little formal education, and disliking farm life, he became an insurance salesman. At the age of twenty-one he suffered a severe attack of laryngitis which resulted in the complete loss of his voice.

Despite medical treatment and several months rest, he remained unable to speak until a travelling hypnotist attempted to cure him. The hypnotist however, in spite of repeated post-hypnotic suggestions, could only succeed in enabling Cayce to speak while under hypnosis: all his efforts to effect a permanent cure failed.

After the professional hypnotist had left the district, a local amateur hypnotist named Layne made a suggestion. He would put Cayce into a trance and then, if able to speak in this state, Cayce would try to describe the nature of his trouble and suggest a possible cure. The sufferer agreed, and when under hypnosis, to Layne's great astonishment said:

'Yes, we can see the body. In the normal physical state this body is unable to speak due to a partial paralysis of the vocal cord, produced by nerve strain. This is a psychological condition producing a physical effect. This may be removed by increasing the circulation to the affected parts by *suggestion* while in this unconscious condition.'

The hypnotist made the suggestions indicated, whereupon Cayce's throat underwent marked changes of colour. After a few minutes he spoke again,

'It's all right now. The condition is removed. Make the suggestion that the circulation return to normal and after that, the body awaken.'

Layne complied, and Cayce, on awakening, was delighted to find that he could speak normally again.

It then occurred to Layne, who suffered from stomach trouble, that if Cayce, with no medical knowledge, could diagnose for himself, he might be able to do the same for others. He therefore rehypnotized Cayce, who then diagnosed Layne's complaint and prescribed certain treatment. Layne followed the advice given and rapidly became well again.

Realizing that Cayce was in possession of a supernormal faculty of some kind, Layne suggested that they should try and see if they could help other sufferers in the same way. Cayce objected that as he knew nothing of medicine, and was not aware of what he said when hypnotized, he might give advice that would do more harm than good. He was, however, eventually prevailed upon to attempt a few experiments, but did so on the firm understanding that he would only help those in genuine need and that no payment of any kind would be accepted.

The first experiments *did* prove successful, and from then onwards Cayce devoted his life to giving what he termed his 'health readings'. These were, in time, to total over thirty thousand, and he became widely renowned as the 'sleeping doctor'.

It was discovered that the patient did not need to be present; in fact, Cayce appears to have made very many accurate diagnoses when the patients concerned were some hundreds of miles away. The only information needed was the patient's name and address and the knowledge that the patient would be at that address at an agreed time. No information concerning symptoms or anything else was required.

Cayce, who by now could practise auto-hypnosis, would lie down at the appointed time and go slowly into a trance. As he was sinking into unconsciousness, Layne would repeat the words which were invariably used.

'You will now have before you (person's name), who is now at (patient's address). You will go over this body carefully, examine it thoroughly, and tell me the conditions you will find at the present time, giving the cause of existing conditions; also suggestions for the help and relief of this body. You will answer the questions as I ask them.'

Cayce would then give a description of the patient, make a diagnosis, and prescribe treatment, using accurate and highly technical medical terminology. He normally began with the words 'We have the body', and often ended the 'reading' with 'The body is leaving now'.

If for any reason the patient was not at home as arranged, Cayce would say 'We do not have the body—we don't find him'. He often gave descriptions of the patient's home and the immediate surroundings, or reported the activities of other people in the house.

He was not always correct, but in the vast majority of cases his 'readings' were incredibly accurate. In one case, for example, that of a girl who had been certified as insane, he said that the trouble was caused by an impacted wisdom tooth impinging upon a nerve in the brain, and that extraction would effect a cure. Dental examination proved him correct, and after its removal the girl was completely restored to sanity.

A case that received wide publicity and close investigation was that of a five-year-old child Aime Dietrich, of Cayce's home town, Hopkinsville, Kentucky. Following an attack of influenza at the age of two, her mind had not developed, and she was frequently seized with convulsions. The best medical opinions had been secured, to the effect that she seemed to be suffering from a rare brain disorder which could only prove fatal.

Cayce's 'reading' was to the effect that prior to the attack of influenza, Aime had been injured in a fall from a carriage, and that her present condition was caused through the influenza germs settling in the injured part. He pronounced that osteopathic treatment could bring about a complete cure. His advice was taken and a few months of such treatment saw an absolute recovery. The girl's father subsequently swore the following statement:

'Our attention was called to Mr Edgar Cayce, who was asked to diagnose her case. By autosuggestion he went into a sleep and diagnosed her case as one of congestion at the base of the brain, stating also minor details. He outlined to Dr A. C. Layne how to proceed to cure her. Dr Layne treated her accordingly every day for three weeks, using Mr Cayce occasionally to follow up the treatment as results developed. Her mind began to clear up about the eighth day and within three months she was in perfect health, and is so to this day. The case can be verified by many of the best citizens of Hopkinsville, Kentucky.'

'Subscribed and sworn before me this
eighth day October, 1910.
Signed, D. H. Dietrich.
Gerrig Raidt, Notary Public,
Hamilton County, Ohio.'

As a result of the publicity following this case, many doctors over a wide area applied to Cayce for help in the diagnosis of difficult cases. He was reported by more than one of them to have been better than ninety per cent accurate in his 'readings' of the cases they submitted.

Later in life, Cayce, while continuing his medical work, began to employ his strange gift in other directions. A wealthy business man named Arthur Lammers, convinced of the genuine nature of Cayce's extraordinary powers, wondered if he could answer questions of a philosophical or religious kind. With some diffidence Cayce, who was a deeply religious Christian, agreed to experiment. As a test Lammers asked if certain events in his own life could be determined by astrology. Cayce, in a trance condition, replied that they were nothing to do with astrology, but connected with a previous life, in which Lammers had been a monk.

When told of this on awakening, Cayce was most distressed, for he knew nothing of such things, and considered them to be in conflict with his own strongly held religious convictions. He was, however, persuaded otherwise by Lammers, and subsequently gave over two thousand 'life readings' as he called them. In a number of these, it was claimed, research proved many statements to be correct.

In one of these readings a man was informed that in a previous life he was a Confederate soldier in the American Civil War, his former name and address being given. It is claimed that historical records verify that a person of that name had lived at the address given at the relevant time, and that he did serve in the Confederate army. Assuming this to be true, it does not, of course, offer much evidence for reincarnation, although it does appear to indicate remarkable clairvoyant ability. This question is discussed more fully in a later chapter.

Cayce, whose name, incidentally, is pronounced as 'Casey', died in 1944, but some time before his death an organization, called the Association for Research and Enlightenment, was formed with the object of carrying out research into his and similar cases. At the Association's headquarters in Virginia all the Cayce readings are filed, together with many reports and records relating to them.

It should not be assumed from these examples that clairvoyance is frequently demonstrated by hypnotic subjects, on the contrary, it is rarely evident, and seldom indeed is it of such a calibre as that evinced in the case just discussed. The ability of the subject to act out, or dramatize a suggestion, often gives the impression that clairvoyance is occurring when it is not, and verification is absolutely essential before any alleged clairvoyance can be accepted as such. That it does occur, however, is undeniable. As Richet puts it:

'It is evident that cryptesthesia (clairvoyance) can exist apart from the hypnotic state; but it is no less well established that hypnosis increases cryptesthesia. Various persons incapable of any trancendental manifestations when their senses are awake, become lucid when hypnotized.'

Before leaving the subject of clairvoyance, it should be reasserted that hypnosis is not the cause of it, but a method by which it can sometimes be enabled to function. In the words of Edmund Gurney and Frederic Myers:

'Mesmerism, if that is indeed the means by which the clairvoyant state is induced, is here no more than the gate which introduces us to an unknown world; and the questions of the method of induction (hypnotic or mesmeric) sink, one might say into insignificance, in comparison with the extraordinary problem presented by the condition itself.'[1]

[1] S.P.R. *Proceedings*, Vol. III, p. 402.

CHAPTER TEN

Telepathy

Telepathy is something that ought not to happen at all if the Materialistic theory were true. But it does happen. So there must be something seriously wrong with the Materialistic theory.

H. H. PRICE

F. W. H. Myers, who originated the term, defined telepathy as 'the communication of impressions of any kind from one mind to another, independently of the recognized channels of sense.'

Telepathy is certainly the best established of all paranormal phenomena. Its existence has been repeatedly demonstrated in the laboratory, and there are few people who, at some time or another, have not had experiences in which it appeared that some telepathic process was involved. In spite of this, our knowledge of how and why telepathy functions is but small, so small in fact that we can only express it in terms of what telepathy is *not*. We know, for instance, that it is not any form of physical force or radiation such as radio, because all these conform to the inverse square law, whereas telepathic communication does not appear to be affected in any way by distance. Dr S. G. Soal, who has carried out hundreds of experiments and written several serious works on the subject, has observed: 'There is no sense in talking about the distance between two minds, and we must consider brains as focal points in space at which Mind produces *physical* manifestations in its interaction with Matter.'[1]

We know that telepathy does not take place between all or any minds and that it happens in different degrees with different people. We know too that in cases where it does occur it is never a reliable means of communication, varying in quality from time to time in a completely unpredictable manner; in fact, when we meet alleged demonstrators of telepathy who do appear to be able to produce results at will, we automatically begin to suspect cheating. We also know that no conscious process is involved and that telepathic communication is at a subliminal or unconscious level of the mind; in other words, it is below the threshold of awareness of the participants, but we do not have more than an inkling of telepathy's true nature.

In considering hypnotically produced telepathy it must be realized that it is often uncertain whether a given phenomenon should

[1] S.P.R. *Journal*, Vol. XXXV, p. 257.

be classed as clairvoyance or as telepathy, and some of the cases described in the last chapter might well be more appropriate to this one. The following examples however, although differing widely in many respects, all have in common the illustration of an apparently direct communication between minds, without any intermediate physical processes, and are therefore truly telepathic in nature.

The condition of *rapport*, or sympathy between hypnotist and subject, is considered by a number of authorities to be more apparent than real, and to be entirely due to the suggestions of the hypnotist. Liébeault for instance, thought that the subject only remained *en rapport* with the operator because he went to sleep while thinking of him, and Bernheim held a similar opinion. Braid claimed that an artificial state was created in which subject and operator merely seemed to be *en rapport*, and Moll believed that *rapport* was caused by the suggestions, direct or indirect, of the hypnotist, or by autosuggestions resulting from the subject's conception of the nature of the hypnotic state.

All or some of which may well be true in many, possibly most, cases, but accepting that telepathy exists, there are strong reasons for believing, and none for disbelieving, that *in some cases* the condition of *rapport* is more than this, that it is in fact a direct linking or communion of two minds. This would appear true for example, in the case of du Potet mentioned in chapter two, in which he caused great confusion in his subject by giving one command verbally and a contradictory one mentally. Another indication that *rapport* is sometimes telepathic in nature is the frequently reported phenomenon known as 'community of sensation', or the perception by the subject of sensations experienced by the hypnotist.

One of the first reliable reports giving experimental evidence of community of sensation is that made in 1850 by Dr Herbert Mayo, F.R.S., a Professor of Physiology at the Royal College of Surgeons. It read:

'The entranced person, who has no feeling or taste or smell of his own, feels, tastes and smells everything that is made to tell on the sense of the operator. If mustard or sugar be put in his (the subject's) own mouth he seems not to know they are there; if mustard is placed on the tongue of the operator the entranced person expresses great disgust and tries to spit it out. The same with bodily pain. If you pluck a hair from the operator's head, the other complains of the pain you have given him.'

William A. Hammond, an American doctor of repute, reported similar results in his experiments. He stated:

'A most remarkable fact is that some few subjects of hypnotism experience sensations from impressions made upon the hypnotizer.

Thus, there is a subject upon whom I sometimes operate whom I can shut up in a room with an observer, while I go into another closed room at a distance of one hundred feet or more with another observer. This one, for instance, scratches my hand with a pin, and instantly the hypnotized subject rubs his corresponding hand, and says, 'Don't scratch my hand so'; or my hair is pulled, and immediately he puts his hand on his head and says, 'Don't pull my hair'; and so on, feeling every sensation that I experience.'

Yet another witness to the reality of these phenomena was the great physicist Sir William Barrett, F.R.S., who marvelled that their significance was so widely overlooked. He considered the reason for this to be that the pioneers of hypnotism confined their attention largely to the study of its therapeutic and anaesthetic uses, and to combating the prejudiced attacks to which they were constantly subjected by the medical profession. Here is his own account of his first experience of hypnotic thought transference.

'My own attention was directed to the subject by witnessing some hypnotic experiments made by a friend whilst staying at his country house in Westmeath, about the year 1870. Fresh from the Royal Institution in London, conversant with and fully sharing the scepticism of the scientific world of that time, as to the genuineness of these alleged marvels, I was interested but unconvinced by the experiments which I witnessed. It was not until my host allowed me to repeat the experiments and to choose the subject myself that my scepticism gave way. Selecting two or three of the village children, they were placed in a quiet room, a scrap of paper was put in the palms of their hands, and they were told to gaze at it steadily. One of their number soon passed into a sleep-waking state, and became susceptible to any suggestion, however absurd, which I might make. The others were dismissed, and the sensitive subject put into a deeper sleep by a few passes of my hand down her face and body. Lifting the eyelid of the subject and touching the eye with my finger, no reflex action, or instinctive contraction, occurred. The eyeball was turned upwards and the subject apparently was in profound slumber. Pricking her hand with a needle, no sign of feeling was evoked. My host had a medical induction coil by which powerful shocks could be administered; the terminals were placed in the hands and on the cheeks of the subject, and the current applied; no notice was taken of shocks that in the normal state it would have been impossible to bear with equanimity. When her name was called loudly by others than myself no reply was given, but when I whispered her name, however faintly, or even inaudibly and outside the room, an instant response was given. Collecting a number of things from the pantry on to a table near me, and standing behind the girl, whose eyes I had securely bandaged, I took up some salt and put it in my mouth; instantly she sputtered and exclaimed, "What for are you putting salt in my mouth?" Then I tried sugar; she said, "That's better"; asked what it was like, she said, "Sweet". Then mustard, pepper, ginger, etc., were tried; each was named, and apparently tasted by the girl when I put them in my own mouth, but when placed in her mouth she seemed to disregard them. Putting my hand over a lighted candle and slightly burning it, the subject, who was still blindfolded and had her back to me, instantly called out her hand was burnt, and showed evident pain. Nor did it make any difference when I repeated these experiments in an adjoining room, nor when every one was excluded from the room but myself and the subject.

'On another occasion, after hypnotizing the girl as before, I took a card at random from a pack in another room, noted what it was, placed it within a book, and giving the closed book to the subject asked her if she could see what was inside. She made no attempt to open the book, but held it to the side of her head and said there was something "with red spots on it". I told her to count the spots, and she said there were "five". The card was, in fact, the five of diamonds. Other cards chosen by me and concealed in a similar way were, for the most part, correctly described, though sometimes she failed, saying the things were dim. One of the most interesting experiments was made when in answer to my request that she would mentally visit London and go to Regent Street, she correctly described the optician's shop of which I was thinking. As a matter of fact, I found, upon subsequent inquiry, that the girl had never gone fifty miles away from her remote Irish village. Nevertheless, not only did she correctly describe the position of this shop, but told me of some large crystals of Iceland spar ("that made things look double") which I knew were in the shop, and that a big clock hung outside over the entrance, as was the case. It was impossible for the subject to gain any information of these facts through the ordinary channels of sense, as there was no conversation about the matter. My friend, the late Mr W. E. Wilson, F.R.S., was present when these experiments were made in his father's house, and in answer to my request he subsequently wrote to me confirming them, saying, "We proved beyond all doubt that the subject was able to read the thoughts of the mesmerizer".'[1]

Sir William Barrett considered such evidence so incontestable that he later read a paper to the British Association for the Advancement of Science, in the hope that this society would appoint a committee to investigate and report on the subject, but the idea was, he

[1] *Psychical Research*, London, 1911.

says, 'received with scorn'. A paragraph from his paper reads:

'In many other ways I convinced myself that the existence of a distinct idea in my own mind gave rise to an image of the idea in the subject's mind; not always a clear image, but one that could not fail to be recognized as a more or less distorted reflection of my own thought. The important point is that every care was taken to prevent any unconscious movement of the lips, or otherwise giving any indication to the subject, although one could hardly reveal the contents of an optician's shop by facial indications.'[1]

A few years later in 1882, the year, incidentally, in which the Society for Psychical Research was formed, Sir William Barrett carried out further experiments to ascertain whether the distance separating the hypnotist and the subject affected the results. This is his report:

'Here the subject was a lad named Fearnley, and the hypnotizer, a complete stranger to him, was a friend, Mr G. A. Smith. On one of two precisely similar cards I wrote the word "Yes", and on the other "No". Placing the hypnotized subject or percipient so that he could not see the cards I held, a request was made that he would open his hand if the card "Yes" was shown to the agent, Mr Smith, or not open it if "No" was pointed to. In this way Mr Smith, who was not in contact with the percipient, silently willed in accordance with the card shown to him. Twenty experiments were made, under the strictest conditions to avoid any possibility of information being gained by the ordinary channels of sense, and only three failures resulted. Then the subject was requested to answer aloud whether he heard me or not. When "Yes" was handed to Mr Smith he silently willed the subject should hear, when "No" that he should not hear. The object was to reduce the experiment to the simplest form to try the effect of increasing distance. In all except the first few experiments, the cards were shuffled by me with their faces downwards, and then the unknown card handed by me to Mr Smith, who looked at it and willed accordingly. This precaution was taken to avoid any possible indication being gained by the percipient from the tone in which I asked the question. After I had noted the reply, and not till then, was the card looked at by me. The percipient remained throughout motionless, with eyes closed and apparently asleep in an arm-chair in one corner of my study; it is needless to repeat that even had he been wide awake he had no means whatever of seeing which card was selected by me. Here are the results, with varying distances between the agent, Mr Smith, and the percipient, Fearnley. It must be borne in mind that not a single word was spoken, nor any sound made by Mr Smith.

[1] *Psychical Research*, London, 1911.

'At 3 feet apart, twenty-five trials were successively made, and in *every case* the subject responded, or did not respond, in exact accordance with the silent will of Mr Smith, as directed by the card selected. At 6 feet apart six similar trials were made without a single failure. At 12 feet apart six more trials were made without a single failure. At 17 feet apart six more trials were made without a single failure. In this last case Mr Smith had to be placed outside the study door, which was then closed with the exception of a narrow chink just wide enough to admit of passing a card in or out, whilst I remained in the study observing the subject.

'A final experiment was made when Mr Smith was taken across the hall and placed in the dining-room, at a distance of about 30 feet from the subject, two doors, both closed, intervening. Under these conditions three trials were made with success, the "Yes" response being, however, very faint and hardly audible to me when I returned to the study to ask the usual question after handing the card to the distant operator. At this point, the subject fell into a deep sleep and made no further replies to the questions addressed to him.

'Subsequently other trials were made under different conditions with the percipient in total darkness, with successful results. Altogether about one hundred trials were made, during which there were only four wrong answers and one doubtful one, and for these Mr Smith blamed himself rather than the percipient. Pure chance would have given about one-half right instead of the ninety-five right actually obtained.

'When the subject was awakened he said he had heard the question each time, but when he gave no answer he felt unable to control his muscles so as to frame the word.'[1]

In the following year, in collaboration with Edmund Gurney, a prominent founder member of the Society for Psychical Research, Sir William Barrett experimented in the mental transference of *pain* from hypnotist to subject. In these tests the same hypnotist, Smith, took part, and the subject was a lad named Wells. Stringent precautions were taken to prevent communication through the normal sense channels. Wells, after being hypnotized, was blindfolded, and the hypnotist stood behind his chair. One of the experimenters then silently pricked or punched the hypnotist in various parts of the body; the only words spoken being the questions to Wells asking what he felt.

Out of twenty-four such tests the exact spot in which the hypnotist had been pricked or punched was correctly given by Wells twenty times. Equally striking results were obtained with another

[1] *Psychical Research*, London, 1911.

subject, who was also successful in a transference of taste experiment similar to those previously described.

Shortly afterwards in France, Pierre Janet, the psychologist, carried out almost identical experiments and attained similar successful results. Even more strict test conditions were observed in the experiments made by Professor and Mrs Sidgwick at Brighton in 1889, some of which were witnessed by Sir William Barrett, and in which the hypnotist Smith again participated. On some occasions hypnotist and subject occupied different rooms without any noticeable effect on the results. It was here observed that the degree of success varied, for no apparent reason, from day to day. The transfer of mental pictures was also carried out with similar results, the tests proving fruitless on one day and astonishingly successful on another. Professor Sidgwick, it should be noted, was the first President of the Society for Psychical Research, and a man whose integrity is beyond question.

A similar experience was reported, unfortunately without any corroboration, by a clergyman, the Rev. C. H. Townshend, whose word there seems to be no reason for doubting. He stated that if he were hurt in any part of his body while he had a young female subject hypnotized, she appeared to suffer pain in a corresponding part of her own body. She also, he claimed, could identify a substance if he tasted it.

James Esdaile, one of the best known early medical hypnotists, who caused a sensation by performing numerous major surgical operations using hypnosis as an anaesthetic, once hypnotized a young Hindu, and then instructed an assistant to pass to him (Esdaile) in whatever order he wished, some salt, a piece of lime, a piece of gentian, and some brandy. As they were tasted by Esdaile, the subject named each one correctly.

Dr Elliotson, a contemporary of Esdaile's, and equally well known as a pioneer hypnotist, reported that he had repeated these experiments with similar success. Professor William Gregory, in his book *Animal Magnetism* wrote 'I have seen and tested the fact of community of sensation in so many cases that I regard it as firmly established'. Further experiments on similar lines were also made by Malcolm Guthrie, who confirmed transference from hypnotist to subject of various smells, pains, tastes and diagrams under exceptionally strict conditions.

It will have been noted that in a number of the cases just referred to, the subject was sometimes separated from the hypnotist by an appreciable distance, and this leads us to the consideration of *telepathic hypnotism*, as Myers termed it, or hypnosis induced by a purely mental process or an effort of will. In passing to this consideration it is appropriate to quote the conclusions in this respect arrived at by the Committee of the French Academy of Medicine appointed to investigate 'magnetism' in 1826. The relevant section of the report, made in 1831, reads thus:

'Lorsqu'on a fait tomber une fois une personne dans le sommeil magnétique, on n'a pas toujours besoin de recourir au contact et aux passes pour la magnétiser de nouveau. La regard du magnétiseur, sa volonté seule, ont sur elle le même influence. Dans ce cas, on peut non-seulement agir sur le magnétisé, mais encore le mettre complètement en somnambulisme et l'en faire sortir à son insu, hors de sa vue, à une certaine distance et au travers des portes fermées.'

One of the earliest reliable reports of the induction of hypnosis by a seemingly telepathic process is that by Esdaile, in which he claims to have succeeded in hypnotizing a blind man on a number of occasions by gazing at him from a distance of twenty yards. To eliminate sensory impressions he used to gaze at the man over a wall, and often experimented at 'untimely hours, when he could not possibly know of my being in his neighbourhood, and always with like results'.

In a paper to the Société de Psychologie Physiologique, in 1885, Pierre Janet, then a young neurologist, stated that he had witnessed and could confirm the claims made by a Dr Gibert of Le Havre that one of his patients could be entranced by an effort of will. Not only had he seen Dr Gibert perform this feat, but he himself had been able to do likewise. On one occasion he had surprised Gibert when the doctor was engaged on other matters and asked him to hypnotize his patient there and then. The patient was not in Gibert's house at the time, but in another building some distance away. In spite of this the attempt was verified by Janet as completely successful.

This report caused such great interest and argument that a few months later a series of experiments were made, under the strictest controlled conditions, by a group of eminent investigators, included among whom were F. W. H. Myers and his brother Dr A. T. Myers. The results of these experiments were so astounding that justice cannot be done to them without quoting the full report. Here therefore is the complete account given by F. W. H. Myers:

'Madame B., the subject of these researches, is of a very different type. She is a heavy, middle-aged, peasant woman, with a patient, stolid expression, and a very limited intelligence and vocabulary. She has, indeed, been more or less somnambulic from childhood, and a Dr Féron, since dead, and other persons, seem to have experimented on her long ago. But she has never made hypnotism her business; she was drawn to Havre by some medical kindness received from Dr Gibert; and care is taken that she shall not make money out of her stay. Her trance-state is never mentioned to her in her normal state; nor does she in any way seek notice as a "sensitive"; on the contrary, she plainly dislikes being sent to sleep from a distance, and has repeatedly tried to prevent it. I have seen her only in the trance-state, and I share the general impression that what she says in that state is naively and sincerely said, and probably gives a true account of her own feelings and actions.

'I will now briefly summarize M. Janet's principal results.

'a. Induction of trance in presence of close proximity of subject.

'Sleep usually induced by holding her hand. She is then only responsive to the operator. He alone can make contractures disappear, &c. Gaze from operator's eye unnecessary. Slight pressure of thumb suffices; but no pressure (except *severe* pressure on thumb) is efficacious without mental concentration—operator's *will* to put her to sleep. "This influence of the operator's *thought*, extraordinary, as it may seem, is here quite preponderant; so much so that it can take the place of all other influences." Will *without* touch induces sleep. Taking precautions to avoid suggestion, it is found that (1) M. Janet, while sitting near her, sends her to sleep when, and only when, he wills it; (2) M. Gibert from adjoining room sends her to sleep, M. Janet remaining near her, but not willing; there is evidence that the sleep is of *M. Gibert's* induction, for she is in *rapport* with him only; whereas had sleep come from suggestion of operator's proximity, the suggestion would probably have been derived from *M. Janet's* close presence. Nevertheless, she did know that Dr Gibert was in the house. (The question as to degrees of proximity will be discussed later on.)

'b. Induction of trance at a distance from subject.

'Oct. 3, 1885. M. Gibert tries to put her to sleep from distance of half a mile; M. Janet finds her awake; puts her to sleep; she says, "I know very well that M. Gibert tried to put me to sleep, but when I felt him I looked for some water, and put my hands in cold water. I don't want people to put me to sleep in that way; it puts me out, and makes me look silly." She had, in fact, held her hands in water at the time when M. Gibert willed her to sleep.

'Oct. 9. M. Gibert succeeds in a similar attempt; she says in trance, "Why does M. Gibert put me to sleep from his house? I had not time to put my hands in my basin." That the sleep was of M. Gibert's induction was shown by M. Janet's inability to wake her. M. Gibert had to be sent for.

'It is observable, however, that MM. Janet and Gibert can *now* (April 1886) operate interchangeably on the subject; her familiarity with both seems to enable either to wake her from a trance which the other has induced.

'Oct. 14. Dr Gibert again succeeded in inducing the trance, from a distance of two-thirds of a mile, at an hour suggested by a third person, and not known to M. Janet, who watched the patient.

'c. Influence exercised from a distance during trance.

'On Oct. 14 she had been put to sleep at 4.15 as aforesaid. At 5, at 5.5, and at 5.10 she rose, exclaimed, "Enough, don't do that," then laughed once, and added, "You can't; if you are the least distracted I recover myself," and fell back into deep sleep. At those moments M. Gibert had attempted to make her perform certain acts in her sleep. Similar results followed from a mental command given in her proximity during her sleep.

'd. Deferred mental suggestion.

'On Oct. 8 M. Gibert pressed his forehead to hers, and gave a *mental* order (I omit details, precautions, &c.) to offer a glass of water at 11.30 a.m. next day to each person present. At the hour assigned she showed great agitation, took a glass, came up from the kitchen, and asked if she had been summoned, came and went often between *salon* and kitchen; was put to sleep from a distance by M. Gibert; said, "I had to come; why will they make me carry glasses? I had to say something when I came in." Two somewhat similar experiments were made October 10th and 13th.

'Thus far M. Janet's account of the autumn experiments, postponing any description of the *stages* through which the subject passed. In February and in April, 1886, Madame B. was again brought to Havre, and some successful experiments (tabulated below) were made before my arrival on April 20th.

'I give next my own notes of experiments, April 20-24th, taken at the time in conjunction with Dr A. T. Myers, and forming the bulk of a paper presented to the Société de Psychologie Physiologique on May 24th.

'I have been asked to write an account of some instances of somnambulic sleep induced at a distance, which I observed at Havre, through the kindness of Dr Gibert and Professor Pierre Janet, April 20-24th, 1886. This account is founded on notes taken by me at the time, and revised on the same or following days by Dr A. T. Myers, who was present at the experiments throughout. Other observers were Dr Gibert, Professor Paul Janet, Professor Pierre Janet, Dr Jules Janet, Dr Ochorowicz, and M. Marillier, some of whom have given, or are about to give, independent accounts.

'I shall confine myself to the cases of production of sleep at a distance by mental suggestion, with one case of deferred mental suggestion of an act to be performed. In order that the phenomenon of *sommeil à distance* may be satisfactory, we have to guard against three possible sources of error, namely, fraud, accidental coincidence, and suggestion by word or gesture.

'The hypothesis of *fraud* on the part of operators or subject may here be set aside. The operators were Dr Gibert and Professor Pierre Janet, and the detailed observations of Professor Pierre Janet, elsewhere published, sufficiently prove the genuineness of Madame B.'s somnambulic sleep. And, in fact, to anyone accustomed to hypnotic phenomena the genuine character of Madame B.'s trance is readily apparent.

'The hypothesis of *accidental coincidence* would be tenable (though not probable) did the events of April 20-24th constitute the whole of the observed series. But the number of coincidences noticed by Dr Gibert, Professor Janet, and others has been so large that the action of mere chance seems to be quite excluded. It is to be observed that, as Professor Janet tells us, the subject has, during an observation of several weeks (maintained by Mlle Gibert when Professor Janet is not present), only twice fallen *spontaneously* into this somnambulic sleep (when no one willed her to do so); once before our arrival, on looking at a picture of Dr Gibert, and once on April 31st, as narrated below. On the other hand, the observed cases of sleep deliberately induced from a distance amount, I believe, to at least a dozen. I exclude, of course, the very numerous occasions when sleep has been induced by an operator present with the patient, by holding her thumbs, looking at her, &c. This, however, brings us to the third source of doubt, whether the sleep may not on *all* occasions have been induced by some *suggestion*, given perhaps unconsciously, by word or gesture. It was thus that I was at first inclined to explain Cases I and II among those that follow, but the other cases here given seem to negative the supposition.

'I still, however, would explain by mere suggestion all the experiments which I saw made with the *magnet*. On one occasion, when I had gone into an adjoining room with the magnet, and this was known to all present, Madame B. followed me, as though attracted. She was taken back to her place, and shortly afterwards I came and sat beside her with the magnet in my pocket, no one knowing that it was there. No effect whatever was produced on the subject. I made some other experiments with the magnet, with a similarly negative result. I would strongly recommend that when magnetic experiments are made with sensitives the following precautions should be used, which our experience in the Society for Psychical Research has shown to be necessary for the exclusion of suggestion.

'1. Only electro-magnets should be employed, in order to effect sudden and noiseless transitions from the presence to the absence of magnetic force.

'2. The operator in charge of the commutator should be in a different room from the subject.

'3. Care should be taken that no indication as to the state of the magnet should be drawn from the "magnetic click" which accompanies the magnetization of the electro-magnet. (The subject's ears may be stopped, or the click repeated many times running, so that it is impossible to tell whether there have been an even or uneven number of clicks, and consequently whether the condition of the instrument is or is not changed.)

'It is not necessary here to go into further detail. Suffice it to say that it is not safe to trust to an apparently lethargic or anaesthetic state in the subject as a guarantee against her gathering suggestions from the words or manner of persons present. If, moreover, she be susceptible of mental suggestion, the effects of such suggestion may be mistaken for the effects of magnetic influence.

'I. I pass on to describe the first case of *sommeil à distance*, April 21st. At 5.50 p.m. (an hour which was selected by drawing lots among various suggested hours), Dr Gibert retired to his study and endeavoured to send Madame B. to sleep in the Pavillon, at a distance of about two-thirds of a mile. She was to fall asleep in the *salon*; whereas she habitually sits in the *kitchen* of the Pavillon (a house occupied by Dr Gibert's sister).

'It was supposed that the command would take about 10 minutes to operate, and at about six Professor Janet, Dr Ochorowicz, M. Marillier, my brother and myself entered the Pavillon, but found that Madame B. was not in the *salon* but in the kitchen. We immediately went out again, supposing that the experiment had failed. A few minutes later Professor Janet re-entered with M. Ochorowica, and found her asleep in the *salon*. In the somnambulic state she told us that she had been in the *salon*, and nearly asleep when our arrival startled her, and had then rushed down to the kitchen to avoid us; had returned to the *salon* and fallen asleep as soon as we left the house. These movements were attested by the *bonne*, but it of course seemed probable that it was merely our arrival which had suggested to her that she was expected to fall asleep.

'On this day she was ill and exhausted from too prolonged experiments on the previous days. In the afternoon she fell asleep of her own accord, and in the late evening (11.35 p.m.), when she had long been in bed, M. Gibert willed that her natural sleep should be transferred into somnambulic, and that she should dress and go into the garden of the Pavillon. Nothing followed on this attempt, unless an unusually prolonged sleep and complaints of unwonted headache next day were to be in any way connected herewith. On the whole, had I left after these experiments only I should have referred the phenomena to suggestion of the ordinary hypnotic kind.

'II. On the morning of the 22nd, however, we again selected by lot an hour (11 a.m.) at which M. Gibert should will, from his dispensary, (which is close to his house,) that Madame B. should go to sleep in the Pavillon. It was agreed that a rather longer time should be allowed for the process to take effect; as it had been observed (see M. Janet's previous communication,) that she sometimes struggled against the influence, and averted the effect for a time by putting her hands in cold water, etc. At 11.25 we entered the Pavillon quietly, and almost at once she descended from her room to the *salon*, profoundly asleep. Here, however, suggestion might again have been at work. We did not, of course, mention M. Gibert's attempt of the previous night. But she told us in her sleep that she had been very ill in the night, and repeatedly exclaimed: "Pourquoi M. Gibert m'a-t-il fait souffrir? Mais j'ai lave les mains continuellement." This is what she does when she wishes to avoid being influenced.

'III. In the evening (22nd) we all dined at M. Gibert's, and in the evening M. Gibert made another attempt to put her to sleep at a distance from his house in the Rue Sery—she being at the Pavillon, Rue de la Ferme—and to bring her to his house by an effort of will. At 8.55 he retired to his study; and MM. Ochorowicz, Marillier, Janet, and A. T. Myers went to the Pavillon, and waited outside in the street, out of sight of the house. At 9.22 Dr Myers observed Madame B. coming half-way out of the garden-gate, and again retreating. Those who saw her more closely observed that she was plainly in the somnambulic state, and was wandering about and muttering. At 9.25 she came out (with eyes persistently closed, so far as could be seen), walked quickly past MM. Janet and Marillier, without noticing them, and made for M. Gibert's house, though not by the usual or shortest route. (It appeared afterwards that the *bonne* had seen her go into the *salon* at 8.45, and issue thence asleep at 9.15: had not looked in between those times.) She avoided lampposts, vehicles, &c., but crossed and recrossed the street repeatedly. No one went in front of her or spoke to her. After eight or ten minutes she grew much more uncertain in gait, and paused as though she would fall. Dr Myers noted the moment in the Rue Faure; it was 9.35. At about 9.40 she grew bolder, and at 9.45 reached the street in front of M. Gibert's house. There she met him, but did not notice him, and walked into his house, where she rushed hurriedly from room to room on the ground-floor. M. Gibert had to take her hand before she recognized him. She then grew calm.

'M. Gibert said that from 8.55 to 9.20 he thought intently about her; from 9.20 to 9.35 he thought more feebly; at 9.35 he gave the experiment up, and began to play billiards; but in a few minutes began to will her again. It appeared that his visit to the billiard-room had coincided with her hesitation and stumbling in the street. But this coincidence may of course have been accidental.

'IV. Later in the evening M. Gibert made to her a *mental suggestion*, by pressing his forehead against hers without other gesture or speech. The suggestion (proposed by me) was that at 11 a.m. on the morrow she should look at a photographic album in the *salon* of the Pavillon. She habitually sat in the kitchen or in her own bedroom and sewed; so this was an unlikely occupation for a morning hour.

'On April 23rd, MM. Marillier and Ochorowicz went to the Pavillon before 11 and ensconced themselves in a room opposite the *salon*. At 11 Madame B. entered the *salon* and wandered about with an anxious, preoccupied air. Professor Janet, Dr Myers and I entered the Pavillon at 11.10 and found her obviously entranced; eyes open, but fixed; anxious, wandering.

'She continued thus till 11.25. We remained in a room where she could not see us, though, by looking through the partially-opened door, we could see her. At 11.25 she began to handle some photographic albums on the table of the *salon*; and at 11.30 was seated on the sofa fixedly looking at one of these albums, open on her lap, and rapidly sinking into lethargic sleep. As soon as the talkative phase of her slumber came round she said, "M. Gibert m'a tourmentée, parce qu'il m'a recommandée—il m'a fait trembler."

"I believe that this was a genuine instance of deferred mental suggestion. But where a suggestion is known to so many persons as was the case here, it is hard to feel sure that no word has been uttered by any one which could give a clue to its nature.

'V. On this same day, 23rd, M. Janet, who had woke her up and left her awake, lunched in our company, and retired to his own house at 4.30 (a time chosen by lot) to try to put her to sleep from thence. At 5.5 we all entered the *salon* of the Pavillon, and found her asleep with shut eyes, but sewing vigorously (being in that stage in which movements once suggested are automatically continued). Passing into the talkative state, she said to M. Janet, "C'est vous qui m'avez fait dormir à quatre heures et demi." The impression as to the hour may have been a suggestion received from M. Janet's mind. We tried to make her believe that it was M. Gibert who had sent her to sleep, but she maintained that she had felt that it was M. Janet.

'VI. On April 24th the whole party chanced to meet at M. Janet's house at 3 p.m., and he then, at my suggestion, entered his study to

No. of Experiments	Date	Operator	Hour when Given	Remarks	Success or Failure
	1885				
1	Oct. 3	Gibert	11.30 a.m.	She washes hands and wards off trance	½
2	,, 9	,,	11.40 a.m.	Found entranced 11.45.	1
3	,, 14	,,	4.15 p.m.	Found entranced 4.30: had been asleep about 15 minutes	1
	1886				
4	Feb. 22	Janet		She washes hands and wards off trance	
5	,, 25	,,	5 p.m.	Asleep at once	1
6	,, 26	,,		Mere discomfort observed	0
7	March 1	,,		,, ,, ,,	
8	,, 2	,,	3 p.m.	Found asleep at 4: had slept about an hour.	1
9	,, 4	,,		Will interrupted: trance coincident but incomplete	1
10	,, 5	,,	5-5.10 p.m.	Found asleep a few minutes afterwards	1
11	,, 6	Gibert	8 p.m.	Found asleep 8.3.	1
12	,, 10	,,		Success—no details	1
13	,, 14	Janet	3 p.m.	Success—no details	1
14	,, 16	Gibert	9 p.m.	Brings her to his house: she leaves her house a few minutes after 9	1
15	April 18	Janet		Found asleep in 10 minutes	1
16	,, 19	Gibert	4 p.m.	Found asleep 4.15	1
17	,, 20	,,	8 p.m.	Made to come to his house	1
18	,, 21	,,	5.50 p.m.	My case I: trance too tardy	0
19	,, 21	,,	11.35 p.m.	Attempt at trance during sleep: see my case I	0
20	,, 22	,,	11 a.m.	Asleep 11.25: trance too tardy: my case II: count as failure	0
21	,, 22	,,	9 p.m.	Comes to his house: leaves her house 9.15: my case III	1
22	,, 23	Janet	4.30 p.m.	Found asleep 5.5, says she has slept since 4.30: my case IV	1
23	,, 24	,,	3 p.m.	Found asleep 3.30, says she has slept since 3.5: my case VI	1
24	May 5	,,		Success—no details	1
25	,, 6	,,		Success—no details	1
					19

will that Madame B. should sleep. We waited in his garden, and at 3.20 proceeded together to the Pavillon, which I entered first at 3.30, and found Madame B. profoundly sleeping over her sewing, having ceased to sew. Becoming talkative, she said to M. Janet, "C'est vous qui m'avez commandée." She said that she fell asleep at 3.5 p.m.

'Professor Janet's paper in the *Revue Philosophique* for August, 1886, enables me to give a conspectus of the experiments on *sommeil a distance* made with Madame B. up to the end of May. M. Janet makes his total 22 trials, 16 successes, but he seems to have omitted the experiments of October, 1885. The distance was in each case between ¼ mile and 1 mile.

'We have thus 19 coincidences and 6 failures—the failures all more or less explicable by special circumstances. During Madame B.'s visits to Havre, about 2 months in all, she once fell into ordinary sleep during the day, and twice (as already mentioned) became spontaneously entranced, one of these times being on April 21, a day of illness and failure. She never left the house in the evening except on the three occasions on which she was willed to do so (experiments 14, 17, 21). Trials of this kind had to be made after dark, for fear her aspect should attract notice. The hours of the other experiments were generally chosen at the moment, to suit the operators' convenience; sometimes, as I have said above, they were chosen by lot.'[1]

Commenting on these experiments at a later date Myers observes:

'Of course it is plain that if one can thus influence unexpectant persons from a distance, there must be sometimes some kind of power actually exercised by the hypnotizer—something beyond the mere tact and impressiveness of address, which is all that Bernheim and his followers admit or claim. Evidence of this has been afforded by the occasional production of organic and other effects in hypnotized subjects by the unuttered will of the operator when near them.'[2]

Another class of phenomenon, almost certainly of a telepathic nature, is that known as Exteriorisation of Sensibility, in which the senses of the subject appear to be transferred to such objects as photographs, wax dolls, or even glasses of water. In 1892, de Rochas recorded that a subject when in a deep trance was touched by a glass of water, and that after the subject had gone to bed the water was put out in the cold, causing the subject to complain next day of feeling bitterly cold in the night. The same subject, if given a wax doll to hold when in trance, later complained of pain in the equiva-

[1] S.P.R. *Proceedings*, Vol. IV, pp. 129-137. [2] *Human Personality*, London, 1903.

lent places when the doll was pricked by a pin. Other famous early hypnotists, notably de Luys and Dupony, achieved the same result using photographs.

Similar experiments to these have been carried out recently by Jarl Fahler, President of the Society for Psychical Research in Finland. Some of these were made in Finland and others at Duke University. Several witnesses and a stenographer were always present. Two similar glasses of water were placed on a table in front of a hypnotized subject. Fahler took one glass and placed it in the subject's hands, suggesting to her that 'all sense of feeling and pain was being drained' from her arms and hands into the water in the glass she was holding, and that her extremities had lost all feeling.

It was then found that when a needle was stuck into the glass the subject reacted, but there were no reactions when her arms and hands were pricked.

The same result was obtained when the glass was taken from the subject and placed on the table. Various people repeated this test with identical results.

Fahler took the glass into another room, from where he could not be seen by anyone in the experiment room. He stuck the needle into the water ten times, and the subject reacted ten times.

Another person then took the glass into the entrance hall and, closing the door behind him, carried out four similar tests. Prior to his return it was observed that the subject reacted strongly four times.

On his return he confirmed that he had pricked the water four times.

Many variations of these tests were made with equally successful results, even when the glass was taken away from the subject and into another room. In one test the subject was observed to smile and move her arms, and when asked why she did this said that someone was blowing warm and then cold air on her arms. When the experimenter who had taken the glass returned, he confirmed that he had been blowing on the surface of the water in the glass.

Further variations included the substitution of different objects for the glass of water, including an apple and even another person, with little effect on the success of the experiment.

Fahler also carried out a further series of tests using post-hypnotic suggestions, in which an article was hidden in one room while the hypnotized subject remained in another. The subject was informed that the article was being hidden and told that when she woke she would go and find it. On awakening, the subject went straight to the hiding place, explaining that she seemed to have been 'dragged towards it'.

The author has repeated some of Fahler's experiments with varying degrees of success, the results being negative in most cases. With one particular subject, however, quite impressive results were obtained in the post-hypnotic tracing of hidden articles. There seemed to be little doubt that in this case the process was telepathic for when the article, a small button, was placed somewhere in the room and the experimenter was aware of its locality, the subject was usually able to find it almost at once; but when the experimenter threw the button into the room over his shoulder, so that he had no idea of its position, the subject was not only unable to find it, but declared, on entering the room, that she would not be able to do so.

Precautions were, of course, taken to ensure that the subject received no visual or auditory clues, and she was never told more than that the button was 'being hidden'. It was found, as in Fahler's experiments, that one particular subject was far more successful than any of the many others tested.

The next, and last two cases to be cited seem so fantastic that the author would have hesitated to include them had they come from a less authoritative source, but Dr Nandor Fodor is a psycho-analyst and parapsychologist of international repute and it is inconceivable that he would report them without good reason for believing in their authenticity.[1] Both illustrate the action of one mind upon another at a distance, not merely to hypnotize, but to bring about the *death* of the subject.

The first concerns a woman who dabbled in 'Black Magic' (she had on one occasion hypnotized a young boy who lived with her and commanded him to 'Go to hell and bring up the devil', with frightening results), and from whose house some silver spoons were missing. She suspected that a former employee, a cook, had stolen them, and angered, voiced the wish that 'Whoever stole the spoons would drop dead—then I would know'. She noticed that the time at which she uttered this imprecation was eleven o'clock. The next day she was informed by her chauffeur that the former servant, who could not have known in the normal way of the curse, had dropped dead in the street at precisely that time.

The other is of a Canadian who in wartime had managed, with an accomplice, to trick a German spy ring out of a large sum of money and had hidden it instead of handing it over to the government. He was suspected by government agents who failed to find the money but who did discover the name of his accomplice. Realizing that this man, if caught, would confess their joint guilt, he concentrated mentally on him, willing him to commit suicide. His attempt almost backfired, however, for the accomplice entered the

[1] *The Haunted Mind*, New York, 1959.

other's house in his absence and shot himself dead with a revolver which he found there. The next day the 'mental killer' was arrested on a charge of murder, but was released when he proved that the accomplice had free access to his house.

'But if there is such a thing as psychic murder,' he told Fodor, 'I was certainly guilty of it.'

There is no proof, of course, that the deaths in these two instances were actually caused by the persons to whom they were attributed, but they bear a striking similarity to the many cases recorded in the literature on witchcraft and black magic, also to recent accounts of killing at a distance by the witch-doctors and clever-men of primitive races.

In assessing the material of which this chapter is comprised, it will be profitable to consider the advice of Albert Moll, probably the greatest and certainly the most scientific of the leading nineteenth century hypnotists. He says:

'In order to understand the gradual development of modern hypnotism we must distinguish two points: first, that there are human beings who can exercise a personal influence over others, either by direct contact or even from a distance; and second, the fact that particularly psychical states can be induced in human beings by certain physical processes.'[1]

Telepathy is not hypnotism, and hypnotism is not telepathy. Both occur independently of each other, but sometimes, rarely it is true, they can and do occur together.

[1] *Hypnotism*, London, 1909.

CHAPTER ELEVEN

Mediumistic Phenomena

Man can learn nothing unless he proceeds from the known to the unknown.
CLAUDE BERNARD

IT is impossible to venture far into the strange world of psychical research without becoming involved, to some degree at least, in the subject of spiritualism, or spiritism as it is sometimes, and more accurately, termed; indeed, to the disinterested layman psychical research and spiritualism are, unfortunately, often regarded as synonymous. Although the so-called spiritualistic phenomena are a proper and important object of enquiry for the psychical researcher, their study, or for that matter their acceptance as factual, does not by any means imply the acceptance of the spiritualistic explanations of them. It is not proposed here to enter into the question of the truth or otherwise of communication with the spirits of the dead, but to examine certain of the phenomena in the light of our knowledge of hypnosis.

These phenomena, termed mediumistic because a sensitive person is alleged to act as an intermediary or *medium* through whom the discarnate are enabled to communicate with the incarnate, are of several kinds, ranging from automatic writing, in which the hand of the medium seems to be controlled by the 'communicator', through clairvoyantly or 'clairaudiently' perceived impressions of those on the 'other side', to deep trance states in which, it is claimed, a 'guide' or control takes charge of the medium's body.

In the early days of the spiritualist 'movement', before the study of psychology had made us aware of the complexity of human personality, it was no doubt reasonable to accept these seeming communications for what they purported to be, but our present knowledge of the phenomena associated with hypnosis, in particular dissociation and multiple personality, lays many of the spiritualist's claims open to question. This is not to say that *all* such claims can be so explained; indeed, in the author's opinion there are many cases in which the 'spirit' hypothesis seems to be the only plausible one.

In passing it is worthy of note that many of the most famous spiritualistic mediums began their psychic careers as hypnotic subjects, and hypnosis has been used with marked success in the development of a number of others. Outstanding among the latter is

Mrs Eileen J. Garrett, regarded by many as the world's finest present-day medium, who, unlike most sensitives, possesses an objective outlook and brings a keen intellect to bear upon the subject. Also unlike the general run of mediums, who object to sitting with serious investigators on the grounds that they 'spoil the conditions' or 'lower the vibrations', Mrs Garrett has submitted to many scientific tests in her desire to further our knowledge of the workings of mediumship, and she, in refreshing contrast to the usual airy-fairy claims of most mediums to 'higher spiritual powers' and such like, boldly asserts that the mediumistic trance is a form of auto-hypnosis. She says:

'In my own case, auto-hypnotic trance developed as part of an innocent escape process in childhood days. I continue to practise it. Perhaps a desire to escape plays a part, having its origin in the day-dreaming and imaginary play of a child who had few close play-mates. Later in life, self-hypnosis developed to a point where it became identified with amnesia. Eventually it grew into a means for perceiving and receiving information from the living—clairvoy-antly, telepathically—and apparently from the dead, through mediumship.

'First, then, what do I mean by self-hypnosis? It is withdrawal from the conscious self into an area of the non-conscious self, where the objective mind can no longer invent nor predict activity. And yet, within this other mind, life is being worked out on a different level—a level not particularly identified with others, nor with the self as such, but a place within, an inner world, where a battery of symbols takes over its own area of rhythmic sound and colour.

'These symbols fall into place, to create an imagery that is un-related to local life feelings or immediate needs of the body. One floats, as it were, as does the unborn infant, in an ocean of colour and light. This can be a frightening experience, if one comes upon it suddenly in one's maturity. I had the good fortune to enter it at an early age, when the mind, not too far removed from the mystery of birth, was able to accept wider dimensions in time and space, with-out being frightened by religious and everyday patterns of maturity. The realm of mystery had not yet departed. What might be re-garded as alien and dangerous by the adult world had no power to inflict doubt on the mind of the child.

'The acts of imitation within an objective world, where youth learns its responses in the process of growth, were not necessary; instead, an effective annihilation of too much dependence on others took place, so that the child became coherent to herself and yet remained "active" within the great field of symbology which finally she learned to bring under disciplined control. By keeping this door open to the inner territory of the self, one continues to live within this instructive wonder world of self-awareness. Within this level of experience one knows that there is a dwelling place for anonymous forms, minute as well as great—and at times overwhelming—from which the objective mind draws, and knows how to create its own colour and strength.

'To-day, in order to place myself in an auto-hypnotic trance, I begin by suggesting to myself that I am withdrawing from the world of reality. In a moment I close my eyes to the external world. I am no longer listening nor taking note of anything. I am going within, within, and within.

'This is more or less an automatic process. Gradually I begin to feel a sense of excitement in the lower areas of the body. As though I had pulled a lever in the mind, a change in perceptiveness enables me to listen to myself speak. And I am speaking from a region that is more basic and authoritative, so it automatically seems to me to sound more definite than if I were speaking with my eyes open.

'I then slow down the speaking process, until the time comes that I withdraw deeper and further away, into a stage of absolute quiet, where I know that everything in the mind will really cease to be of any particular importance.

'Then comes the moment when I have finished shifting gears. I become aware that I now have to produce, as it were, a new method of breathing. Eventually I will want to take more oxygen and I will yawn the conscious mind out of existence and begin to operate on another level.

'I am often asked whether it is easier to go into an auto-hypnotic mediumistic trance than it is to be placed under hypnosis by a physician. In the auto-hypnotic trance there is a sense of travel, of getting away from everything. On the other hand, when placed under hypnosis by the physician, I am always peculiarly mentally alert. I am listening to what he tells me; at the same time, I am telling myself that I must be in contact with him on another level, so that I will be ready, anxious and willing to obey.

'Nevertheless, as he talks to me I am fast losing active consciousness and I am setting up, as it were, two gateways: one through which his words may reach me all the time; and another, through which my own mind will not function. So, working with a hypnotist gives me a much more restricted area than I have when I work auto-hypnotically.

'The mediumistic trance utilizes more than just the normally automatic consciousness that operates through known senses. It calls upon an additional consciousness, seems to insist on examining taking in everything, even though it may not be comprehended.

Now, when we let that idea of the consciousness emerge, it displays so much energy, it has so much more "life", so much more to give of energy, that there is the tendency for internal drama to be personified, that the inner excitement may show itself through all kinds of histrionics that are difficult to discipline. The mind, released from what we would call the ordinary "normal" way of our thinking, is frisking about like a young dog ready to fetch and carry all kinds of the most exciting bits of stuff that it finds on the way.

'Our minds, like the atmosphere, would seem to be loaded with bits and pieces of thought or fact. We are like birds, going out to gather oddments from which to make what we might call "the nest of the mind". This process goes on, whether under auto-hypnosis, or hypnosis from the outside. The essential difference is that, under hypnosis, I am subject to the hypnotist's wish and will, as soon as a condition of empathy has been established.

'Auto-hypnosis, on the other hand, places me under my own suggestion. In a sense, it permits me to roam more widely. But this is largely a matter of degree. In both instances, the same reactions and mechanisms are at work. Indeed, in self-hypnosis, I will address myself as would an outsider, saying "Eileen, you will now slowly relax, you will grow more passive, etc".'[1]

Psychological experiments, in particular word association tests, indicate that in some cases at least, the 'guides' and controls of the entranced medium are no more than secondary personalities, whilst in many instances the medium merely 'acts out' self given suggestions. Anyone who has had to listen to many of the 'inspirational' trance addresses given regularly by run of the mill mediums at spiritualist churches will agree that most of these fall into the latter category. Here again it must be stressed that the fact that a 'guide' is only a product of the medium's subconscious mind does not preclude the possibility that the actual information given is from a discarnate source.

It is obvious, however, that many of the cases of clairvoyance and telepathy described in the two previous chapters could easily be dressed up by a spiritualistically inclined sensitive, without any conscious attempt at fraud, to appear as messages from the departed. In this connection it must be borne in mind that most sensitives, in the course of their 'training' or 'development', are indoctrinated with all the traditional beliefs and practices of religious spiritualism, and imitative auto-suggestion can therefore be held to account for the prevalence of 'guides' who claim to be Red Indians, Sisters of Mercy, and ancient Chinese philosophers. That the truth of this did not escape the early pioneers of psychical research is shown by the

[1] 'Roads to Greater Reality', *Tomorrow*, Vol. 6, No. 4, Autumn, 1958.

following quotation from a paper published in an early edition of the Proceedings of the Society for Psychical Research. Discussing trance-speaking and inspirational mediumship, the author, who is anonymous, says:

'In these cases we have obviously states very nearly and probably quite identical with the hypnotic sleep. But the medium goes into trance first, and then speaks afterwards whilst in the trance, if this be really due to self-suggestion, the suggestion of speaking would probably be made before the medium is actually in the trance. That is to say, the medium would suggest to himself that he is going to sleep, and is going to speak when he is asleep. Hence to produce identical phenomena by suggestion, I must suggest to the subject what he is to do when asleep before he is sent to sleep. I tried it as follows: I told M. that I should send him to sleep, and that when he was asleep he would get up and write his name and address on a piece of paper. I then sent him to sleep. I may mention that I usually send my subjects to sleep by a simple command to "sleep" and the effect is generally practically instantaneous. I did nothing else. Twelve or fifteen seconds after he went to sleep he got up, wrote his name and address on the paper, and then sat down again. I repeated this form of experiment several times, making him perform various actions; for instance, I have several times made him give me spoken messages from my spirit-brother.

'These messages were very similar to those which I have heard from trance mediums. I may mention that I do not possess a spirit-brother. Hence by suggestions given in the waking state a subject may be sent to sleep and made to speak on a given subject while actually asleep. This, therefore, can probably be done by self-suggestion. There are also certain other facts which point to self-suggestion as the explanation of trance-speaking mediumship. I have met many trance-speaking mediums, only one of them being a professional. The most striking fact about them was that they seemed to have different ways of going into a trance. Some seemed to go off always with violent convulsions, others quite quietly. The explanation seems to have been this. Six who went off in convulsions had, I found, seen others go off in a similar way before they became mediums themselves. The others who went off quietly had seen mediums go off quietly before. I did not see all of these persons in the trance myself; I only saw eight of them; and from the rest I had only what they told me to depend on. Here self-suggestion seems to have been a powerful factor. In fact, they imitated the mediums whom they had seen.

'One case was a curious one. He was a lad of about eighteen; he could be sent into convulsions or into the quiet state before going into the speaking state. If he wished to go into the convulsive state he asked someone to hold his hand. In a few seconds he would be seized with violent epileptiform convulsions, which gradually passed off, and then he would speak, and eventually slowly recover himself. If he wished to go off quietly he simply shut his eyes and sat still and quietly went to sleep; then he would speak and gradually come round again.

'It is instructive to note how he first went into a trance. Some friends of his had seen a medium go off in convulsions and were telling him about it and describing it, when he was suddenly seized himself with a similar attack. He afterwards saw a medium who went off in convulsions when his hands were held by another person, and he also saw another who sent himself to sleep quietly in the way I have described. These facts lend additional support to the theory of self-suggestion.'[1]

Whilst the foregoing is, without doubt, true in probably the majority of cases, there are nevertheless a number of well attested reports of subjects going into spontaneous trance and giving quite evidential 'messages', although they have had no prior knowledge of common mediumistic practices or even of psychic matters generally. The fact that some of these subjects were young children is also significant. The evidential nature of some of the 'communications' received through certain mediums when the possibility of fraud was completely eliminated demonstrates, if not the truth of the spirit hypothesis, at least the possession of quite fantastic supernormal powers. A few of the best attested of these cases are now described.

One of the most celebrated of the early mediums was William Stainton Moses, 1839-1892, a clergyman of unquestioned integrity, whose life was described by F. W. H. Myers as one of the most extraordinary of the nineteenth century. He is most widely known for his prolific automatic writings, allegedly emanating from a group of exalted spirits, many of which were published in a famous book, *Spirit Teachings*, often referred to as the spiritualist's bible. Whatever the real source of these writings, they are remarkable for the amazing differences in calligraphy shown by the various 'communicators'. The originals are now a treasured possession of the College of Psychic Science in London, and are open for inspection to any serious enquirer.

Moses's trance sittings, however, were even more astounding. At a séance in the Isle of Wight in August 1874, a 'spirit' spoke through him and claimed to be that of a man named Abraham Florentine,

[1] 'The Connection of Hypnotism and Spiritualism', S.P.R. *Proceedings*, Vol. V, pp. 284-6.

who said that he had died at Brooklyn, U.S.A., on August 5th, at the age of eighty-three years, one month and seventeen days, and who gave details of events in his life. None of the sitters knew of such a man, but inquiries made in America revealed that someone of that name had, in fact, died in Brooklyn on the day stated, and that all the details given were correct except that the seventeen days should have been twenty-eight.

On another occasion in London, during dinner, Moses said that he felt an unpleasant influence, and later obtained the impression of a horse and some kind of vehicle, together with the statement: 'I killed myself—killed myself to-day—Baker Street—medium passed —killed myself to-day—under a steam-roller.' Moses had been in Baker Street earlier that day, but knew nothing of such an occurrence, but it was found later that a man had committed suicide in Baker Street that afternoon by throwing himself in front of a steam-roller. The front of the roller carried a brass representation of a horse, which presumably accounted for Moses's earlier impression. The incident was reported in the evening paper, but neither the medium nor the sitters had seen a copy at the time of the sitting.

There can be little doubt that the messages received through Moses were recorded by him in good faith as emanating from the sources claimed, but, to quote Myers, himself a firm believer in survival and spirit communication, 'As to whether they did really proceed from those personages or no there may in many cases be very grave doubt—a doubt which I, at least, shall be quite unable to remove.'

An even more remarkable medium than Stainton Moses was the famous American sensitive, Mrs Leonora Piper, to whom goes the distinction of being the first medium to submit to serious scientific investigation. First among these investigators (chronologically) was Professor William James, of Harvard, who, in addition to a number of personal sittings, sent many people, most of them anonymous. He reported, 'In the trances of this medium I cannot resist the conviction that knowledge appears which she has never gained by the ordinary waking use of her eyes and ears and wit. What the source of this knowledge may be I know not, and have not the glimmer of an explanatory suggestion to make; but from admitting the fact of such knowledge, I can see no escape'.[1] Later he wrote, 'Taking everything that I know of Mrs Piper into account, the result is to make me as absolutely certain as I am of any personal fact in the world that she knows things in her trances which she cannot possibly have heard in her waking state, and that the definite philosophy of her trances is yet to be found.'

[1] S.P.R. *Proceedings*, Vol. XII, pp. 5-6.

Professor James Hyslop also made a close study of Mrs Piper's trances and became convinced that some of the messages were from his dead father. In a check of over a thousand items of information received during fifteen sittings he found that 77 per cent were correct and only 5 per cent definitely incorrect.

Extraordinary precautions were taken by Dr Richard Hodgson, who went to America specially to investigate Mrs Piper on behalf of the Society for Psychical Research. For some time he employed a detective to check on her movements, and on the days when sittings were held she was not even allowed to see a newspaper.

When she came to England in 1889, Mrs Piper was personally escorted from the liner by Sir Oliver Lodge, in order that she could have no opportunity to make contact with any sources of information. She gave a large number of successful sittings to S.P.R. investigators, whose report, edited by Sir Oliver Lodge, Dr Walter Leaf and F. W. H. Myers, contained the following statement:

'On certain external or preliminary points, as will be seen, not we three alone, but all who have had adequate opportunity of judgment, are decisively agreed. But on the more delicate and interesting question as to the origin of the trance-utterances we cannot unite in any absolute view. We agree only in maintaining that the utterances show that knowledge has been acquired by some intelligence in some supernormal fashion; and in urging on experimental psychologists the duty of watching for similar cases, and of analysing the results in some such way as we have endeavoured to do.'[1]

Mrs Piper's first psychic experience seems to have occurred at the age of eight, when, while playing in the garden, she felt a sudden blow on her right ear, followed by a strange hissing noise. She then heard the words, 'Aunt Sarah, not dead, but with you still.' Naturally frightened by what had occurred, she ran and told her mother, who wisely noted the date and time. Several days later the news was received that an aunt named Sarah had died on the same date and at the exact time of the child's experience. Shortly afterwards she became unable to sleep at night, complaining of a 'bright light in the room with many faces in it'. This trouble soon passed, and from that time onwards she appears to have enjoyed a perfectly normal childhood.

During her early twenties Mrs Piper, who had recently married, consulted a Boston medium named Cocke, and during the sitting she herself fell into a trance. At a second sitting, in a 'developing circle' held by Cocke, she saw what she described as 'a flood of light in which many strange faces appeared.' Then, falling into a trance, she stood up, handed the paper on which she had written to a

[1] S.P.R. *Proceedings*, Vol. VI, p. 436.

member of the circle, a Judge Frost, who asserted that the message could only have come from his deceased son.

The news of this amazing young medium spread rapidly, and Mrs Piper was soon overwhelmed with requests for sittings. Fortunately she was brought to the notice of Professor William James, who, following an impressive personal sitting, took over complete control of her séances. Several years later Dr Richard Hodgson assumed responsibility, and it was during his supervision that the messages comprising the famous George Pelham case were received.

George Pelham was the assumed name under which a young lawyer friend of Hodgson had a sitting with Mrs Piper in 1888. She was never told of his real identity. Four years later he died, and a month afterwards communications purporting to be from him were received through Mrs Piper. These communications continued for six years, comprising a total of over 150 sitters, some of whom he had known when living, and he recognized 30 of the latter, although they were quite unknown to the medium. Further, on no occasion did he claim acquaintance with a sitter whom he had never known. The associations with and between his former friends were discussed with accuracy and dramatic realism; as Hodgson recorded, 'through the years the manifestations behaved like a continuous, living and persistent personality, the only observable changes being not of disintegration, but rather of integration and evolution.' The sitters were all introduced anonymously or pseudonymously.

In all these cases names were given correctly and the right degree of intimacy was indicated. In one doubtful case, that of a Miss Warner, Pelham failed at first to recognize the sitter, but as he had only known her slightly when she was a child, some years before the sitting, this non-recognition seems perfectly natural. Correct information was also given concerning Miss Warner's relatives. Of the large number of sitters who had not known him during his life, Pelham showed no knowledge whatsoever.

In contrast to the extravagant claims made by the vast majority of mediums, Mrs Piper herself was not convinced that the information obtained through her came from discarnate sources or that her 'controls' were, in fact, the spirits they purported to be. One of her early controls, who called himself Phinuit, was obviously fictitious, for although he claimed to be the spirit of a French doctor who had lived in Marseilles, he knew but little of French and still less of medicine. All attempts to verify his statements met with failure. One investigator invented a dead niece whom he named Bessie Beale, and requested Mrs Piper's control to contact her spirit. Messages from the non-existent 'spirit' were duly given.

It is interesting to note that Mrs Piper was hypnotized by William

James on several occasions, but hetero-hypnosis never produced results comparable with those obtained during her own auto-hypnotic trances.

Of the many instances of mediumship in the form of writing and other kinds of automatism, one of the best known and most puzzling is the phenomenon of 'Patience Worth'. In 1913 a Mrs Pearl Curran, a normal, healthy American woman with no special abilities or ambitions, was induced, somewhat against her will, to take part in some experiments with a ouija board. After a few sittings a 'communicator' who gave the name of Patience Worth, and claimed to be the spirit of an English girl who had lived during the seventeenth century took control. These communications continued for many years, Patience graduating from the slow and clumsy method of the ouija board, first to automatic writing, and later to direct dictation from the lips of the medium to a note taker.

In this manner a large number of poems, considered by many reputable critics to be of high quality, were produced, also no less than six full length novels. These were in addition to numerous discourses, particularly on philosophy and religion, and conversations with the many observers, many of them well known public figures, who witnessed her work. A strong religious flavour is evident in all her writings. A consistent feature is the inclusion of a much greater proportion of sixteenth century English than is found in any other American writer's works. This is most marked in *Telka*, one of the best known of Patience Worth's novels. Ruby Yeatman, Secretary to the College of Psychic Science, London, who has made an intensive study of this case, says:

'*Telka* is a story of English country life written in dialect—a dialect that cannot be claimed to belong to any one county or period. It has been studied in detail by learned philologists, who estimate that no word of it has come into the English language since the sixteenth century. It appears to be made up of many types of old English words, 90% of which are Anglo-Saxon. There are some very rare words and some archaic words and, of course, many that are now obsolete but which may still be in use although they are employed by Patience in an obsolete sense. The dialect would seem to be mainly from the southern part of England—Wessex—King Alfred's country, and Sir J. A. H. Murray says: "the direct descendant of Alfred's English is now to be found in the non-literary rustic speech of Wilts and Somerset." To write in archaic English without committing anachronisms is, to say the least, extremely difficult, but Patience Worth does it. Or, if you prefer it, here is a very ordinary American housewife, with no knowledge of English literature, and certainly no knowledge of old English dialects, with no previous experience of writing, spelling out from interior dictation a tale of English life of long ago, consistent throughout, with wisdom, wit and beauty that would do justice to a Shakespeare.'

Of the case as a whole Ruby Yeatman says:—'The problem is this: Who or what is Patience Worth? Is she who she says she is—the spirit of a seventeenth century peasant girl, returning to earth to be about her Father's business, even as the Christ she adored—a "putter" of words, a singer of songs, who comes with a purpose and a message? Or is she a secondary personality built up by Mrs Curran, or the content of the subconscious of Mrs Curran which, released from inhibitions, rises to the surface and produces all this original and outstanding literature which apparently the conscious mind of Mrs Curran has not had the necessary material to build with?'[1] She then quotes Dr Walter Franklin Prince's book *The Case of Patience Worth*, a detailed authoritative discussion of the case. 'Either our concept of what we call the subconscious must be radically altered, so as to include potencies of which we hitherto have had no knowledge, or else some cause operating through but not originating in the subconsciousness of Mrs Curran must be acknowledged.'[2]

Outstanding among British mediums, not only for the quality of her mediumship, but also for her honesty and sincerity, is Mrs Gladys Osborne Leonard. She took part in many tests with leading members of the Society for Psychical Research, all of whom were in agreement concerning her complete integrity, and many of whom expressed their appreciation of her desire to assist in, and submit to, the scientific precautions taken by them. Her 'control' purports to be the spirit of a young Indian girl named Feda.

Her career as a medium began shortly before the first World War at the insistence of 'Feda' who predicted that 'something big and terrible would happen', and that 'Feda must help many people through you'. (Feda always spoke in the third person.) Mrs Leonard became famous overnight when Sir Oliver Lodge, convinced that his son, killed in the war, had communicated through her, published the story in his book *Raymond*. The most striking demonstrations of her mediumship, however, were the many 'book tests' in which she scored outstanding success. One of the best examples is now summarized.

In 1917 a Mrs Hugh Talbot, who had never consulted a medium before and who was completely unknown to Mrs Leonard, had two sittings with her. Neither her name nor her address were disclosed

---

[1] 'The Phenomenon of Patience Worth', *Light*, December, 1956.
[2] *The Case of Patience Worth*, Boston, 1927.

at the time. Feda gave an accurate description of Mrs Talbot's deceased husband, who then purported to speak directly through the medium. Suddenly Feda broke in with the description of a book, which, she said, was made of dark coloured leather, and indicated its size by movements of the medium's hands. It was not a printed book; it contained writing and a diagram of Indo-European, Aryan, Semitic and other languages. There were also, said Feda, a number of lines, the shape of which the medium's finger traced. The sitter knew of no such book, but at Feda's insistence promised to look for it afterwards. Feda then said, 'Look at page twelve or thirteen. *If it is there it will interest him after this conversation.*' Quite convinced that Feda was 'off the beam', and bored by this apparent nonsense, Mrs Talbot left and went home.

Her niece, to whom she gave an account of the sitting, persuaded her to search for the book, and eventually she discovered several of her husband's old notebooks. One, bound in black leather, was of the size the medium had indicated, and to her astonishment she saw on the front page the words 'Table of Semitic or Syro-Arabian Languages'. Unfolding the table, which was a larger sheet pasted in the book, she read on the reverse side, 'General Table of the Aryan and Indo-European Languages', together with a diagram containing lines arranged in the manner Feda had described. Turning to page 13, she found the following, apparently an extract from a book entitled *Post Mortem*:

'I discovered by certain whispers which it was supposed I was unable to hear and from certain glances of curiosity or commiseration which it was supposed I was unable to see, that I was near death. ...

'Presently, my mind began to dwell not only on happiness which was to come, but upon happiness which I was actually enjoying. I saw long-forgotten forms, playmates, school-fellows, companions of my youth and of my old age, who one and all, smiled upon me. They did not smile with any compassion—that I no longer felt that I needed—but with that sort of kindness which is exchanged by people who are equally happy. I saw my mother, father, and sisters, all of whom I had survived. They did not speak, yet them communicated to me their unaltered and unalterable affection. At about the time when they appeared, I made an effort to realize my bodily situation ... that is, I endeavoured to connect my soul with the body which lay on the bed in my house. ... The endeavour failed. I was dead. ...'

A systematic series of book tests, spread over many years, were made by The Rev. Charles Drayton Thomas. Another excellent report on Mrs Leonard's mediumship is that by Miss Radclyffe-Hall and (Una) Lady Troubridge.[1]

Even the briefest outline of outstanding feats of mediumship would be sadly incomplete without mention of the world famous Eileen Garrett 'R 101' séance; indeed, its importance warrants a fuller account than is usually to be found, for it is generally recognized to be one of the cases most difficult to explain by any hypothesis other than that of survival and spirit communication.

On the 2nd of October, 1930, Harry Price, at that time director of the 'National Laboratory of Psychical Research', engaged Mrs Garrett for a séance to be held on the 7th October. In the early hours of Sunday, the 5th October, the great new airship, R101, crashed on a hillside in France, with the loss of all but six of her passengers and crew. The séance took place as arranged on the following Tuesday afternoon, its object being the attempt to establish communication with the late Sir Arthur Conan Doyle.

As soon as Mrs Garrett had gone into a trance her 'control', allegedly the spirit of an Arab, named Uvani, announced that someone named Irving or Irwin was anxious to speak. The medium's voice changed, and in short, sharp phrases, as if labouring under great difficulties, announced that Flight Lieutenant Irwin, captain of the R101, was speaking. He went on to give a detailed, accurate and highly technical account of the disaster and of the events preceding it, together with a description of the many faults of design and construction which were the cause of the crash. Among his statements were the following:

'Whole bulk of the dirigible was too much for her engine capacity.' 'Engines too heavy.' 'Useful lift too small.' 'Oil pipe plugged.' 'Load too great for long flight.' 'Never reached cruising altitude.' 'Airscrews too small.' 'Gross lift computed badly.' 'Impossible to rise.' 'Too short trials.' 'Fabric waterlogged and ship's nose down.' 'Severe tension on the fabric, which is chafing.' 'Cruising speed bad and ship swinging badly.' 'No one knew ship properly.' 'Starboard strakes started.' 'Elevator jammed.' 'Added middle section entirely wrong.' 'Superstructure of envelope contained no resilience and far too much weight on envelope.' 'This exorbitant scheme of carbon and hydrogen is entirely and absolutely wrong.' 'We almost scraped the roofs of Achy. Kept to railway.'

At the subsequent inquiry into the circumstances of the crash practically all these statements were shown to be correct, although none of those who attended the séance, and emphatically not Mrs Garrett, had the slightest knowledge of aviation. None of the remaining statements were proved incorrect and may well have been true,

[1] S.P.R. *Proceedings*, Vol. XXX, pp. 339-554.

while several were shown to be probably correct. The statement concerning the roofs of Achy is of special interest, for although it is such a small village that no ordinary maps show it and it is not named in guide books, it *was* shown on the special large scale flying maps used in the navigation of the airship. Evidence was given at the inquiry that the R101 passed over Achy at a height of not more than three hundred feet from the ground.

Concluding a personal account of this séance, Harry Price states:

'It is inconceivable that Mrs Garrett could have acquired the R101 information through normal channels, and the case strongly supports the hypothesis of "survival". As an argument for spirit communication it is much more convincing than the evidence provided by "Raymond" through various mediums. Telepathy between the living will not cover the facts, though some sort of nexus between the living and the dead would. No one present at the séance was consciously thinking of the R101 disaster, and no one had any technical knowledge of airships.'[1]

As an indication of the complexity of the problems involved in attempts to find the true explanation of mediumistic phenomena, mention must be made of the classic Gordon Davis case, in which 'spirit messages' were received from a man who was afterwards found to be alive and well. This case was reported by a well-known English researcher, Dr S. G. Soal.[2]

The medium concerned was Mrs Blanche Cooper, through whom, at a number of sittings, Dr Soal's deceased brother purported to communicate. A childhood friend, Gordon Davis, believed by Soal to be dead also, was another 'communicator'. In addition to recalling incidents of their youth, some of which Soal was able to recall and others which he subsequently confirmed, 'Davis' sent messages for his family, describing in detail the interior of the house in which he said they were then living.

Several years afterwards, Soal discovered that Davis was still living and paid him a visit. He was astonished to find that the furnishings and interior arrangements of Davis's house were exactly as the medium had described, and still more surprised when he learned that his friend had not lived in the house until *twelve months after the sitting* at which it was described.

This case appears to throw doubt on many others that are put forward as 'proof' of spirit communication, and indicates that a large proportion of them are purely examples of clairvoyance and/or telepathy dressed up in spiritualist trappings. There is no doubt,

---
[1] *Fifty Years of Psychical Research*, London, 1939.
[2] S.P.R. *Proceedings*, Vol. XXXV, pp. 471-594.

however, that in all the cases mentioned the mediums did transmit information acquired in a paranormal manner; there is no doubt also that the mental states in which these phenomena are manifest are auto-hypnotic ones.

Lest it be assumed by the newcomer to psychic matters that all or even most of the many practising mediums produce phenomena such as have been described, it must be stressed that mediumship of this calibre is a very, very rare thing. Apart from fraud, and there is much of this, particularly in the case of so-called 'physical mediums', an overwhelming proportion of the alleged phenomena of spiritualism is attributable to self delusion on the part of both mediums and sitters, heightened in many cases by varying degrees of self-hypnosis, and coupled with a large measure of unconscious 'cheating'. Even when an element of genuine psychic perception is present, it is often overlaid with 'padding' to such an extent that it is distorted almost out of recognition.

This is particularly true of the public demonstrations given at spiritualistic propaganda meetings and of the 'clairvoyance' that forms a major part of their religious services. In these cases there is always a highly emotional, tense atmosphere, of which the medium is the centre, and the 'will to believe' is strongly present in the members of the audience, many of whom are pathetic in their eagerness to acknowledge any 'message', however banal, as evidence that their departed friends and relations continue to exist.

At séances where the medium goes into a really deep trance the normal phenomena of hypnosis are accountable for much that appears at first to be paranormal. The ability to 'act out' suggestions with a startling degree of realism is well known, and the marked increase in sensitivity of sight, smell and hearing which hypnosis brings about in many subjects has already been noted. Sensory clues are often obtained in this manner without sitter or medium being consciously aware of the fact.

Automatic writing also rarely contains any matter that appears to emanate from any source beyond the unconscious of the writer, and for every example that is remotely comparable to the products of 'Patience Worth', there are many thousands consisting of nothing more than ill-assembled strings of platitudinous banalities. So great is the vanity, and so strong the will to believe, of many of the deluded authors of these 'Messages from Great Teachers in the Unseen World', that certain unscrupulous publishers make a speciality of printing them, having first, of course, extracted payment, often to the tune of several hundred pounds for a small book, from their misguided authors. The author of this book, who, as a member of Council of one of the leading psychical research societies has been unfortunate enough to have to read many of them, owns to rather strong feelings on this subject.

Of the few outstanding examples of automatic writing, in which some paranormal factor is definitely present, mention should be made of the 'cross-correspondences' of the 'SPR group' and of Miss Geraldine Cummins.

The cross-correspondences were the result of an attempt, first suggested by F. W. H. Myers, to receive messages which bore references to the same subjects, or which taken individually were meaningless but when assembled together became coherent. The automatists comprising the group were Mrs A. W. Verral, her daughter Mrs W. H. Salter, 'Mrs Holland' (Alice Kipling), and 'Mrs Willett' (Mrs Coombe-Tennant). A great deal of highly evidential matter was produced in these experiments.

Miss Geraldine Cummins is famous as the author of a number of books written while in auto-hypnotic trance. The quality of her work is all the more extraordinary when it is realized that much of it is produced at the remarkable speed of nearly 2000 words to the hour. Her earlier books, *The Scripts of Cleophas*, *Paul in Athens* and *The Great Days of Ephesus*, deal with the early history of the Christian Church, while her later works, *Beyond Human Personality*, and *The Road to Immortality*, are, it is claimed, communicated from the spirit of F. W. H. Myers.

As stated at the beginning of this chapter, it is not intended to discuss the question of the reality or otherwise of survival and spirit communication; indeed, such discussion would be out of place in a book of this nature, but a closing word on the subject is felt to be permissible and even desirable. There is a school of thought which holds, as did Charles Richet, that 'if we accept the two facts—that some mediums are aware of things that normal channels cannot convey—and that they tend to group both normal and supernormal knowledge round real or imaginary personalities, that amply suffices to explain everything.'[1]

But does it? If the 'higher phenomena of hypnotism—telepathy, clairvoyance, precognition, etc., and the auto-hypnotic phemonena of mediumship—occur, and they *do* occur, then the conclusion that there is some non-material aspect of existence, some extra-physical aspect of man, is difficult to avoid. And, accepting this conclusion, may it not well be that this non-material—astral, etheric, extra-physical, even spiritual, call it what you will—aspect of human personality survives the death of its material component, and is able, sometimes, to demonstrate its survival?

[1] *Thirty Years of Psychical Research*, London, 1923.

CHAPTER TWELVE

Reincarnation?

In knowledge, that man only is to be condemned and despised who is not in a state of transition.
MICHAEL FARADAY

THE claim has often been made that proof of, or at least strong grounds for a belief in the theory of reincarnation, can be obtained by regressing a hypnotized subject back to a period in time before the beginning of his present life, and it is true that a large number of subjects, when regressed in this manner, will give highly plausible accounts of what purport to be experiences in previous lives.

Although many cases had been recorded of such memories occurring to persons in spontaneous states of dissociation or auto-hypnosis, the first experimental work along these lines seems to have been carried out by a French hypnotist, Colonel Albert de Rochas, at the beginning of the present century. The results of these experiments were published in his book *Les Vies Successives*. De Rochas claimed that by the use of passes in different directions he could take the mind of a subject either backwards or forwards in time. Transverse passes sent the subject back into the past, whilst longitudinal ones facilitated precognition of future events. By means of the latter, he once caused a widow aged thirty-five, who at the time had no intention of remarrying, to predict in dramatic detail the birth of two children, one when she was thirty-seven and the other two years later. She described the second birth as happening 'on the water'. Both events took place at the times predicted, the second occurring on a bridge over a river.

Another of de Rochas's subjects, a young orphan named Mlle Mayo, was sent into a 'past life' in which she claimed that she was a fisherman's daughter named Lina. Regressed still further, she professed to be a man, calling herself Charles Mauville, and saying that she worked as a clerk in the Ministerial offices of Louis XVIII. A third subject, Mme J., re-enacted events from a large number of alleged previous lives, and de Rochas was able to confirm the descriptions of places she claimed to know in one of the less remote incarnations.

Replying to criticisms that suggestion was at the root of the memories claimed by his subjects, de Rochas insisted that the suggestions could not have emanated from him, as he had not only taken great care to avoid guiding the subjects in any way, but had even attempted to lead them astray by deliberate suggestions. He also stressed the unanimity of nearly all his subjects' descriptions of the 'grey period' preceding birth, which they referred to before reporting the last stages of a previous life. A very fair assessment of his work is that by another Frenchman, Geley, the famous Psychical Researcher. He says:

'The experiences of de Rochas on regression of the memory are only sufficient to encourage further research. They are in no sense conclusive. It seems impossible to eliminate mental suggestion on the part of the operator when face to face with the subject, or of autosuggestion on the part of the latter. ... The experiments of de Rochas do not offer so much a precise proof as a unanimous testimony on the part of the subjects to the truth of reincarnation. All, irrespective of birth, education, intellectual grade and religious principles, declared spontaneously that they had passed through other lives. Upon this they very often build romances, of varying worth, but usually unverifiable. But the fact of the unanimity and spontaneity of their assertion relative to the plurality of their lives is by no means negligible.'[1]

Geley's comments are also applicable to most of the other alleged proofs of incarnation obtained by hypnotic age regression, and even in cases where some verifiable information concerning the past is given, as, for instance, that of Edgar Cayce mentioned on page 93 they may well be partially true. Dramatization of clairvoyantly acquired information is considered by many to be a simpler explanation than reincarnation. Before passing to the discussion of the most famous if all such cases, that of 'Bridey Murphy', it may be well to note an illuminating experiment made by Eric Cuddon.

'In hypnosis the subject was told that (Cuddon) had been able to ascertain who she was in a previous incarnation! She had been born of poor parents at Ostia, near Rome, and had eventually found her way to the slave market where she had been purchased for the Emperor Nero and had subsequently become his favourite concubine; further he had taken her with him on a trip to Egypt. The subject purported to remember the incident of being purchased in the slave market quite clearly and stated that the Emperor had fallen for her lovely long hair. (Note: She has often stated that she had lovely long hair when a girl.) About a week later she was asked by someone, in the course of conversation, whether she believed she had lived before; her answer was that she was quite certain that she had been the favourite slave of the *Egyptian* Emperor Nero!'[2]

[1] *Reincarnation*, London, 1924.
[2] *Hypnosis, its Theory and Practice*, London, 1955.

To return to Bridey Murphy; the story is briefly this. Morey Bernstein, a Colorado businessman who is also an experienced and accomplished hypnotist, had his attention drawn to various attempts to demonstrate the truth of reincarnation by means of hypnotic age regression. After reading most of the literature concerning the subject he decided to carry out experiments himself, using one of his subjects, a young married woman named Virginia Tighe—referred to in his subsequent book as 'Ruth Simmonds'—whom he knew to be an exceptionally good somnambule. The experiment consisted of six sessions in each of which, as soon as she was deeply hypnotized, Virginia was regressed to early childhood, and then instructed to go further back into a past life, and to describe events from it. From her statements, in the main replies to questions posed by the hypnotist, the following picture was constructed.

Virginia had formerly been, she claimed, an Irish woman named Bridget (usually corrupted to Bridey) Kathleen Murphy, who was born in Cork in 1798. Her father was a barrister, Duncan Murphy, and she had a brother named Duncan Blaine Murphy. Another brother had died soon after birth. As a child she lived at 'The Meadows', and went to a school run by a Mrs Strayne, whose daughter later married Bridey's brother. At the age of four, her earliest 'recollection', she had been spanked for scratching the paint off her bed. When she was twenty she married Sean Joseph McCarthy, whose father was also a Cork barrister, in a Protestant church, she being of that faith whilst he was a Catholic. They moved to Belfast and there went through a second marriage ceremony, performed by a Catholic priest, Father John Joseph Gorman. Her husband taught law at Queen's University, Belfast. Bridey died childless in 1864, and was buried at Belfast.

Much more information was given, including the names of friends and relations, her likes and dislikes concerning food, books, music and clothes, descriptions and names of places, and of various business houses and shops. She spoke with an Irish brogue, and used many words peculiar to Ireland, although neither she nor Bernstein had ever been to that country. Bernstein checked on a number of 'Bridey's' statements and seemed to find confirmation of some of them. A verbatim report of the sittings, which had been recorded on tape, together with an account of Bernstein's enquiries and his conclusions, were published in 1956 in his book *The Search for Bridey Murphy*, which rapidly became a best seller.

The controversy that followed was stormy. It was joined by psychiatrists, journalists, psychical researchers, folklore experts, theosophists, clergymen and philologists, whose opinions, as often as not, were more in conflict with each other than with those of

Bernstein. Most of them were, of course, biased by preconceived ideas, and many did not scruple to twist and distort any facts not in accordance with their own pet theories. Although opinions were freely forthcoming, the only extensive field research of a really objective nature appears to have been that carried out by Dr E. J. Dingwall, a world-famous and much respected English parapsychologist, and by William J. Barker, a journalist on the staff of the *Denver Post*. The findings of the latter, who went to Ireland and made on-the-spot enquiries, were published in later editions of *The Search for Bridey Murphy* under the title 'The Case for Bridey in Ireland'. Of the self-styled experts who interest themselves in the case, Barker comments:

'Since then [the publication of his report], many articles purporting to give "the inside facts" on the case have bobbed up in a variety of magazines and journals. Inevitably the debunking, scoffing line has been exploited, but the incredible aspect of so many of these 'exposes' has been the apparent willingness to substitute so-called experts' opinions for researchers' findings.'[1]

Dingwall's scrupulously honest findings[2] are, in the main, negative, but Barker unearthed a number of facts which were in conformity with 'Bridey's' statements; facts with which, it appears, Virginia Tighe could not have become acquainted in the normal way of things. Many of her statements concerning obscure facts, which were at first thought to be quite incorrect, were corroborated by subsequent investigations.

A masterly analysis of this case, in which all the pro and anti arguments so far published are listed and discussed, has recently been made by Professor C. J. Ducasse. Its study is urged, not only for the information to be gained concerning the Bridey Murphy case, but for its indictment of the muddled headed and myopic attitude towards hypnosis displayed by so many psychiatrists who pontificate in the name of science. His conclusions on the Bridey Murphy controversy are these:

'The outcome of our reviews and discussion of the Bridey Murphy case may now be summarily stated. It is, on the one hand, that neither the articles in magazines and newspapers which we have mentioned and commented upon, nor the comments of the authors of the so-classed "Scientific Report" and of other psychiatrists hostile to the reincarnation hypothesis, have succeeded in disproving, or even in establishing a strong case against, the possibility that many of the statements of the Bridey personality are genuinely memories of an earlier life of Virginia Tighe over a century ago in Ireland.

[1] *The Search for Bridey Murphy*, Pocket Books Edition, New York, 1956.
[2] 'The Woman Who Never Was', *Tomorrow*, Vol. 4, No. 4, Summer, 1956.

'On the other hand, for reasons other than those which were advanced by those various hostile critics, but which there is no space here to develop, the verifications summarized by Barker, of obscure points in Ireland mentioned in Bridey's six recorded conversations with Bernstein, do not prove that Virginia is a reincarnation of Bridey, nor do they establish a particularly strong case for it. They do, on the other hand, constitute fairly strong evidence that, in the hypnotic trances, *paranormal* knowledge of one or other of several possible kinds concerning these recondite facts of nineteenth century Ireland, became manifest.'[1]

Following the publication of Bernstein's book, numerous attempts were made to duplicate his experiments, none, so far as can be ascertained, with very convincing results. An American doctor is said to have hypnotized a hard-headed journalist on a television programme and regressed him to a life in Germany two hundred years ago. The subject spoke fluent German, although he disclaimed all knowledge of that language when in his normal waking state. He claimed to have been a leather worker and gave a detailed account of his job. Another report was of a subject who was regressed to a time when she was a little girl being burned at the stake. Another subject claimed to have been a red fox, and yet another a horse.

There is little doubt that in most of these cases the explanation is nothing more than the dramatisation of matter which has at some time been known to the subject but is not consciously remembered, with no paranormal factors whatsoever involved. A good illustration of this is the case, recently cited by Dr Harold Rosen of Toronto, in which a hypnotized patient began speaking in Oscan, a language not in use since the third century B.C. No one present could understand what he was saying, so he was asked to write it out. This he did, carefully printing each word. 'This made identification possible. He was reciting in Oscan one of a series of magical curses which usually were inscribed on lead plates thin enough to be rolled up and thrown in graves, so the thrower could gain control over various of the infernal deities. Our patient had never studied Latin, had never heard of Oscan, and on non-hypnotic levels was completely unaware of what he had said or written.'[2] Subsequent enquiries elicited the information that some time previously the patient had been sitting in a library preparing for an examination when he began to daydream. His eyes wandered to a book which was lying open on the table. On the open page were the words 'The Curse of Vibia', and under it the Oscan curse printed in that language. These became, as

---

[1] 'How the Case of *The Search for Bridey Murphy* Stands Today', A.S.P.R. *Journal*, Vol. IV, p. 22, also *A Critical Examination of the Belief in a Life after Death*, Springfield, Ill., 1960. [2] *Toronto Star Weekly*, 9th June, 1956.

it were, photographically imprinted upon his mind, although he was not consciously aware of it, and would have taken an oath that he knew nothing of the matter.

On the other hand, there are a few cases on record for which, at first sight, the reincarnation hypothesis seems to offer the only explanation, and of these the example now instanced, although not connected with the subject of hypnotism, is one of the most puzzling. A young Indian girl named Shanti Devi, who lived at New Delhi, had, from the age of four, made references to a former life in Muttra, a city she had never visited. When she was eleven she stated that she had died twelve years previously after bearing her second child, and that her former husband's name was Kedar Nath Chaubey. A group of people, including her teacher, a lawyer and a well-known publisher, became interested, and ascertained that her alleged former husband was still living at Muttra. They arranged a series of tests in which the girl successfully described the house in which she claimed to have lived and a number of people she had known. Most startling of all, however, were the descriptions she gave to her 'husband' of their former life together, which included details that no one but a wife could have known. He, moved to tears, commented that 'It were as if that wife, now twelve years dead, stood again beside him.' She also told him the exact location of a box containing money which she had hidden in his parents' house. When taken to the house she pointed to the hiding place and then dug up the box. It was found to be empty, whereupon the husband stated that he had discovered the box and removed the money after his wife's death.[1]

Several similar cases were recently reported in the *Indian Journal of Parapsychology*,[1] and are under investigation by the Seth Sohan Lal Memorial Institute of Parapsychology, the leading Indian psychical research authority. From the same source comes the report of a boy from Rasulpur named Jasbir, who, four years ago, at the age of seven, had died in the night. The next day, as his body was about to be removed, he astonished his parents by showing signs of life, and within two days appeared to have recovered completely. He began to behave strangely, however, and refused to eat any food in his own house. He claimed to be a Brahmin boy, saying that he was the son of Shankar Lal Tyagi, a resident of Vehedi, a village over twenty miles away.

For about eighteen months the boy was fed on food cooked by a Brahmin woman, refusing to eat anything else. When a school teacher from Vehedi, to which Jasbir had never been, visited

[1] Ranhauat Banshi Dhar, 'Study of Spontaneous Cases', *Indian Journal of Parapsychology*, Vol. I, pp. 76-80, June, 1959.

Rasulpur, the boy instantly recognized him and began to talk of places and people in Vehedi, including Shankar Lal Tyagi, the contents of whose house he was able to describe. As a result he was taken to Vehedi, where he recognized a number of its residents. There it was discovered that Shankar Lal Tyagi's son, who had been killed accidentally at the age of twenty-five, had died at the exact time that Jasbir had undergone his strange 'resurrection'. It is stated that Jasbir is still living in Rasulpur, but is not reconciled with his parents.

A case more closely related to hypnotism in that it concerns sleep-walking, a form of self induced, spontaneous hypnosis, was recently made public by Nandor Fodor.[1] It concerns Violet Tweedale, the well-known novelist. During a somnambulistic trance she walked out of her house into the garden, where she cut her foot on a sharp stone. Awakened by the pain she suddenly recalled vivid memories of a former life in Sicily, when she had been a barefooted gipsy girl. So strong was the impression that she decided to go to Sicily, which she had never previously visited, and investigate. There she found the place she had seen as she awoke from her trance, and the memory proved so exact that when she came to a blind corner she was able to predict precisely what she would see after turning it.

No discussion of the alleged proofs of reincarnation by means of hypnosis would be adequate without mention of the celebrated Swiss psychologist Theodore Flournoy, and of his work in connection with the medium Helene Smith (pseudonym).[2] Brought up in the reincarnationist beliefs of most Continental spiritists, she would never consciously permit herself to be hypnotized although, as Flournoy states, 'she does not realize that although avoiding the word she accepts the reality, for her spiritist exercises really consist of an auto-hypnosis which inevitably degenerates into hetero-hypnosis because she comes under the special influence of certain of the sitters'. Her 'guide', who called himself Leopold, claimed to be a reincarnation of Joseph Balsamo, otherwise the notorious juggler Count Cagliostro, who lived in the eighteenth century.

The most sensational of Helene's 'communications' purported to be from a young man who had been reincarnated on the planet Mars. Some time before the 'Martian Cycle', as Flournoy termed it, began, a colleague, Professor Lemaitre, had remarked to Helene that it would be wonderful if during the séances they could hear from some of the planets. Then, at a séance at which Lemaitre was present, the medium had a sensation as if she were leaving her body. She found herself in a dense fog, which changed colour from blue to

---

[1] *The Haunted Mind*, New York, 1956.
[2] *Des Indes a la Planéte Mars*, Paris, 1900.

a vivid rose, to grey and then to black. She seemed to be floating, and saw a star, growing larger and larger, until it became 'as big as our house'. She then found herself walking 'on a world—Mars'. She then began to describe some of the strange things she could see, 'Carriages without horses or wheels, emitting sparks as they glided by: houses with fountains on the roofs; a cradle having for curtains an angel made of iron with outstretched wings, etc. What seemed less strange were people exactly like the inhabitants of our earth, save that both sexes wore the same costume, formed of trousers very ample, and a long blouse, drawn tight about the waist and decorated with various designs. The child in the cradle was exactly like our children, according to the sketch which Helene made from memory after the séance.'

There followed a 'communication', allegedly from the deceased son of one of the ladies present, saying that he was reincarnated on Mars. After the message had been given, Helene returned to consciousness.

This was the first of a long series of similar séances, in which a vast amount of information was given, including the 'Martian' alphabet and numerous samples of the language. The following specimen, which accompanied the vision of a 'Martian' house, is supposed to mean 'this is the house of the great man Astane, whom thou hast seen'.

Dodé né ci haudan té mess méche métiche Astané ké dé mé véche.

Much of the information given in, and concerning this language was by automatic writing, and, over a long period, showed a remarkable consistency in the use of various terms. Flournoy's analysis proved, however, that it bore a marked structural likeness to the French language, from which he concluded that it was purely a subconscious invention on the part of Helene. For a woman of her limited background it is, nevertheless, a quite fantastic achievement.

Helene also gave remarkable impersonations of Marie Antoinette and of a Hindu princess, Simandini, both of whom she claimed were former incarnations of herself. There were, however, a number of anachronisms in both stories, and a sample of handwriting allegedly by Marie Antoinette bore no resemblance to that of the real Queen. Flournoy made a brilliant analysis of the case as a whole, tracing the origin of the trance personalities back to Helene's own latent inclinations, her experiences, temperament and standards. He showed quite clearly that there was no question of the phenomena being conscious productions of the medium's imagination or fancy, but that they were purely the result of subconscious mental processes.

Further, or more general, consideration of the question of reincarnation would be out of place in a book on hypnotism. For a scholarly appraisal of the value of cases such as those just instanced as evidence of reincarnation, the reader is referred to a paper by Dr Ian Stevenson, of Virginia University, entitled 'The Evidence for Survival from Claimed Memories of Former Incarnations.'[1]

[1] A.S.P.R. *Journal*, Vol. LIV, pp. 51-71 and 95-117 (April and June, 1950).

CHAPTER THIRTEEN

Hypnotism and Crime

Il est d'autant plus important a établir, ce fait, que mille faits négatifs ne prouvent rien contre un seul fait positif.

CHARLES RICHET

THE consideration of crime in connection with hypnotism may conveniently be divided into two sections:

(a) The possibility of a hypnotized subject being compelled by the hypnotist to carry out an illegal act.

(b) The possibility of the hypnotist performing an illegal act against a hypnotized subject.

Question (a) is one about which there is probably more dispute by the experts than any other aspect of hypnotism. Some assert emphatically that crimes *will* be committed by hypnotized subjects, and instance controlled experiments which appear to prove it, whilst others equally knowledgeable deny just as vehemently that such a thing is possible, and cite other carefully arranged experiments which seem to substantiate their case.

Most writers on hypnotism appear to support the latter school of thought, whose general belief is that no hypnotized person will ever carry out a suggestion which is in conflict with his or her moral or ethical standards. They seem to ignore the fact that hypnotic suggestions act upon the inner or subconscious mind, in which to some extent the seeds of all the desires and vices are always present, although normally held in check by the conscious standards of morals, ethics, religion, etc. There is strong evidence, however, that hypnotic suggestions can sometimes break through these conscious restrictions and be effective in spite of them.

It seems to the author that another important fact is overlooked by the 'will do nothing against their moral standards' school. We know so little of the real nature of hypnotism, or of man for that matter, that it is surely rash and unwarranted to say that because in *some* cases *some* people have refused to act on suggestions contrary to their better natures, *all* hypnotized subjects are bound to behave in the same way?

A favourite argument of the 'will do nothing against etc.' protagonists is that in experiments the subjects know they are not committing real crimes, and merely indulge in subconscious play-acting.

Another is that the hypnotized person sees hypersensitively and is able to detect safety devices incorporated in an experimental 'set-up' The classic American case to be quoted seems to dispose of these contentions.

A series of tests were made in which the hypnotized subjects were instructed to throw sulphuric acid in the face of one of the experimenters. A clean and apparently invisible sheet of plate glass was interposed between them, and the subjects invariably would pick up the acid and throw it at the experimenter. The objection was raised that a subject's hyper-sensitivity of vision enabled him to see the glass and he therefore knew that he would not cause any injury. The experiment was thereupon modified. The glass was dispensed with and it was arranged that at the moment when the subject was about to throw the acid his attention would be distracted and a harmless liquid substituted. The subjects continued to throw what they believed to be acid at the experimenter. The objectors then said that the subjects must realize that the experimenter would not allow himself to be injured, and only threw the 'acid' because they knew it was a trick and that in some way the experimenter was protected.

But on one occasion something went wrong, the usual 'switch' was not made and the subject actually threw the acid into the experimenter's face. The unfortunate man was severely burnt and badly disfigured, but although he had seen this the same subject, in subsequent tests, continued to throw 'acid' as obediently as ever.

The truth concerning this question is probably that while *some* people cannot be made to carry out hypnotic suggestions contrary to their principles, there are certainly *some* who can. Repeated hypnosis and a considerable amount of conditioning might be necessary, and the hypnotist would need to be a highly skilful one. It is of course agreed that the practical difficulties entailed are sufficient to ensure that the number of actual crimes carried out by such methods must be very small.

A paper to the Society for Psychical Research by F. W. H. Myers throws a great deal of light on this question. It refers to the work of Professor Liégeois, a colleague of Liébeault, who compelled a number of the latter's patients to commit a variety of experimental 'crimes'. Here is an extract,

'Professor Liégeois, whose speciality is medical jurisprudence, has taken much pains to induce Dr Liébeault's patients to commit a number of crimes—as murder, theft, perjury, etc., and has made them give him receipts for large sums of money which he has never really lent them. I abridge a passage from his careful and conscientious tractate.

' "I have spoken of my friend M.P., a former magistrate. I must accuse myself of having endeavoured to get him murdered, and this moreover in the presence of the *Commissaire Central* of Nancy, who witnessed the occurrence.

' "I provided myself with a revolver and several cartridges. In order to prevent the Subject, whom I selected at random from among the five or six somnambules who happened to be at M. Liébeault's house on that day, from supposing that the thing was a joke, I charged one of the barrels and fired it off in the garden, showing a card which the ball had pierced. In less than a quarter of a minute I suggested to Mme G. the idea of killing M.P. by a pistol-shot. With perfect docility Mme G. advanced on M.P. and fired at him with the revolver. Interrogated immediately by the *Commissaire Central*, she avowed her crime with entire indifference. 'She had killed M.P. because she did not like him. She knew the consequences. If her life was taken, she would go to the next world, like her victim, whom she saw (by hallucination) lying before her, bathed in blood'. She was asked whether it was not *I* who had suggested to her the idea of the murder. She declared that it was not so—that she alone was guilty, and that she would take the consequences." (It had not been *suggested* to her that her act was due to *suggestion*.)

'Similarly Mlle A.E. (a very amiable young person) was made by Professor Liégeois to fire on her own mother with a pistol which she had no means of knowing to be unloaded. She was also made to accuse herself before a *juge d'instruction* of having assassinated an intimate friend with a knife. When she thus accused herself she appeared to be in a perfectly normal waking state. And even the most *bizarre* actions, performed under suggestion, *look* perfectly spontaneous when the subject carries them out. The action may be *deferred* for hours or days after the suggestion is given. Professor Liégeois gave to M.N. a paper of white powder, informing him that it was arsenic, and that on his return home he must dissolve it in a glass of water and give it to his aunt. In the evening a note from the aunt arrived as follows: "Madame M. has the honour to inform M. Liégeois that the experiment has completely succeeded. Her nephew duly presented her with the poison".

'In this case the culprit entirely forgot his action, and was unwilling to believe that he had endeavoured to poison a relative to whom he was much attached.

'Experiments like these will produce in the minds of many readers a feeling of moral shock and alarm. In the first place, they may naturally feel that a power like this may be abused for evil purposes, and the subject induced to commit real as well as imaginary crimes. And in the second place, they may suspect that even if no actual crime is committed, the mere fact of the subjection of the will to temptation must leave some stain on the moral nature of the Subject who has thus acted out a guilty dream. I do not account the first of these apprehensions as chimerical, nor the second as squeamish; nay, I consider on the other hand that the advocate of hypnotic experiment is bound in candour to exhibit as fully as I have done the grounds for moral demur.

'But speaking from the experience of those best qualified to judge, I feel justified in replying that there is little fear that cases like these will ever be more than the harmless curiosities of the lecture-room. As regards the danger of the suggestion of real acts of crime, it must be remembered in the first place that Professor Liégeois's subjects were the picked specimens of a sensitive nation, and that among thousands of English men and women perhaps not one case of similar susceptibility would be found. Again, there is a simple precaution which the French experimenters recommend as effectual. If a subject feels that he is becoming too sensitive, let him get some trustworthy friend to hypnotize him, and to suggest to him that no one else will be able to do so. This suggestion, it appears, fulfils itself like the rest, and the bane works its own antidote without further trouble.

'For my part, especially where a female subject was concerned, I should recommend the still further precaution of not allowing any one except a trustworthy friend to hypnotize her at all. As to the second ground of apprehension, the possible tarnishing of the moral sense, or weakening of the moral fibre, by the mere performance, in however abnormal a state, of immoral acts, the requisite precautions are, I think, very easy to take. In the first place, the subject, unless told to remember the acts, will absolutely forget them—*always* when they are performed in the hypnotic trance, and *generally* when (like the poisoning of the aunt) they are performed by the subject after he has been awakened from the trance, and in a condition apparently normal. They remain no more in the subject's mind than if he had read them in a book and forgotten them. Certain precautions, nevertheless, may well be taken. I should avoid, for instance, making any suggestion which at all resembled a possible temptation of the subject's waking state. I should not myself like to dream of injuring some real personal enemy, but should feel no compunction if I dreamt that I had killed the Emperor of China. Now when the dutiful and affectionate Mlle A.E. shot at her mother, it was not like a dream of yielding to a temptation, it was like the purely fantastic dream which has no root in the moral nature.'[1]

It will have been noted that Liégeois was able to compel some of

[1] 'Human Personality in the Light of Hypnotic Suggestion', S.P.R. *Proceedings*, Vol. IV, pp. 9-11.

his subjects to give him receipts for money they imagined had been lent to them, and this is a convenient point on which to turn to the question (b), of whether an unscrupulous operator could perform an illegal act against, or to the disadvantage of, his hypnotized subject.

The receipts obtained by Liégeois would appear to make the answer 'yes', and other cases are on record where subjects have handed over money or signed cheques in a similar manner. A real criminal hypnotist would no doubt use post-hypnotic suggestions, in order that innocent witnesses might be present and thus make the transaction seem genuine. The author has certain knowledge of a case where the subject, by this means, was induced to buy an article, and to pay far more for it than its true value.

It is certainly probable that a hypnotist could cause the serious injury or even the death of a subject, and do so in such a manner that it would appear to be accidental. Here again, it could not be done by a direct suggestion that the subject should take his own life or perform a suicidal act, but if, for example, a somnambule were told that an open window on a top floor was the entrance to say, a lift, there is little doubt but that he would walk obediently through it into space.

Two extremely good illustrations are made by Cuddon, a barrister as well as an authority on hypnotism:

'Be it remembered that in the case of a good Deep Stage Subject any of the phenomena which can be evoked during Hypnosis can be made to occur at a later time by means of post-hypnotic suggestion. It is, however, essential that the Inner Mind of the Subject should accept the suggestion and hence this must be couched in a form agreeable to the Subject. Suppose that the person, whose death was desired, chanced to be a fine swimmer and diver; it could be suggested in Hypnosis that at a certain time the Subject would find that whatever he was standing upon was in fact a diving board and that he would forthwith take a glorious dive into the deep water below him. If the suggested time at which this would occur were made to fall within the probable period that the Subject would be travelling home by bus or train, it is possible that the dive might be made under the wheels of one or the other. Again, if the Subject were habitually taking, say, Luminal Sleeping Tablets, it might be possible to persuade him to take a fatal overdose by such suggestions as "They will do you no harm. Take lots and lots and have a lovely deep refreshing sleep. You will then feel so much better".'[1]

Another question over which there is much misunderstanding is the possibility of the hypnotist committing a sexual offence against his subject, and when considering this question it is important to

[1] *Hypnosis, its Theory and Practice*, London, 1955.

differentiate between what would constitute a criminal act and what might be looked upon as morally wrong. While a direct attempt at rape would almost certainly have no effect beyond causing the subject's immediate return to consciousness, it is possible that the subject might be tricked into submission by means of a suggested hallucination that the hypnotist was her husband or possibly her lover. The more subtle misuse of hypnotism however, could certainly be of great assistance to the philanderer, although to what extent this could be regarded as criminal is by no means clear. Cuddon has said,

'... if the Subject had any amorous feelings towards the hypnotist when normally conscious, it would, I believe, be a simple matter to increase the intensity of those feelings by suggestion in hypnosis to the point at which consent to intercourse might be willingly given in the normal state. It will be appreciated that in the present state of our criminal law the last example would result not in a rape but in enthusiastic acquiescence!'[1]

It is not intended to suggest that any lecherous minded individual who buys a do-it-yourself book on hypnotism can become a Casanova overnight; on the contrary, he would probably never become a hypnotist, but there is no doubt that a knowledge of hypnotism could be of inestimable value to a *coureur des femmes*.

The argument often advanced that 'no virtuous woman can be seduced by hypnosis, and that in other cases hypnosis is an unnecessarily involved and roundabout method', is not founded on fact. It is utterly ridiculous and quite impossible to attempt to divide women into two simple classes of those who will and those who will not.

An important question to the reputable consultant hypnotist is the possibility of an untrue accusation of improper conduct being made against him by a patient. Such an accusation might allege indecent behaviour or even rape, and be followed by threats of prosecution or even worse, blackmail. Although innocent, and despite the fact that no such charge could be pursued far in the absence of corroborative evidence, the unfortunate consultant might well suffer irreparable harm to his reputation if an allegation of this nature became public knowledge.

It has long been accepted therefore, that the presence of a reliable witness is most desirable at consultations when the patient is a woman, but unfortunately many patients are loath to discuss their problems when a third party is present. The author has found that the use of a recording machine provides a most effective solution to this difficulty, but considers it wise to ensure that an assistant is

[1] 'Hypnotism and the Law', *Light*, September, 1957.

immedately available at the touch of a button. An incidental advantage of using a recorder is that it obviates the need for taking voluminous notes, a process frequently found 'off-putting' by the patient. It is of considerable help also to have a clean transcript of the consultation which can be made at any convenient time afterwards.

So far the criminal activities discussed have been either hypothetical cases or laboratory experiments, but hypnosis is known to have been used in the perpetration of real crimes, some of them major ones.

Without doubt the most authentic and carefully documented example of the use of hypnosis for criminal purposes is that generally referred to as the Heidelberg Case. It is important not only for the light it throws upon many technical aspects of the subject, but because it appears to offer proof of the fallacy of the widely held belief that it is impossible to cause a hypnotic subject to perform any act not in accord with his or her moral or ethical standards.

The report of this case by Dr Ludwig Mayer, who was called in by the police, runs into a thousand pages and was the result of nineteen months intensive work.

In 1934 a man complained to the Heidelberg police that his wife had been defrauded of large sums of money by a man who, posing as a doctor, had hypnotized her repeatedly in the treatment of various illnesses. The husband suspected that not only were the illnesses suggested to his wife in order to extract payment, but that the hypnotist, who had since disappeared, had had sexual relations with her during the hypnosis without her knowledge or consent.

Dr Mayer examined the woman and found no illness of an organic nature, but a complete loss of memory concerning her sickness and all matters connected with the hypnotist. On other matters her memory was perfectly normal. She was, however, able to tell the doctor that the man always placed his hand on her forehead in order to hypnotize her and that when he did this she became tired and remembered nothing. She consented to be hypnotized by the doctor, and using the same technique he soon produced a light trance. After a number of sessions she eventually remembered, while in a trance, that before she was married she had met the man on a train. He had offered to cure her of some stomach pains and hypnotized her. He instructed her to go and see him at a later date for 'treatment'. On this and subsequent occasions he met her and took her by the hand through the streets, suggesting that everything was dark around her so that she had no idea where they went. She was taken to a small room and deeply hypnotized and she could still remember nothing of what took place then.

The post-hypnotic suggestions that she had obviously been given to make her forget these events were almost impossible to overcome, but suggesting during hypnosis that the man was standing in front of her caused her to have an hallucination of his face which she was able to describe. Her description was found to resemble that of a man named Franz Walter who had recently been arrested in another town for posing as a doctor, and when she saw this man she confirmed that it was he who had hypnotized her. Walter denied that he knew anything of her or of hypnosis and was kept under arrest.

By a long series of hypnoses, Dr Mayer was able gradually to remove the post-hypnotic blockage Walter had imposed on her memory. His method was to find a few stimulus words which could cause associations in her mind. One of these, for example, the term 'bathing-pool', enabled her to recollect some towels of an unusual colour and pattern which she had seen in Walter's room, and these were then found by the police.

In order to find suitable stimulus words the woman was told under hypnosis to mention automatically any words that came into her mind. In this way the following were obtained. 'Shoe — Shuhmacher—5 Mark', 'Leichtbino', 'Auto—6071', 'Combarus', 'Loxitiv', and '17—to write—Walter—not come—dark—19-3'. In a later hypnosis she was asked what associations she had with these expressions—she had none during the waking state—and here is a summary of her answers.

The expression beginning 'Shoe' recalled an occasion when Walter had bought some yellow shoes, leaving his old ones at the shop and paying an additional 5 Marks. 'Leichtbino' was a code word which Walter had said would come into her mind if ever she was about to say anything that might incriminate him. She would then feel unwell until she began to speak in his favour. 'Auto—6071' was the number of a car in which she had once been driven by Walter. (The police verified the purchase by Walter of the shoes, and also that he had once hired a car bearing that number.)

'Combarus' was another code or 'trigger' word. Walter used to take money from other men for allowing them to have sexual intercourse with her, and he told her that when these men wanted anything she would think of the word and then go into such a deep trance that she would remember nothing of what they did to her. 'Loxitiv' was another imaginary word used to send her quickly into deep hypnosis, and the other expression indicated the address to which she was to write, and other action to be taken if for any reason she was ever unable to go to see Walter as ordered. He had told her that if ever she remembered these things she would immediately fall dead.

Another method used to lift the memory blockage was that of regression. The woman was told she was back with Walter at a certain time and place, and made to relive, as it were, these things. In this way she described the manner in which Walter had abused her sexually, the contents of letters he had written to her, and the fictitious operations he had pretended to carry out in order to extract more money from her.

In spite of the post-hypnotic and other precautions he had taken, Walter became suspected by the woman's husband and family, and she, in all innocence, informed Walter of this suspicion. He thereupon attempted, by various ruses, to cause her to murder her husband and even to take her own life. On one occasion she tried to shoot him with a revolver which, unknown to her, was fortunately not loaded, and several times she attempted, under Walter's detailed instructions, to poison him. He was nearly killed when his motor-cycle crashed after Walter had ordered her to tamper with its brakes. Her powers of judgment were so reduced by hypnotic influence that although she was a motor cyclist herself, she was made to believe that severing the handbrake control and slackening the footbrake adjustment of her husband's machine was actually a safety measure.

Walter ordered her to take a large quantity of a certain kind of tablet, and when this plan failed because she could not obtain them he instructed her to 'end her torment' by jumping from a moving train. She was only restrained from doing this by other passengers, in whom she had confided about her feelings of distress. When told to drown herself she attempted to do so, but her housekeeper was able to prevent her at the last moment.

After preliminary examinations and enquiries which had taken nearly two years, and a trial lasting for three weeks, Franz Walter was convicted and sentenced to ten years imprisonment.

Medical evidence confirmed that the victim of this unique crime was a well integrated woman showing no signs of being a psychopath, a hysteric or morally unbalanced. This opinion was endorsed by specialists from the leading psychiatric and nerve clinics of the country, who were unanimous in excluding any possibility that she was in any way unstable or morbidly suggestable. Walter had been able to make her do things by hypnosis which were contrary to her whole nature.

What has been described as a classic case in the history of modern crime took place in Copenhagen, Denmark, in 1951. A man walked into the Landmandsbank, took a revolver from his briefcase and fired it at the ceiling. Throwing the case on the counter he ordered the cashier to fill it with money. When the cashier hesitated the man shot him dead. He then turned to the manager and told him to fill the case. The manager attempted to reach the alarm switch, but before he could do so he too was shot dead. Another bank employee did manage to sound the alarm, whereupon the raider turned and ran out of the building, threatening to shoot anyone who stood in his way. Leaping on to a bicycle he rode away, eluding all his pursuers except a fourteen-year-old boy who managed to keep on his tail until the gunman entered an apartment house. The lad informed the police, who searched the house. They found the killer, who admitted he was the man they wanted, and accompanied him into the flat which he had been about to enter.

In the flat they found a filthy, drunken old woman, who told them that the arrested man was a friend of her nephew, a man named Nielsen, who was away in the country with her tenant, a night club dancer. She gave the police a photograph of her nephew and their files showed that he had a bad criminal record, having spent a number of years in prison. The arrested man, whose name was Hardrup, insisted however that his friend had no part in the hold-up, and as he was away at the time no suspicion fell upon him, the gunman being sent for trial.

Then the police received an anonymous letter. The sender claimed to be in possession of important evidence concerning the case and asked for a detective to meet him at a local bar. A detective kept the appointment and met a man who told an astounding story. He claimed that he had spent several years in prison and that Nielsen and Hardrup were serving sentences for treason at the same time, in fact they shared the same cell. Nielsen, he claimed, was a hypnotist, who had reduced Hardrup to such a state that he became virtually his slave, giving up all his personal possessions and even much of his prison food to him. The code, or trigger sign which always sent Hardrup into a deep trance was the sign of an X, and Nielsen had so conditioned his subject that whenever this sign was made he went straight into a state of somnambulance. The informant insisted that although Hardrup had carried out the raid, Nielsen's was certainly the mind controlling him at the time.

On the strength of this the police reopened their enquiries, and Hardrup was examined by three psychiatrists. They noticed that although he repeatedly and emphatically denied that his 'friend' was involved in the crimes, his protests seemed unreasoned, mechanical reiterations of the same simple statements. He did however admit that the bicycle he had used belonged to Nielsen. A famous psychologist, Dr Max Schmid, was then called in. He asked Hardrup what he knew of hypnosis, and whether he had ever been hypnotized. Hardrup became very agitated, saying that his 'good angel' would not allow him to answer, and repeated his admissions of guilt, adding the request to 'get it over'.

The police visited Nielsen again, who denied lending his bicycle to Hardrup. They next decided to interrogate Hardrup in Nielsen's presence. The same questions were asked as before, and the same admissions of guilt and denials of Nielsen's complicity were received. It was noticed however, that Nielsen was sitting forward with elbows on knees, arms crossed and hands on shoulders, thus making a clear X sign. When told to sit properly he changed his position for a more upright one, but immediately crossed his legs. For the duration of the interrogation, a matter of some three hours, he stared intently into Hardrup's eyes. It was observed that whenever Nielsen made an X sign Hardrup renewed his own confessions and protestations of Nielsen's innocence, but when Nielsen was prevented from making an X, Hardrup ceased to remember anything. When Nielsen was removed from the room Hardrup began to say that his 'good angel' would not allow him to talk.

This, of course, was not sufficient evidence to enable the police to take further action, and the case seemed to have reached a deadlock when it came to their notice that a raid on a bank in another town seven months before had followed an almost identical pattern, with the importance difference that it had been successful. Witnesses were able to identify Hardrup as the raider, but when accused of this hold-up he denied all recollection of it. His 'good angel', he said, told him when to remember and when to forget.

By now the police were satisfied that Hardrup was being made to act under a series of post-hypnotic suggestions, but were still unable to find any means of proving this. Eventually they re-questioned Hardrup's wife. She confessed that she was terrified of Nielsen, who had once stripped and beaten her unconscious in front of her husband when she had tried to persuade him to break away from Nielsen's influence. She had seen Nielsen hypnotize her husband on many occasions by making the sign of an X, and had suspected that he was involved in the first bank raid.

Next the police discovered that Hardrup was receiving letters daily, seemingly innocent, but each marked in some way with the X sign. They also obtained an admission from another prisoner that he had been bribed by Nielsen to mark X signs on the walls where Hardrup was certain to see them. Removal to a solitary cell and precautions to ensure that no Xs were visible, enabled Hardrup, after five days, to break away from Nielsen's hypnotic influence. He then called for pen and paper and began to set down his story.

He and Nielsen had met in 1947 when they were both in prison for collaborating with the Nazis. Nielsen hypnotized him and told him that as his 'good angel' he would protect him. God, he told Hardrup, had commanded him to be his leader, and that when he saw the X sign it was God talking to him. After they were released from prison Nielsen continued to hypnotize him in the same way, and had instructed him to raid the banks, playing on Hardrup's political fanaticism by making the 'good angel' say they were carried out in this cause.

Nielsen was convicted of murder and imprisoned for life. Hardrup was found guilty but not responsible for his actions, and was sent to a psychiatric hospital.

Of the fact that hypnosis was a major factor in the two cases outlined there can be no doubt, and Myers was wrong for once when he prognosticated that the criminal uses of hypnotism would never be more than 'the harmless curiosities of the lecture-room'. It stands out clearly that hypnotic suggestion can be and has been misused for criminal purposes, although by the nature of things such misuses can never be common. As Hammerschlag puts it,

'In individual instances this misuse may overstep the boundaries of what seems rationally intelligible. Out of a bond between one person and another, a powerful relationship can result which is not explicable in terms of reason. This relationship, because of an enhanced suggestive influence and dependence, in certain circumstances leads inevitably to situations in which the suggestor is endowed with almost uncanny powers. But we can also establish that such an outcome is only conceivable under exceptional conditions and that the criminal use of suggestion and hypnosis therefore belongs to the rarities of crime.'[1]

[1] *Hypnotism and Crime* (English translation by Prof. John Cohen), London, 1956. Dr Hammerschlag's book also contains a detailed account and an exhaustive psychological examination of the Heidelberg case and several others of equal interest.

CHAPTER FOURTEEN

Miscellany

It will always be sufficient to my fame that I have been able to open out a vast field of research to the speculations of science, and that I have, so to say, traced out the path of this new highway.

FRANZ ANTON MESMER

DURING his researches into the sources of the material for this book, the author noted a number of items which he felt should be included but for which a suitable place could not be found in the preceding chapters. They are therefore set down here in somewhat random order, without any special reference to their relationships with each other.

HYPNOTISM OF ANIMALS

Many of the early mesmerists, and a few present-day hypnotists, have made the claim that the hypnotic state can be induced in certain animals; indeed, it has been stated that the possibility of influencing animals is evidence of some mesmeric or magnetic fluid, since the effects could not be ascribed to imagination or suggestion. Many cases are recorded in the early literature, but few seem to be at all well authenticated. There are reports in *Zoist* of the mesmerization of savage dogs, a bear, a mad bull and many less dangerous creatures. One case, which attracted much attention at the time, was the cure of a sick cow which had been pronounced incurable by the veterinary surgeon. The treatment was said to consist of passes made across the chest and along the spine. Two horses suffering from lockjaw were reported to have been cured by similar methods, passes being made daily for several hours. Another horse was allegedly relieved of inflammation of the eye by passes without contact, and yet another of a leg inflammation in the same manner.

Lafontaine, who introduced Braid to mesmerism, is said to have mesmerized a lion at the London Zoo, and Moll records that in Austria army horses were required by law to be mesmerized before they were shod. It is generally accepted nowadays however, that the so-called hypnotism of animals is quite a different phenomenon from hypnosis in man. It usually takes the form of catalepsy and appears to be due either to paralysis through fear, or to a simulation of death in the instinctive knowledge that many animals and birds of prey will not attack the dead. Replying to the contention that animals, birds, frogs, insects and even young alligators can be hypnotized by methods similar to those employed with human subjects, Milne Bramwell comments:

'The only argument in favour of this is drawn from the fact that these animals, after certain physical stimuli have been applied to them, present the phenomenon of catalepsy. ... If, for example, you turn a beetle over on its back it will remain motionless and apparently cataleptic with its legs sticking rigidly in the air. The moment you turn away, however, it scrambles to its feet and resumes its journey. Here death or catalepsy was in all probability only shammed, and doubtless the insect was keenly watching your every movement and anxiously waiting for your departure. Again, catalepsy is only one, and a comparatively unimportant, phenomenon of hypnosis. One of the main characteristics of the hypnotic state is the rapidity with which one phenomenon can be changed into its opposite. Have we any evidence of this in the so-called hypnosis of animals? I think not. Again, is it logical to conclude similarity of cause from similarity of effect? ... It is possible that in some instance the phenomenon is genuine, and then, according to Preyer, the condition is one of paralysis resulting from fright. Now fear is not necessary for the induction of hypnosis; and, before concluding that the condition is a hypnotic one, it would be wise to exclude this factor from the equation. To do this experimentally would not be difficult; it would only be necessary to get rid of the disproprotion between the size and strength of the operator and the animal, a disproprotion which, in the experiments referred to, has always existed in favour of the hypnotizer. Instead of a young alligator, let one of greater age and larger growth be chosen and the experiment repeated. I am inclined to think that in such a case the roles would be reversed, the operator would become cataleptic and the subject uncommonly and disagreeably mobile.'[1]

MASS HYPNOTISM

A term describing an important aspect of the subject, but which has been degraded by common misuse to the status of a mere cliché, is the expression 'mass hypnotism'. It is true that the emotional atmosphere of the political meeting or of the revivalist gathering is conducive to a state of heightened suggestibility, in which the politician or preacher is able to 'put across' ideas which, under normal circumstances, his audience would be far less likely to accept; indeed, the stage hypnotist deliberately strives to build up a

[1] 'What is Hypnotism?', S.P.R. *Proceedings*, Vol. XII, pp. 213-4.

similar atmosphere in order to make his performance more impressive, and the ability to produce and control such conditions is, of course, the hall-mark of the first-class orator. In this sense a man such as Hitler, who was able to rouse vast crowds to the point of hysteria, and to place a whole nation under his spell, might be described as a great mass-hypnotist, but this is going somewhat beyond the limits normally connated by the term hypnotism.

True mass hypnotism is the simultaneous induction of hypnosis in a group of people, as for example, when Mesmer's patients gathered round the *baquet*, and whilst it is certainly possible to hypnotize a large number of selected subjects together, the novelist's conception of the master hypnotist who is able to perform such feats with all and sundry, has no real foundation in fact. Mass hypnotism is often put forward as the explanation of the famous Indian rope trick, the suggestion being that the *fakir* hypnotizes the complete audience and then suggests the hallucination of a boy climbing up a rope, disappearing, etc. The odds against any casual audience being composed entirely of people sufficiently suggestible to enable this to be done are, of course, overwhelming, and the theory is not therefore, tenable. In point of fact, no well authenticated record of a performance of the Indian rope trick exists. Incidentally, this reminds the author of a delightful *Punch* joke which is not all a joke. The scene is India, Sahib and Memsahib walk stolidly past a brilliant exposition of the Rope Trick. Says Sahib to Memsahib, 'He only thinks he does it.'

A MASTER HYPNOTIST

An American professor of psychology, Donald Powell Wilson, has, however, recorded that while carrying out research in an American prison he investigated the case of a convict who, besides being a master hypnotist, could influence groups of people by telepathy, place himself in a state of suspended animation, and while in this condition cause the twelve signs of the Zodiac to appear on various parts of his body purely by an effort of will.

The convict, named Hadad, who was part Hindu and part Senegalese and had a reputation among the other prisoners and prison staff as a magician and escapist, first came to the psychologist's notice when he was found hanging by the neck, apparently dead, in his cell. He had hypnotized a warder without that man's knowledge, taken his belt, given the warder a post-hypnotic suggestion that the belt would not appear to be missing from his waist, and then used it to hang himself. A doctor pronounced him dead and he was removed to the prison mortuary.

Three days later, when an autopsy was about to be performed and the surgeon picked up his knife to commence work, the three doctors present suddenly heard the sound of breathing from the 'corpse', and saw his muscles begin to ripple. Then he rose to a sitting position, opened his eyes, and said: 'Gentlemen, I would rather not, if you do not mind'.

The doctors, all highly qualified and experienced men, while agreeing that catatonic trances of such duration were not unheard of, considered Hadad's ability to retain consciousness and memory throughout the trance, so that he was able to awaken just before the autopsy began, to be unique.

When interviewed later in the prison hospital, Hadad stated that the purpose of this astounding feat was merely to draw the attention of the doctors to him, and then declared that he would give an even more startling demonstration of his strange powers. In the hospital's psychopathic ward were a number of epileptics, among them some hopeless cases who through severe brain deterioration, suffered frequent seizures. After obtaining the doctors' agreement that such seizures could not, by any means known to them, be delayed for more than a few hours, Hadad announced that as a demonstration of the use of telepathy in healing at a distance, he would cause a delay of all seizures in the ward for three days and nights, and would then cause them to re-commence at a given time.

Incredulous, the doctors arranged for the prisoner to be kept locked in a solitary cell, and a close watch was kept both on him and on the psychopathic ward. As predicted, there were no seizures whatever for the duration of the three days, right up until the time given, after which they commenced again.

Before putting his promise into practice, Hadad produced other equally astonishing, if less useful phenomena. He undressed and announced that after he had gone into a trance the twelve signs of the Zodiac would appear on his body, with Aries on the forehead, Cancer on the breast, Sagittarius on the thighs and the rest in appropriate places.

Sure enough, soon after he had placed himself in a state of autohypnosis, hive-like patches began to appear, which in some places were clearly recognizable as the signs appropriate to those parts of the body.

One of the doctors checked Hadad's condition, and pronounced that by all tests the man was dead. Even when a vein was punctured there was no flow of blood, but when it was mentioned that some of the Zodiacal signs were not clear, Hadad 'awoke', and told them the signs would be seen more distinctly through a magnifying glass. He then relapsed into his strange trance, and remained in this state until a glass had been brought and several more of the signs verified. On awakening, and in answer to questions, he merely said: 'Suspended animation, Doctor; it is simple.'

The doctors admitted to themselves that although science might offer an explanation of the phenomena in psychological terms, it could not reproduce it, and that in the case of the epileptics all their training and knowledge could not enable them to interrupt seizures even for a short time. To quote:

'We were struck by the incongruity of the fact that here was modern science epitomized in a research hospital with the last word in equipment, and with the best consultants in the country only five telephone minutes away. But no X-ray machine could penetrate, no microscope reveal, no surgery excise, no cosmic ray illuminate, no test tube break down the rationale of a black man in a dungeon five hundred feet away, quietly working the ancient mysteries of the world outside the body and the senses, quietly reflecting the ancient philosophic victory of mind in the impingement of the unknown and feared upon the known.'[1]

HYPNOTISM AND PRIMITIVE RACES

While on the subject of the remarkable understanding of the uses of hypnotism by coloured people, mention should be made of a recent report of an investigation into the psychic practices of the Australian aborigines by an American parapsychologist, Ronald Rose, who, with his wife, lived among these primitive people for many weeks. He records that they employ hypnotism in many of their ritual practices, and that their witch-doctors, or 'clever-men' possess a surprising appreciation of its power and applications.

These clever-men employ hypnotism extensively in healing the sick, and some of the methods by which they induce hypnosis is remarkably similar to those employed by more 'civilized' practitioners. One such method, almost identical with that favoured by the British pioneer hypnotist Braid, is to make the subject gaze intently as some bright object, in this case the witch-doctor's 'clever-stone', a piece of highly polished quartz, such as is the prized possession of every clever-man. But these comparatively simple methods are by no means the only ones. Hypnosis induced telepathically by an effort of will and concentration is far from rare. The following example, told to Rose by an old native woman, is typical of many cases reported.

When she was a girl, a clever-man had told her that he could

[1] *My Six Convicts*, London, 1951.

'will' a person to come to him. Thinking he was merely 'showing off', she laughed and replied that she did not believe him. Thereupon he sat down and gave a sort of groan, much as if he were ill, whereat a stranger who had been walking along a path some distance away suddenly stopped, looked round and then came across to them, saying that he had 'felt' the clever-man calling him.

Another native described how his grandfather hypnotized a man from a distance in order to kill him. 'In the old days my grandfather was very clever. He was so clever that a Queensland "doctor" was trying to catch him to show he was cleverer. My grandfather thought he had better catch this other fellow first. He couldn't get close enough him ordinarywise, so he sat down and sang a song that made this Queensland fellow come to him. This was at Boonah, near the border. When this other fellow came up my grandfather said, "I made you come. You bin trying to catch me." Then he killed this fellow.'

A third aborigine recounted what had happened when his uncle stole something from a clever-man. He was working with him pulling potatoes when he suddenly complained 'I don't feel good. Some fellow's watching us.' Shortly afterwards he said, 'I got to lie down. Someone's doing something to me.' The uncle lay down, and shortly afterwards a man came into the paddock, walked up to him and said, 'This fellow pinched a thing belonging to me. I've come to get it.' The man took something from the uncle's coat and said, 'He'll wake up soon. You tell him not to pinch things.' When the uncle awoke and was told of what had occurred he said, 'I should have knowed not to take anything from a doctor fellow.'

Mass hypnotism, says Ronald Rose, is of paramount importance in much of the phenomena of aboriginal magic. This, he thinks, is due largely to the fact that the tribal initiation rites of the young include hypnotic tests and instruction, and, as novices who fail the initiation trials do not survive, those remaining are predisposed to subsequent hypnotic influence.

The clever-men are also masters of the art of auto-hypnosis, and frequently throw themselves into a state of trance. While entranced they often 'go travelling', and on awakening, give accounts of happenings many miles away, accounts which, in some cases, are subsequently confirmed. Instruction in this travelling clairvoyance is an important part in the training of prospective 'doctors', so also is the technique of 'pointing', or willing a person to die, Rose gives a number of examples of the latter, one of the most impressive being a case in which a man, who claimed to possess magic power, forced two young girls to go off into the bush with him; threatening to use his 'magic' against them if they refused. The girls' people went to an old clever-man for help, and he promised to 'point' the kidnapper and thus kill him.

The clever-man, white haired and white bearded, and so aged that he could hardly walk, took a piece of fencing wire about a foot long and with one of his clever-stones hammered one end of it into a point. To the other end of the wire he attached a piece of wax from the nest of some wild bees. He walked a short distance from the camp, sat down and began to 'sing the curses' of the kidnapper, all the while pointing and jerking the 'bone'[1] in various directions.

'Every night he did this at his camp-fire, a short distance from the main camp of the tribe. He held the "bone" over the fire and it became very hot; and every night he sang the "bone" away into the bush seeking out the man who had taken the two girls. For more than a week he did this, while the old men looked and the women held their heads. Then one night he put the "bone" down and said: "I got that fellow".'

Two days later the girls returned safely, saying that one day the kidnapper had complained that he felt sick. Within a few days he was having to lie down for most of the time, and then he had died. His death occurred at about the time when the old clever-man said that he had 'got him'.

Rose's report, incidentally, is not entirely concerned with hypnotism. Sorcery, hauntings, premonitions of death, rainmaking and many other aspects of the psychic background of this remarkable race are dealt with in a very thorough and comprehensive manner. He sums up thus:—'It is certainly true that aborigines have not developed a mode of reasoned thought in any substantial way resembling ours. But could it not also be true that aborigines have plumbed depths of the mind, rich in their peculiar rewards, that we have left relatively unexplored? And might it not also be true that, while they find it difficult to adapt themselves to our way of thought, we might indeed find it impossible to achieve theirs.'[2]

'DO-IT-YOURSELF'

The author's first introduction to hypnotism was by the accidental discovery when clearing out a lumber-room during his early teens, of a tattered old booklet bearing the modest title, *Professor*

---

[1] The wire was a substitute for the piece of human bone normally used in ritualistic killing by 'willing to death'. Rose says that among tribes who were in contact with white culture various other articles, including rifle barrels and even sheets of tin are reported to have been used; indicating that the bone or other object was merely a symbol, and not an essential part of the killing process.

[2] *Living Magic*, London, 1957.

Williams' Complete Hypnotism Comprising Twenty Lessons. This book, undated but obviously Victorian, seems to have been the fore-runner of the numerous correspondence courses on hypnotism now regularly advertised in a wide variety of periodicals. The 'professor's' opening paragraphs typify the style in which the 'course', of seventy pages, is written.

'You now approach Hypnotism in the character of a student, and I trust with all a student's eagerness and docility. You will find in this Course of Lessons easy and complete directions for hypnotizing others, as well as counsel and guidance on the exhibition of hypnotic phenomena. I have aimed to give the actual truth about this wonder-working force, and it is the opinion of all experts that my lessons on its applications are the very best the world has yet produced. You may therefore have full confidence that no amount of money could produce you better instructions. I give you all the secrets of the art in plain language, without omitting one point or word that could be helpful to a complete understanding of the subject. I have nothing else in this connection to offer or sell, and thus I have no motive to hold back a single thing that would make you a practical operator.'

It will be appreciated that a mere seventy pages of such flowery phraseology can provide but little opportunity for the complete exposition of hypnotism, yet what little information is given is remarkably sound. The course concludes:

'I am always pleased to hear from my students. When you find (as you surely will) that I have given you the true secrets of the art, and when your success calls forth a natural display if enthusiasm, I will feel deeply honoured by a knowledge of the same.

'Trusting and believing that the knowledge you have received from these instructions will be the means of benefiting you in many ways, and advancing yourself intellectually, socially, and financially,
           I remain,
               Most sincerely yours,
                   Prof. WILLIAMS,
                       London.'

The self-styled professor's literary style may now seem archaic, but his method of obtaining a handsome income (his 'course' was priced at 18/6) is still successfully practised by a legion of 'master hypnotists' offering their 'jealously guarded secrets' at fees ranging from a few shillings to a useful number of guineas. That such 'master hypnotists' have a wide understanding, not only of human suggestibility, but of human credulity and gullibility, is evident from the manner in which their advertisements are couched. An

American 'Ph.D.', for instance, runs the following advertisement in a magazine with a world-wide circulation.

HYPNOSIS UNAWARES

LEARN to hypnotize others while they sleep. You can—easily—with my new copyrighted Home-Study Course! Jealously-guarded professional secrets of 'natural sleep hypnosis'; cases, examples, exciting instructions. Complete self-study course, cautiously offered to ADULTS ONLY $5.00. (Sorry, no C.O.D.)

Another American, who disdains to use letters after his name, and contents himself with the modest description, ———— 'the Hypnotist', words his advertisement thus:

HYPNOTIZE *the First Day*

Instantaneous hypnotic sleep the *first* day or your money back. This method has been a closely guarded secret for years. Now revealed for the first time. Here is what you get: 'How to Hypnotize the First Day'. 'Hypnotism Can Help You' and the famous ———— hypnograph. Only $2.00. Complete. *Supply Limited*.

The most extravagant claims are made in a frequently seen advertisement by the publisher of a 'Hypnotism Handbook', who states that hypnosis can be induced merely by asking the subject to gaze at a spiral pattern while 'word for word hypnotic techniques' are read from the handbook. 'As soon as he is hypnotized', states the advertisement, 'READ TO HIM the particular WORD FOR WORD therapy which applies to his particular problem. Many such therapies are given, always in the exact WORD FOR WORD form, which is essential in any scientific or professional use of hypnosis.' Were it not for the regularity with which this advertisement continues to appear it would be difficult to believe that even the most naive person would be taken in by such absurdly baseless claims. Indeed, it is an interesting, if sad, reflection on human nature that the 'suckers' who are thus induced to waste their money are the last people in the world likely to become hypnotists.

The foregoing examples are, needless to say, of American origin, and probably few British journals would accept advertisements in which such outrageous claims appear. The 'racket' in this country more often takes the form of a dubious 'institute' which issues worthless diplomas, usually associated with an equally doubtful society or federation, whose elaborate certificates of membership again have no value except for the impression they may make on the uncritical. The author recently saw a grubby card on which the advertiser proclaimed his membership of what purported to be a responsible society of hypnotherapists, displayed on a Chelsea advertisement board in company with notices describing the allurements of various 'call-girls'.[1]

WHO SHOULD PRACTISE HYPNOTISM?

The preceding paragraphs indicate that a large measure of fraud and charlatanism still besmirches the name of hypnotism, and no reasonable person would deny that some degree of control and protection is, from many points of view, desirable. The question thus presented is that of who should be permitted to practise hypnotism. The official viewpoint of the medical profession is that none but qualified medical men should be allowed to use hypnosis, and this attitude is understandable and, in many respects, quite reasonable. Before considering the question further, however, it is interesting to note that many of the people who seek consultations with the author, do so on the advice of their own doctors. This is also true in the case of several other hypnotists well known to the author.

The medical profession's claim that it should have the exclusive right to use hypnotism falls down on several counts, not the least of which is its past, and, in some quarters, its present, attitude towards the subject, an attitude which has persisted right from the time of Mesmer. It should be pointed out also that much, if not most, of our present knowledge of hypnosis is due to the work of non-medical men. Braid probably would never have become interested had it not been for Lafontaine, and the value of the work of Myers and Gurney, neither of whom was a doctor, is unquestioned.

This is certainly not to say, however, that any Tom, Dick or Harriet who is able to induce hypnosis is qualified to practise medical hypnotism. On the contrary, it has been shown that many such operators lack the educational, technical and ethical standards rightly insisted upon in registered members of the medical profession.

---

[1] Since writing this chapter the author has noted the following in the classified advertisements of a British spiritualist newspaper:

"Send 4½d. stamp for free lesson on hypnotism and how to attract money. Adults only."

The address given was, needless to say, an accommodation one, imposingly prefixed by the words '——— House'.

There would seem to be no real objection though to some arrangement whereby a responsible hypnotist treats patients under the direction or on the advice of a qualified doctor, in the same manner as various 'medical auxiliaries' work; or, as so often happens professionally, two men, each a specialist in his own field, combine their knowledge and efforts. Although officially unrecognized, such collaboration between doctor and hypnotist is not uncommon to-day.

The foregoing remarks refer to the use of hypnosis in the treatment of disease. In the field of psychotherapy, however, the hypnotist who has received proper training can claim, with complete truth, that he is better qualified to practise than the average medical man; indeed, with the increasing complexity of both psychological and medical science the need for specialization becomes ever more apparent. It is surely no more necessary for a man who intends to practise hypnotism in clinical psychology to learn to use a stethoscope or a hypodermic syringe than for a Cornish fisherman to be familiar with the technique of harpooning a whale.

Dr Robert Laidlow, Chief of the Psychiatric Service at the Roosevelt Hospital, New York, has stated the position wisely and well. When questioned on the desirability of outlawing the non-medical use of hypnotism he replied:

'I feel very deeply that hypnosis should be regarded as a medical technique and should be utilized only under proper medical auspices. One shouldn't permit its use by laymen any more than the layman should be permitted to give intravenous drugs or perform minor surgery.

'Certainly I would advocate the banning of hypnotic entertainment. *I would use the word "non-medical" in a broad sense, however. There are trained clinical psychologists who use hypnosis wisely and well.* I would decry the amateur use of hypnosis as contrasted with the professional use. The amateur should be rightly banned.'[1]

The author, in common with all responsible hypnotists, would welcome the elimination of the charlatan and the fool, by the establishment of certain standards of knowledge, ability and ethics, conformity with which would be a legal requirement; but, with due respect to a great profession, insists that the monopolistic claims of certain medical men are not warranted by the facts. There is more than a grain of truth in the comment by H. J. D. Murton, who, referring to attempts by South African doctors to ban 'lay' hypnotists, says:

'Of course, there wouldn't *be* any hypnosis but for the pioneer and research work of laymen. Would it be unfair, I wonder, to suggest that the medical profession, when a "band-wagon" they have tried

[1] 'Psychiatric uses of Hypnosis', *Tomorrow*, Autumn, 1958.

to wreck proves successful, jump on the wagon and try to push everyone else off?"[1]

MEDICAL APPLICATIONS OF HYPNOTISM

As was stated at the beginning, it is not the purpose of this book to deal extensively with medical hypnosis as such. This ground is already well covered in the literature, and the author particularly recommends *A Handbook of Medical Hypnosis* by Drs Gordon Ambrose and George Newbold, and *The Healing Voice* by Dr A. Philip Magonet, to those who wish to study this aspect of the subject more fully. Mention of some of the medical uses in which hypnosis has proved outstandingly successful may not, however, be out of place. Its use in obstetrics, gynaecology and dentistry is rapidly becoming widespread, and the disorders treated with conspicuous success include skin diseases, blushing, stammering, headache, insomnia, obesity, sterility, impotence, frigidity, asthma, and many other complaints. Homosexuality, exhibitionism, masturbation, flagellation and similar sexual abnormalities have also proved amenable to hypnotic treatment, as have many kinds of neuroses, including hysterical paralysis, hysterical deafness, hysterical amnesia and various phobias, obsessions and impulses. Shyness and self-consciousness, smoking, drinking, sea-sickness and nail-biting have also been cured by hypnotic therapy.

In most cases complaints must be traced to the source; the mere removal of symptoms rarely being sufficient. Hypnosis, it must be emphasized, is not a cure-all or a magic elixir; it is, however, a priceless addition to the armamentarium of the doctor and the clinical psychologist.

MILITARY APPLICATIONS—'BRAIN-WASHING'

There has been much conjecture, and a certain amount of experimental work, on the possible uses of hypnotism in warfare, and the imaginative reader will readily visualize situations in which much of the phenomena already described could be put to military use.

It is said, for instance, that during the First World War a famous hypnotist offered to hypnotize a captured German U boat captain and to make him, while entranced, pilot a submarine through the network of enemy minefields, with the object of attacking the German grand fleet. This offer apparently, was not accepted.

Estabrooks[2] suggests that hypnotized subjects could easily be used for spying, sabotage and the transmission of secret messages. As an

[1] Editorial, *Prediction*, September, 1960.   [2] *Hypnotism*, London, 1959.

example of the last he cites the hypothetical case of a selected subject hypnotized, say, in America and made subconsciously to memorize a long and complicated message—a simple matter with a good subject—and also told that no one else can possibly hypnotize him except a named person in, perhaps, Australia, to whom, under hypnosis, he will repeat the message. As the subject will have no conscious knowledge of his mission or of the message, no amount of interrogation or even torture by possible captors could make him reveal it.

Hypnosis undoubtedly plays a prominent part also in the technique of so-called 'brain-washing', and the remarks of Estabrooks in this connection have already been noted on page 33. The knowledge that prior hypnosis could be a means of protecting certain men against these ghastly processes is, at least, of some comfort.

DANGERS OF HYPNOTISM

Whilst it is true that most of the supposed dangers of hypnotism are misconceptions arising from sensational reports in the popular press and weird notions in the minds of novelists, it is at the same time certainly true that the misuse of hypnotism, either through ignorance or with deliberate intent, can be the cause of very real harm. But, surely, this is true of anything? Misuse of drugs can kill a patient or degrade the addict, but few would advocate the abolition of pharmacy on these grounds. Many women have died as the result of illegal operations, but this would not constitute a sound argument against the general practice of surgery. Yet, many people, including doctors, still condemn the use of hypnotism for reasons which are no more logical.

CHAPTER FIFTEEN

Conclusion

The final conclusion is that we know very little, and yet it is astonishing that we know so much, and still more astonishing that so little knowledge can give us so much power.

WALTER GRIERSON

THIS book has not been written for the advanced student of either hypnotism or psychical research, and, as was stated at the beginning, its purpose is not to make any original contribution to our knowledge of these subjects. It is an effort to give an honest and unprejudiced survey and to make certain information, already on record but widely distributed throughout an extensive literature, more accessible, particularly to the newcomer to these fields of enquiry.

Many of the accounts of clairvoyance, telepathy and mediumistic phenomena will seem unbelievably fantastic to the reader unacquainted with psychical research, and indeed, were it not for the eminence and unquestioned integrity of the investigators concerned, might well be dismissed as fiction. But, Sir William Barrett, F.R.S., M.I.E.E., M.R.I.A., is universally recognized as having been one of our greatest physicists; Charles Richet, winner of a Nobel prize for medicine and a former editor of the *Revue Scientifique*, was the most celebrated European physiologist of his day and also President of the Société pour l'Arbitrage entre nations; Henri Bergson achieved equal fame as a philosopher and was another Nobel prizewinner; William James has been described as 'the most renowned of the thinkers of America',[1] and these are but representative of the large body of famous men who have borne testimony to the occurrence of such phenomena. Most of them stood to gain nothing, and to lose a great deal, by their insistence that these things must be recognized as scientific facts.

It is a sorry reflection on human nature that whilst the findings of such men as these concerning more prosaic matters are generally accepted without question, their reported observations on less easily explained phenomena are received, more often than not, with hostility and derision, and this attitude is, unfortunately, typical of many of their fellow scientists from whom, surely, we have a right to expect an objective and rational outlook, yet who frequently evince

[1] *Encyclopaedia Britannica.*

a woeful degree of emotional bias and prejudice. Indeed, Professor Eysenck has rightly said that 'Scientists, especially when they leave the particular field in which they have specialized, are just as ordinary, pig-headed, and unreasonable as anybody else, and their unusually high intelligence only makes their prejudices all the more dangerous because it enables them to cover these up with an unusually glib and smooth flow of high-sounding talk.'[1]

Even the illustrious Thomas Huxley, who wisely enjoined the enquirer to 'Sit down before fact as a little child, be prepared to give up every preconceived notion, follow humbly wherever and to whatsoever abysses Nature leads', was not above reproach in this respect, for when invited to sit on the Committee of the London Dialectical Society, the forerunner of the Society for Psychical Research, he scornfully declined, refusing even to consider the possibility of there being any truth in the alleged facts under investigation.

Although the early workers suffered through this attitude towards hypnotism itself, this did not always prevent them from adopting it in turn towards the claims of some of their colleagues that supernormal phenomena sometimes occurred. Not the least of the offenders in this respect was the oft quoted Milne Bramwell, whose *Hypnotism, its History, Theory and Practice* is, without doubt, the best known and most authoritative work on medical hypnosis yet published. But when Bramwell deals with such things as clairvoyance and telepathy, he shows himself to be just as prejudiced and reactionary as those members of his profession whom he rightly condemns for refusing to consider the claims of the pioneers of hypnotism.

When the findings and views of such authorities as Myers and Gurney tend to support his own beliefs, Bramwell quotes them profusely but, when they pronounce themselves convinced of the reality of phenomena in the existence of which he does not believe, he does not hesitate to accuse them of mal-observation, self deception, and every fault and failing short of rank dishonesty. His attitude to all the psychic or 'higher' phenomena, however well attested, is virtually 'I have not experienced them, therefore I do not believe they can be possible'. And from Milne Bramwell onwards, medical hypnotists have, in general, taken the same line. It has been left largely to the non-medically qualified hypnotists, those whom many doctors would see banned from practising, to further our knowledge of these things.

Whilst no thinking person would deny that an attitude of healthy scepticism is infinitely preferable to one of unquestioning gullibility, if we earnestly desire to learn more concerning the real nature of

[1] *Sense and Nonsense in Psychology*, London, 1957.

human personality and man's place in the scheme of things, surely the only attitude must be one of unbiased, scientific objectivity. Hamlet's oft quoted words to Horatio may be hackneyed, but their truth nevertheless, cannot be gainsaid.

The author is always happy to receive constructive correspondence concerning any matter relating to hypnotism or psychical research. Letters should be addressed c/o the Publishers, and if a reply is desired, a stamped addressed envelope should accompany such letters.

APPENDIX I

The Hypnotism Act, 1952

Reproduced by permission of H.M. Stationery Office

BE it enacted by the Queen's most Excellent Majesty, by and with the advice and consent of the Lords Spiritual and Temporal, and Commons, in this present Parliament assembled, and by the authority of the same, as follows:

1. (1) Where under any enactment an authority in any area have power to grant licences for the regulation of places kept or ordinarily used for public dancing, singing, music or other public entertainment of the like kind, any power conferred by any enactment to attach conditions to any such licence shall include power to attach conditions regulating or prohibiting the giving of an exhibition, demonstration or performance of hypnotism on any person at the place to which the licence relates.

(2) In the application of this section to Scotland, for the reference to places kept or ordinarily used for public dancing, singing, music or other public entertainment of the like kind there shall be substituted a reference to theatres or other places of public amusement or public entertainment.

2. (1) No person shall give an exhibition, demonstration or performance of hypnotism on any living person at or in connection with an entertainment to which the public are admitted, whether on payment or otherwise, at any place in relation to which such a licence as is mentioned in section one of this Act is not in force unless the controlling authority have authorized that exhibition, demonstration or performance.

(2) Any authorization under this section may be made subject to any conditions.

(3) If a person gives any exhibition, demonstration or performance of hypnotism in contravention of this section, or in contravention of any conditions attached to an authorisation under this section, he shall be liable on summary conviction to a fine not exceeding fifty pounds

(4) In this section, the expression 'controlling authority' means—

    (a) in relation to a place in any such area as is mentioned in section one of this Act, the authority having power to grant licences of the kind mentioned in that section in that area;

(b) in relation to a place in any other area in England, the council of the county borough, borough, or urban or rural district where the place is, and in relation to a place in any other area in Scotland, the council of the county or burgh where the place is.

3. A person who gives an exhibition, demonstration or performance of hypnotism on a person who has not attained the age of twenty-one years at or in connection with an entertainment to which the public are admitted, whether on payment or otherwise, shall, unless he had reasonable cause to believe that that person had attained that age, be liable on summary conviction to a fine not exceeding fifty pounds.

4. Any police constable may enter any premises where any entertainment is held if he has reasonable cause to believe that any act is being or may be done in contravention of this Act.

5. Nothing in this Act shall prevent the exhibition, demonstration or performance of hypnotism (otherwise than at or in connection with an entertainment) for scientific or research purposes or for the treatment of mental or physical disease.

6. In this Act, except where the context otherwise requires it, the following expression shall have the meaning hereby assigned to it, that is to say:

'hypnotism' includes hypnotism, mesmerism and any similar act or process which produces or is intended to produce in any person any form of induced sleep or trance in which the susceptibility of the mind of that person to suggestion or direction is increased or intended to be increased but does not include hypnotism, mesmerism or any such similar act or process which is self-induced.

7. (1) This Act may be cited as the Hypnotism Act, 1952.

(2) This Act shall not extend to Northern Ireland.

(3) This Act shall come into force on the first day of April, nineteen hundred and fifty-three.

APPENDIX II

The 'Baquet'

THE following instructions for the building of a *baquet* are by Deleuze, one of the most reliable recorders of early mesmeric practices.

'Magnetized reservoirs, or troughs, are vessels filled with magnetized materials, and provided with conductors to direct the fluid which they contain. The most common mode of constructing them is the following:

'Take a wooden vessel, two feet high, larger or smaller according to the number of persons to be placed round it, having the bottom elevated an inch from the floor by the projection of the sides. Place an iron rod in the centre, to serve as the principal conductor, having a diameter of half an inch, or of one inch, descending to within two inches of the bottom, and rising above the trough two or three feet. The lower end of this iron rod should be firmly fixed in a glass foot, or in a jug, so that it may retain its vertical position. Put into the vessel bottles of magnetized water, or other magnetized substances, cork them, and run through each cork a piece of iron wire projecting two or three inches; and arrange them in such a manner that the neck may be near the central conductor, and communicate with it by the iron wire which pierces the cork. Then place a second range of bottles above the first. If the *baquet*, or trough, is large, you can put two ranges of bottles in the same order; the neck of one being placed in the bottom of the other. This being done, you will fill the vessel with water, white sand well washed, pounded glass, and iron filings, all well magnetized. Place upon it a cover in two pieces, fitted closely together, having an opening in the middle for the central conductor. At a short distance from the circumference, at points corresponding to the spaces between the bottles, you will pierce several holes, for the purpose of thrusting into the reservoir iron conductors, bent and movable, which are raised and lowered at pleasure, so that one may direct them against any part of the body, and pass the hands above them, to draw off the fluid. And, lastly, you will attach to the central conductor cords of cotton or wool, which the patients may twine around their bodies.

Although everything that is placed in the reservoir has been magnetized beforehand, the reservoir is to be regularly magnetized, when its construction has been completed, before the cover is placed upon it. When this operation is first performed, it takes a considerable time—nearly an hour. It is even proper to repeat it three or four days in succession. But when once the reservoir has been well charged, it is readily charged again, by the magnetizer's holding the central conductor in his hands several minutes. I do not know whether reservoirs filled with water are more easily charged with the magnetic fluid than those which contain between the bottles only pounded glass, iron filings, or simply sand; but it is certain that these last are more proper and convenient, and for this reason I give them the preference. It is difficult to prevent the water's escaping from the *baquet,* and it might become foul in the course of time. The same magnetizer ought always to charge the reservoir.'

From *Animal Magnetism*, Second Edition, 1846.

APPENDIX III

Bibliography

THE following works have been consulted. Where substantial quotations are made the sources are indicated by footnotes throughout the text. Most of the books and bound volumes of many of the periodicals mentioned are to be found in the libraries of the Society for Psychical Research and the College of Psychic Science, both in London. Periodicals which have ceased publication are marked with an asterisk.

PERIODICALS

American Society for Psychical Research *Journal*, New York.
American Society for Psychical Research *Proceedings*.
Annales des Sciences Psychiques,* Paris.
*Annals of Psychical Science,** London.
Boston Society for Psychical Research *Bulletins,** Boston.
British Journal of Medical Hypnotism, London.
Indian Journal of Parapsychology, Rajasthan.
International Journal of Parapsychology, New York.
Journal of Abnormal and Social Psychology, New York.
Journal of Parapsychology, Durham, N.C.
Light, London.
*Occult Review,** London.
Parapsychology Foundation *Newsletter*, New York.
*Psychic Science,** London.
Revue Métapsychique, Paris.
Society for Psychical Research *Journal*, London.
Society for Psychical Research *Proceedings*, London.
Tomorrow, New York.

BOOKS

Publishers' names are only given in the case of books published from 1940 onwards. The dates and places of publication given are those of the actual books consulted. British editions of a number of the French and American works mentioned are in existence.

AMBROSE, GORDON (with NEWBOLD, GEORGE)
   A Handbook of Medical Hypnosis, Baillière, Tindall & Cox Ltd., London, 1956.

BARRETT, SIR WILLIAM FLETCHER
Psychical Research, London, 1911.
On the Threshold of the Unseen, London, 1918.

BAUDOUIN, ALFRED
Suggestion and Autosuggestion, London, 1920.

BERNHEIM, H.
Hypnotisme, Suggestion, Psychotherapie, Paris, 1891.

BERNSTEIN, MOREY
The Search for Bridey Murphy, Doubleday, New York, 1956.
The Search for Bridey Murphy, Pocket Books Inc., New York, 1956.

BINET, ALFRED
Etudes de Psychologie Experimentale, Paris, 1888.

BRAID, JAMES
Neurypnology; or the Rationale of Nervous Sleep, London, 1843.

BRAMWELL, J. MILNE
Hypnotism; its History, Practice and Theory, London, 1903.

CLECKLEY, HERVEY M. (with THIGPEN, CORBETT H.)
The Three Faces of Eve, Secker & Warburg, London, 1957.

COATES, JAMES
Human Magnetism, London, 1897.

COLQUHOUN, J. C.
An History of Magic, Witchcraft, and Animal Magnetism, London, 1851.

CORIAT, ISADORE H. (with WORCESTER, ELWOOD and McCOMB, SAMUEL)
Religion and Medicine, New York, 1908.

CUDDON, ERIC
Hypnosis; its Meaning and Practice, Bell, London, 1955.

DELEUZE, J. P. R.
Histoire Critique du Magnetisme Animal, Paris, 1813.
Animal Magnetism, New York, 1846.

ERSKINE, ALEX
A Hypnotist's Case Book, London, 1932.

ESTABROOKS, GEORGE H.
Hypnotism, Museum Press, London, 1959.

EYSENCK, H. J.
Uses and Abuses of Psychology, Penguin, London, 1953.
Sense and Nonsense in Psychology, Penguin, London, 1957.

FLAMMARION, CAMILLE
Mysterious Psychic Forces, Boston, 1907.

FLOURNOY, THEODOR
Des Indes à la Planète Mars, Paris, 1900.

FODOR, NANDOR
  Encyclopaedia of Psychic Science, London, 1934.
  The Search for the Beloved, Hermitage Press, New York, 1949.
  The Haunted Mind, Helix Press, New York, 1959.
FOREL, AUGUST
  Hypnotism; or Suggestion and Psychotherapy, London, 1906.
GARRETT, EILEEN J.
  Telepathy; In Search of a Lost Faculty, Creative Age Press, New York, 1941.
GELEY, GUSTAV
  From the Conscious to the Unconscious, London, 1920.
  Reincarnation, London, 1924.
GINDES, B. C.
  New Concepts of Hypnosis, Allen & Unwin, London, 1953.
HADFIELD, J. A.
  Functional Nerve Diseases, London, 1920.
HAMMERSCHLAG, HEINZ E.
  Hypnotism and Crime, Rider, London, 1956.
HART, BERNARD
  The Psychology of Insanity, London, 1912.
HOLLANDER, BERNARD
  Methods and Uses of Hypnosis and Self-Hypnosis, London, 1928.
HORSLEY, J. STEPHEN
  Narco-Analysis, Oxford University Press, London, 1943.
HUDSON, THOMAS J.
  The Law of Psychic Phenomena, London, 1895.
HULL, C. L.
  Hypnosis and Suggestibility, New York, 1933.
HYSLOP, JAMES HERVEY
  Borderland of Psychical Research, London, 1906.
  Enigmas of Psychical Research, Boston, 1906.
JANET, PIERRE
  L'Automatisme Psychologique, Paris, 1899.
  The Major Symptoms of Hysteria, New York, 1920.
  Psychological Healing, New York, 1925.
JOIRE, PAUL
  Psychical and Supernormal Phenomena, London, 1936.
KLINE, MILTON V.
  Freud and Hypnosis—The Interaction of Psycho-Dynamics and Hypnosis, Julian Press, New York, 1958.
KRAFFT-EBING, R. VON
  An Experimental Study in the Domain of Hypnotism, New York, 1899.

LANCASTER, EVELYN (with POLING, JAMES)
Strangers in my Body or The Final Face of Eve, Secker & Warburg, London, 1958.

LE CRON, LESLIE M.
Hypnotism Today, Macmillan, New York, 1947.
Experimental Hypnosis (Editor), Macmillan, New York, 1952.

LODGE, SIR OLIVER JOSEPH
Raymond; or Life After Death, London, 1916.

MAGONET, A. PHILIP
The Healing Voice, Heinemann, London, 1959.

MASON, R. OSGOOD
Telepathy and the Subliminal Self, London, 1897.

MCCOMB, SAMUEL (with WORCESTER, ELWOOD and CORIAT, ISADORE H.)
Religion and Medicine, New York, 1908.

MITCHELL, ALAN
Harley Street Hypnotist, Harrap, London, 1959

MOLL, J. ALBERT
Hypnotism, London, 1909.

MOTT, FRANCIS J.
Creative Consciousness, Boston, 1937.

MYERS, FREDERIC W. H.
Human Personality and its Survival of Bodily Death, London, 1903.

NEWBOLD, GEORGE
Medical Hypnosis, Gollancz, London, 1953.
A Handbook of Medical Hypnosis (with Ambrose Gordon), Baillière, Tindall & Cox, London, 1956.

OSTY, EUGENE
Supernormal Faculties in Man, London, 1923.

PODMORE, FRANK
Modern Spiritualism, London, 1902.
Mesmerism and Christian Science, London, 1909.

POLING, JAMES (with LANCASTER, EVELYN)
Strangers in my Body or The Final Face of Eve, Secker & Warburg, London, 1958.

PRICE, HARRY
Fifty Years of Psychical Research, London, 1939.

PRINCE, MORTON
The Dissociation of a Personality, New York, 1906.
The Nature of Mind and Human Automatism, Philadelphia, 1885.
The Unconscious, New York, 1914.

PRINCE, WALTER FRANKLIN
The Case of Patience Worth, Boston, 1927.
QUACKENBOS, J. D.
Hypnotic Therapeutics in Theory and Practice, New York, 1908.
RICHET, CHARLES
Thirty Years of Psychical Research, London, 1923.
Notre Sixième Sens, Paris, 1928.
Traité de Métapsychique, Paris, 1922.
ROCHAS, ALBERT DE
L'Extériorisation de la Motricité, Paris, 1906.
L'Extériorisation de la Sensibilité, Paris, 1895.
Les Vies Successives, Paris, 1911.
ROSE, RONALD
Living Magic, Chatto & Windus, London, 1957.
ROSENTHAL, RAYMOND (with WOLFE, BERNARD)
Hypnotism Comes of Age, Bobbs-Merrill, New York, 1948.
SALTER, ANDREW
What is Hypnosis? Athenaeum Press, London, 1950.
SCHOFIELD, ALFRED TAYLOR
The Force of Mind, London, 1903.
SHIRLEY, THE HON. RALPH
The Problem of Rebirth, London, 1936.
SIDIS, BORIS
The Psychology of Suggestion, New York, 1898.
SUDRE, RENE
Traite de Parapsychologie, Editions Payot, Paris, 1956.
THIGPEN, CORBETT H. (with CLECKLEY, HERVEY M.)
The Three Faces of Eve, Secker & Warburg, London, 1957.
TUCKEY, C. LLOYD
Psycho-Therapeutics, London, 1889
VAN PELT, S. J.
Hypnotism and the Power Within, Skeffington, London, 1950.
Hypnotic Suggestion, Wright, Bristol, n.d.
WEST, DONALD J.
Eleven Lourdes Miracles, Duckworth, London, 1957.
Psychical Research Today, Duckworth, London, 1948.
WILSON, DONALD POWELL
My Six Convicts, Hamish Hamilton, London, 1951.
WINGFIELD, H. E.
Introduction to the Study of Hypnotism, London, 1920.
WINSLOW, FORBES
On the Obscure Diseases of the Brain and Disorders of the Mind, New York, 1900.

Index

ABORIGINES, 155-7
Abortion, 47
Abreaction, 41
Age regression, 41-3, 130, 147
Alcohol, 23, 34, 39
Ambrose, Gordon, 32, 162
American Society for Psychical Research, 75, 79
Amnesia, 16, 49
Anaesthesia, 6, 7, 45-6
Analgesia, 22, 45-6
Animal magnetism, ix, 4, 5, 6
Animals, whether hypnotizable, 151-2
Augustine, Saint, 37
Automatic writing, 53, 114, 123-4
Auto-hypnosis, x, 91, 115, 116, 117, 123, 154, 156, *see also* self-hypnosis
Auto-suggestion, 13, 56-64, 96, 117, *see also* self-suggestion
Avicenna, 2

Baquet, 4, 153, 169
Barker, William J., 133
Barrett, Sir William Fletcher, 4, 9, 78, 79, 97, 99-101, 164
Baudouin, Charles, 56
'Beauchamp, Sally', 71-5
Beaunis, 28, 47, 49, 51-2
Behavourist school, 19
Bergson, Henri, 1, 43, 164
Bernard, Claude, 114
Bernheim, H., 8, 9, 10, 18, 28, 33, 34, 49, 96, 110
Bernstein, Morey, 132-4
Bertrand, Alexandre, 6
Birth control, 47
Bjorkhem, John, 86
Black magic, x, 11, 112, 113
Body temperature, regulation by hypnotic suggestion, 47
Boirac, E., 83-4
Book tests, 125
Bordeaux, J., 25
Bourne, Ansel, 66-8
Bowel action, regulation by hypnotic suggestion, 47
Boyle, Robert, 2
Braid, James, 7, 17, 28, 29, 44, 47, 151, 155
Brain washing, 162-3
Bramwell, J. Milne, 10, 14, 16, 18, 20-23, 28-9, 34, 44, 47, 49, 52, 56, 152, 165
British Association for the Advancement of Science, 8, 98
British Medical Association, 10, 62, 63
Brown, William, 10, 82

CAGLIOSTRO, Count, 136
Catalepsy, 37, 151-2
Catherine of Siena, Saint, 57
Cayce, Edgar, 90-93, 131
Charcot, Jean, 8, 17
Chloroform, 8
Chowrin, 88
Christ, 1, 7, 57, 58
Christian Church, 2, 3, 7, 60, 82
Christian 'Science', 60, 61-2, 64
Church, Christian, *see* Christian Church
Clairvoyance, 6, 7, 80, 81-94, 117, 129, 165
'Clever-men,' 1, 113, 155-7
Collaboration between doctor and hypnotist, 161
College of Psychic Science, 80, 119, 123
Colours, effect on induction of hypnosis, 25
Community of sensation, 6, 7, 96
Conception, prevention of, 47
Conditioned reflexes, 19
Confusional technique, 32
Convulsions, 4, 5, 118-19
Cooper, Blanche, 127
Coué, Emile, 13, 56
Criminal uses of hypnotism, 139-150
Cross-correspondence, 129
Cuddon, Eric, 23, 131, 143, 144
Cummins, Geraldine, 129
Curran, Pearl, 123-4

DANGERS of hypnotism, 163
'Davis, Gordon', 127
Delboeuf, 22
Deleuze, 169-170
Delusions, 41
Devi, Shanti, 135
Dingwall, Eric J., 78, 133
Dissociation, 22, 65-77
Distance, influencing at, 6, 7, 106-113, 156
Divination, 1
'Do-it-yourself', 157-160
Doyle, Sir Arthur Conan, 126
Drugs, 33, 34
Ducasse, C. J., 133-4
Dufay, 89-90
Duke University, 79
Dupuys, Sylvain, 85

INDEX

Ebers papyrus, 1
Eddy, Mary Baker, 61-2
Elliot, Hugh, 24
Elliotson, John, 6. 7, 45, 101
Emerson, R. W., 48, 65
Erickson, M. H., 42, 49
Erskine, Alex, 32, 47, 82
Esculapius, 1
Esdaile, James, 7, 17, 27-8, 45-6, 47, 100, 102
Estabrooks, George H., 33, 42, 49, 50, 52, 65, 162-3
Evil Eye, 58
Exorcism, 2, 3
Exteriorization of sensibility, 110-112
Extra-sensory-perception, 80
Eysenck, H. J., 38, 165

Fahler, Jarl, 111-12
Fakirs, 1, 153
Faraday, Michael, 130
Faria, the Abbé, 5
'Feda', 124-6
Ferenczi, Sandor, 20
Fischer, Doris, 75-6
Fishman, Charles, 42
'Florentine, Abraham', 119-120
Flournoy, Theodore, 136-7
Fluid, magnetic, *see* magnetic fluid
Fodor, Nandor, 42, 112-13, 136
Forel, August, 10, 34, 43, 47, 57
Fractionation technique, 31
Freud, Sigmund, 9, 19, 41

Garrett, Eileen J., 11, 79, 115-17, 126-7
Gassner, Johann, 3
Geley, Gustav, 131
Genius, 58
Gibert, 82. 102-110
Greatrakes, Valentine, 2
Gregory, William, 101
Grierson, Walter, 164
Gurney, Edmund, 9, 10, 29, 53, 93-4, 100-101, 160, 165
Guthrie, Malcolm, 101

Hadfield, J. A., 10
Hallucinations, 18, 38-43, 50
Hammerschlag, Heinz E., 150
Hammond, William A., 96
Hand clasping test, 27
Hand levitation test, 27
Hardrup, Pelle, 147-150
Healing, 1, 60, 62-4, 78, 90-93, 154, *see also* 'spiritual' healing
Hehl, Father, 3
Heidelberg case, 145-7
Helmont, van, 3
Herschell, Sir John, 80
Hetero-suggestion, 13

'Higher phenomena', ix, 7, 80, 81, 82, 129, 165
Hippocrates, 1
Hitler, Adolf, 153
Hodgson, Richard, 121-2
Huxley, T. H., x, 165
Hyperaesthesia, 43, 44
Hypno-analysis, 10
Hypnotherapy, 10
Horsley, J. Stephen, 34
Hypochondria, 58-9
Hyslop, James, 121
Hysteria, 17, 21-2, 147

Illusions, 18
Indian rope trick, 153
'Inner Mind', 23, 143
Irwin, Flight Lieutenant, 126-7

James, William, 9, 20, 66, 120, 123, 164
Janet, Pierre, 10, 19, 68, 82, 101, 102-110
Jar-phoonk, 1
Johnson, Samuel, 2

Koestler, Arthur, 56
Krafft-Ebing, R. von, 10, 25, 47, 57

Lafontaine, 7, 151, 160
Laidlow, Robert E., 25, 161
Lancet, the, 7
Lateau, Louise, 57
Layne, A. C., 90-92
Leaf, Walter, 121
Leonard, Gladys Osborne, 124-6
Liébeault, A. A., 8, 10, 28, 47, 51-2, 57, 96, 140
Liégeois, Jules, 40, 41, 51-2, 140-143
Lindner, Robert, 42
Lodge, Sir Oliver Joseph, 121, 124
London Dialectical Society, 79, 165
Louis XVI, 5
Lourdes, 60
Luys, J., 28, 33

Madow, L. W., 14
Magic, 58, 156, *see also* black magic
Magnet, 3-4, 8, 105
Magnetic fluid, ix, 3, 4, 5, 16, 17, 151, 169-170
Magnetism, ix, 61, 151, 169, *see also* animal magnetism
Magonet, A. Philip, 162
Mail order courses in hypnotism, 157-9
'Martian language', 137
Mason, R. Osgood, 84
Mass hypnotism, 152-3, 156
Mayer, Ludwig, 145-7
Mayo, Herbert, 89, 96
McComb, Samuel, 59
McDougall, William, 10, 20

INDEX

Mechanical aids to induction, 33
Medical applications of hypnosis, xi, 162
Mediumistic phenomena, 114-129
Menstruation, regulation by hypnotic suggestion, 47
Mesmer, Franz Anton, 2, 3, 4, 5, 27, 81, 82, 152, 153
Mesmerism, ix, x, 5, 6, 7, 93-4, 151, 168, 169
Methods of hypnotizing, 26-35
Military applications, 162-3
Milk, secretion of regulated by hypnotic suggestion, 47
Miracles, 1, 2, 7, 60 63, 78
Mitchell, T. W., 9, 53
Moll, J. Albert, 10, 24, 28, 34, 44, 49, 96, 113, 151
Monoideism, 17, 18, 19
Morel, Madame, 83-4
Moses, William Stainton, 119-120
Multiple personality, 65-77
'Murphy, Bridie', 131-4
Murton, H. J. D., 161-2
Myers, A. T., 102-110
Myers, Frederic W. H., 9, 10, 13, 20, 29, 57, 60, 68, 80, 84, 93-4, 95, 101, 102-110, 119, 121, 129, 140-43, 150, 160, 165

NANCY school, 8, 18, 29
Neumann, Therese, 58
Newbold, George, 32, 162
Nielsen, Björn, 147-150

OD light, 8
Odylic forces, 16, 17
Opposition to mesmerism and hypnotism, 7, 46
Origin of terms 'hypnosis' and 'hypnotism', x, 7, 11
Osty, Eugene, 10, 82-4
Oswald, Ian, 35
Ouija Board, 123

PAGENSTECHER, G., 86-7
Painless surgery, 45-6
Parapsychology, 10, 79, 80
Parapsychology foundation, 79
Passes 27, 28, 70, 130
Pavlov, L. P., 19
'Pelham, George', 122
Peracelsus, 2
'Phinuit', 122
Pincher, Chapman, 35
Piper, Leonore E., 120-123
Platanof, 39
Podmore, Frank, 9
Points de repère, 43
Polydeism, 19
Pomponatius, 2, 60

Post-hypnotic phenomena, 48-55
Post-hypnotic suggestion, 22, 48, 50, 57, 111, 147, 153
Postural Sway test, 26
Potet, Baron du, 6, 96
Precognition, 80, 129
Price, Harry, 126-7
Price, H. H., 95
Primitive races, hypnotism amongst, 155-7
Prince, Morton, 10, 71
Prince, Walter Franklin, 75-6, 87, 124
Prophecy, 1, 78
Psychic phenomena, definitions of various kinds, ix, x, 78-80
Psychical Research, 10, 164
Psychical research societies, *see* Society for Psychical Research, American Society for Psychical Research, College of Psychic Science, Parapsychology Foundation, London Dialectical Society, and Seth Sohan Lal Memorial Institute of Parapsychology
Psycho-analysis, 9, 20, 112
Psychokinesis, 80
Psychometry, 86-8
Psychotherapy, 9, 161
Puysegur, The Marquis de, 5, 82

QUIMBY, Phineas, 61

R101 Airship, information concerning given at seance, 126-7
Rape, 144
Rapport, 16, 26, 32, 34, 81, 96
Reichenbach, Baron Karl von, 8
Reincarnation, 130-138
Reversed effort, law of, 14
Rhine, J. B., 79
Richet, Charles, 10, 28, 82, 89, 93, 129, 139, 164
Richter, Paul, 58
Rochas, Albert de, 110, 130
Rorchach tests, 14
Rose, Louis, 62
Rose, Ronald, 155-7
Rosen, Harold, 134-5
Royal Touch, 2, 4

SACRED sleep, 1
Salpêtrière, 8, 18, 33
Sarbin, T. R., 14
Schmid, Max, 148
Schofield, A. T., 13
Schrenck-Notzing, Freiherr Albert von, 33
Scott, Sir Walter, 66
Second sight, 78, 81
Secondary personality, 124
Seduction, hypnosis an aid to?, 143-4

INDEX

Self-hypnosis, 16, 20, 56, 115, 168, *see also* auto-hypnosis
Self-suggestion, 60, 118, 119, *see also* auto-suggestion
Seth Sohan Lal Memorial Institute of Parapsychology, 135
Sexual offences, 143-4, 146, 147
Shell-shock, 10, 82
Sidgewick, Henry, 9, 101
Sidis, Boris, 10, 43, 65
'Simmonds, Ruth', 132-4
Sleep-walking, 66
Sleep-walking, 12, 136
Smith, G. A., 99-100
'Smith, Helene', 136-7
Soal, S. G., 95, 127
Society for Psychical Research, ix, 9, 60, 79, 99, 101, 118, 121, 124, 140, 165
Solon, 27
Somnambulism, 5, 6, 12, 49, 58, 66, 78, 136-7
Soothsaying, 1
Spencer, Herbert, x
Spiegel, John P., 42
'Spirit guides', 114, 117, 136
Spiritism, *see* spiritualism
'Spiritual' healing, 62-4, *see also* healing
Spiritualism, 62, 75, 78, 79, 114, 128, 136
Spofford, D., 61-2
Stage performances, x, 11, 41, 44, 50, 167-8
Stages of hypnosis, 5, 15
Stevenson, Ian, 138
Stigmata, 2, 57-8
Subliminal consciousness, 20-23, 75
Suggestion and suggestibility, 12-16, 18, 33, 90, 130, 152, 153, 168
Susceptibility, 14, 15, 26
Suspended animation, 153, 155
'Svengalis', x

TACITUS, 1
Talbot, Mrs Hugh, 124-5
Telepathy, 6, 43, 80, 95-113, 117, 129, 153, 154, 165

Telka, 123
Termination of hypnosis, 35, 36
Tests of hypnotizability, 26, 27
Theories, 16-23
Thomas, Charles Drayton, 125
Thought reading, 7
Thought transference, 43, 80
Three Faces of Eve, 76
Tighe, Virginia, 132-4
Time, appreciation of passage of, 6, 52-5
Townshend, C. H., 101
Trance, 5, 11, 15, 16, 23, 31, 48, 103, 114, 116, 119, 121, 123, 168
Travelling clairvoyance, 82, 156, *see also* clairvoyance
Tweedale, Violet, 136

URINE, secretion of regulated by hypnotic suggestion, 47
'Uvani', 126

VOLUNTARY muscular system, changes in, 37, 38

WAKING hypnosis, 32
Walter, Franz, 145-7
Wells, W. R., 32
West, Donald J., 60
Wetterstrand, 28, 34, 47
White, R., 19
Who should practise hypnotism? 160-162
Will power, 3, 13, 14, 35
Wilson, Donald Powell, 153-5
Wilson, W. E., 98
Witch-doctors, 1, 58, 78, 113
Witches, 58, 113
Wolberg, Lewis M., 42
Wolfart, Carl, 5
'Worth, Patience', 123-4, 128

YEATMAN, Ruby, 123-4
Yogis, 1

Zoist, 7, 151

MELVIN POWERS SELF-IMPROVEMENT LIBRARY

ASTROLOGY

____ ASTROLOGY: HOW TO CHART YOUR HOROSCOPE *Max Heindel*	3.00
____ ASTROLOGY: YOUR PERSONAL SUN-SIGN GUIDE *Beatrice Ryder*	3.00
____ ASTROLOGY FOR EVERYDAY LIVING *Janet Harris*	2.00
____ ASTROLOGY MADE EASY *Astarte*	3.00
____ ASTROLOGY MADE PRACTICAL *Alexandra Kayhle*	3.00
____ ASTROLOGY, ROMANCE, YOU AND THE STARS *Anthony Norvell*	4.00
____ MY WORLD OF ASTROLOGY *Sydney Omarr*	5.00
____ THOUGHT DIAL *Sydney Omarr*	4.00
____ WHAT THE STARS REVEAL ABOUT THE MEN IN YOUR LIFE *Thelma White*	3.00

BRIDGE

____ BRIDGE BIDDING MADE EASY *Edwin B. Kantar*	5.00
____ BRIDGE CONVENTIONS *Edwin B. Kantar*	5.00
____ BRIDGE HUMOR *Edwin B. Kantar*	3.00
____ COMPETITIVE BIDDING IN MODERN BRIDGE *Edgar Kaplan*	4.00
____ DEFENSIVE BRIDGE PLAY COMPLETE *Edwin B. Kantar*	10.00
____ HOW TO IMPROVE YOUR BRIDGE *Alfred Sheinwold*	3.00
____ IMPROVING YOUR BIDDING SKILLS *Edwin B. Kantar*	4.00
____ INTRODUCTION TO DEFENDER'S PLAY *Edwin B. Kantar*	3.00
____ SHORT CUT TO WINNING BRIDGE *Alfred Sheinwold*	3.00
____ TEST YOUR BRIDGE PLAY *Edwin B. Kantar*	3.00
____ WINNING DECLARER PLAY *Dorothy Hayden Truscott*	4.00

BUSINESS, STUDY & REFERENCE

____ CONVERSATION MADE EASY *Elliot Russell*	2.00
____ EXAM SECRET *Dennis B. Jackson*	3.00
____ FIX-IT BOOK *Arthur Symons*	2.00
____ HOW TO DEVELOP A BETTER SPEAKING VOICE *M. Hellier*	3.00
____ HOW TO MAKE A FORTUNE IN REAL ESTATE *Albert Winnikoff*	4.00
____ INCREASE YOUR LEARNING POWER *Geoffrey A. Dudley*	2.00
____ MAGIC OF NUMBERS *Robert Tocquet*	2.00
____ PRACTICAL GUIDE TO BETTER CONCENTRATION *Melvin Powers*	3.00
____ PRACTICAL GUIDE TO PUBLIC SPEAKING *Maurice Forley*	3.00
____ 7 DAYS TO FASTER READING *William S. Schaill*	3.00
____ SONGWRITERS RHYMING DICTIONARY *Jane Shaw Whitfield*	5.00
____ SPELLING MADE EASY *Lester D. Basch & Dr. Milton Finkelstein*	2.00
____ STUDENT'S GUIDE TO BETTER GRADES *J. A. Rickard*	3.00
____ TEST YOURSELF—Find Your Hidden Talent *Jack Shafer*	3.00
____ YOUR WILL & WHAT TO DO ABOUT IT *Attorney Samuel G. Kling*	3.00

CALLIGRAPHY

____ ADVANCED CALLIGRAPHY *Katherine Jeffares*	7.00
____ CALLIGRAPHER'S REFERENCE BOOK *Anne Leptich & Jacque Evans*	6.00
____ CALLIGRAPHY—The Art of Beautiful Writing *Katherine Jeffares*	7.00
____ CALLIGRAPHY FOR FUN & PROFIT *Anne Leptich & Jacque Evans*	7.00
____ CALLIGRAPHY MADE EASY *Tina Serafini*	7.00

CHESS & CHECKERS

____ BEGINNER'S GUIDE TO WINNING CHESS *Fred Reinfeld*	3.00
____ BETTER CHESS—How to Play *Fred Reinfeld*	2.00
____ CHECKERS MADE EASY *Tom Wiswell*	2.00
____ CHESS IN TEN EASY LESSONS *Larry Evans*	3.00
____ CHESS MADE EASY *Milton L. Hanauer*	3.00
____ CHESS MASTERY—A New Approach *Fred Reinfeld*	3.00
____ CHESS PROBLEMS FOR BEGINNERS *edited by Fred Reinfeld*	2.00
____ CHESS SECRETS REVEALED *Fred Reinfeld*	2.00
____ CHESS STRATEGY—An Expert's Guide *Fred Reinfeld*	2.00
____ CHESS TACTICS FOR BEGINNERS *edited by Fred Reinfeld*	3.00
____ CHESS THEORY & PRACTICE *Morry & Mitchell*	2.00
____ HOW TO WIN AT CHECKERS *Fred Reinfeld*	3.00
____ 1001 BRILLIANT WAYS TO CHECKMATE *Fred Reinfeld*	3.00
____ 1001 WINNING CHESS SACRIFICES & COMBINATIONS *Fred Reinfeld*	3.00
____ SOVIET CHESS *Edited by R. G. Wade*	3.00

COOKERY & HERBS

CULPEPER'S HERBAL REMEDIES *Dr. Nicholas Culpeper*	3.00
FAST GOURMET COOKBOOK *Poppy Cannon*	2.50
GINSENG The Myth & The Truth *Joseph P. Hou*	3.00
HEALING POWER OF HERBS *May Bethel*	3.00
HEALING POWER OF NATURAL FOODS *May Bethel*	3.00
HERB HANDBOOK *Dawn MacLeod*	3.00
HERBS FOR COOKING AND HEALING *Dr. Donald Law*	2.00
HERBS FOR HEALTH—How to Grow & Use Them *Louise Evans Doole*	3.00
HOME GARDEN COOKBOOK—Delicious Natural Food Recipes *Ken Kraft*	3.00
MEDICAL HERBALIST *edited by Dr. J. R. Yemm*	3.00
NATURAL FOOD COOKBOOK *Dr. Harry C. Bond*	3.00
NATURE'S MEDICINES *Richard Lucas*	3.00
VEGETABLE GARDENING FOR BEGINNERS *Hugh Wiberg*	2.00
VEGETABLES FOR TODAY'S GARDENS *R. Milton Carleton*	2.00
VEGETARIAN COOKERY *Janet Walker*	3.00
VEGETARIAN COOKING MADE EASY & DELECTABLE *Veronica Vezza*	3.00
VEGETARIAN DELIGHTS—A Happy Cookbook for Health *K. R. Mehta*	2.00
VEGETARIAN GOURMET COOKBOOK *Joyce McKinnel*	3.00

GAMBLING & POKER

ADVANCED POKER STRATEGY & WINNING PLAY *A. D. Livingston*	3.00
HOW NOT TO LOSE AT POKER *Jeffrey Lloyd Castle*	3.00
HOW TO WIN AT DICE GAMES *Skip Frey*	3.00
HOW TO WIN AT POKER *Terence Reese & Anthony T. Watkins*	3.00
SECRETS OF WINNING POKER *George S. Coffin*	3.00
WINNING AT CRAPS *Dr. Lloyd T. Commins*	3.00
WINNING AT GIN *Chester Wander & Cy Rice*	3.00
WINNING AT POKER—An Expert's Guide *John Archer*	3.00
WINNING AT 21—An Expert's Guide *John Archer*	3.00
WINNING POKER SYSTEMS *Norman Zadeh*	3.00

HEALTH

BEE POLLEN *Lynda Lyngheim & Jack Scagnetti*	3.00
DR. LINDNER'S SPECIAL WEIGHT CONTROL METHOD *P. G. Lindner, M.D.*	1.50
HELP YOURSELF TO BETTER SIGHT *Margaret Darst Corbett*	3.00
HOW TO IMPROVE YOUR VISION *Dr. Robert A. Kraskin*	3.00
HOW YOU CAN STOP SMOKING PERMANENTLY *Ernest Caldwell*	3.00
MIND OVER PLATTER *Peter G. Lindner, M.D.*	3.00
NATURE'S WAY TO NUTRITION & VIBRANT HEALTH *Robert J. Scrutton*	3.00
NEW CARBOHYDRATE DIET COUNTER *Patti Lopez-Pereira*	1.50
PSYCHEDELIC ECSTASY *William Marshall & Gilbert W. Taylor*	2.00
QUICK & EASY EXERCISES FOR FACIAL BEAUTY *Judy Smith-deal*	2.00
QUICK & EASY EXERCISES FOR FIGURE BEAUTY *Judy Smith-deal*	2.00
REFLEXOLOGY *Dr. Maybelle Segal*	3.00
REFLEXOLOGY FOR GOOD HEALTH *Anna Kaye & Don C. Matchan*	3.00
YOU CAN LEARN TO RELAX *Dr. Samuel Gutwirth*	3.00
YOUR ALLERGY—What To Do About It *Allan Knight, M.D.*	3.00

HOBBIES

BEACHCOMBING FOR BEGINNERS *Norman Hickin*	2.00
BLACKSTONE'S MODERN CARD TRICKS *Harry Blackstone*	3.00
BLACKSTONE'S SECRETS OF MAGIC *Harry Blackstone*	3.00
COIN COLLECTING FOR BEGINNERS *Burton Hobson & Fred Reinfeld*	3.00
ENTERTAINING WITH ESP *Tony 'Doc' Shiels*	2.00
400 FASCINATING MAGIC TRICKS YOU CAN DO *Howard Thurston*	3.00
HOW I TURN JUNK INTO FUN AND PROFIT *Sari*	3.00
HOW TO PLAY THE HARMONICA FOR FUN & PROFIT *Hal Leighton*	3.00
HOW TO WRITE A HIT SONG & SELL IT *Tommy Boyce*	7.00
JUGGLING MADE EASY *Rudolf Dittrich*	2.00
MAGIC MADE EASY *Byron Wels*	2.00
STAMP COLLECTING FOR BEGINNERS *Burton Hobson*	2.00

HORSE PLAYERS' WINNING GUIDES

BETTING HORSES TO WIN *Les Conklin*	3.00
ELIMINATE THE LOSERS *Bob McKnight*	3.00

____HOW TO PICK WINNING HORSES *Bob McKnight* 3.
____HOW TO WIN AT THE RACES *Sam (The Genius) Lewin* 3.
____HOW YOU CAN BEAT THE RACES *Jack Kavanagh* 3.
____MAKING MONEY AT THE RACES *David Barr* 3.
____PAYDAY AT THE RACES *Les Conklin* 3.
____SMART HANDICAPPING MADE EASY *William Bauman* 3.
____SUCCESS AT THE HARNESS RACES *Barry Meadow* 3.
____WINNING AT THE HARNESS RACES—An Expert's Guide *Nick Cammarano* 3.

HUMOR
____HOW TO BE A COMEDIAN FOR FUN & PROFIT *King & Laufer* 2.
____HOW TO FLATTEN YOUR TUSH *Coach Marge Reardon* 2.
____JOKE TELLER'S HANDBOOK *Bob Orben* 3.
____JOKES FOR ALL OCCASIONS *Al Schock* 3.
____2000 NEW LAUGHS FOR SPEAKERS *Bob Orben* 3.
____2,500 JOKES TO START 'EM LAUGHING *Bob Orben* 3

HYPNOTISM
____ADVANCED TECHNIQUES OF HYPNOSIS *Melvin Powers* 2.
____BRAINWASHING AND THE CULTS *Paul A. Verdier, Ph.D.* 3.
____CHILDBIRTH WITH HYPNOSIS *William S. Kroger, M.D.* 3.
____HOW TO SOLVE Your Sex Problems with Self-Hypnosis *Frank S. Caprio, M.D.* 3.
____HOW TO STOP SMOKING THRU SELF-HYPNOSIS *Leslie M. LeCron* 3
____HOW TO USE AUTO-SUGGESTION EFFECTIVELY *John Duckworth* 3.
____HOW YOU CAN BOWL BETTER USING SELF-HYPNOSIS *Jack Heise* 3.
____HOW YOU CAN PLAY BETTER GOLF USING SELF-HYPNOSIS *Jack Heise* 3.
____HYPNOSIS AND SELF-HYPNOSIS *Bernard Hollander, M.D.* 3.
____HYPNOTISM (Originally published in 1893) *Carl Sextus* 5.
____HYPNOTISM & PSYCHIC PHENOMENA *Simeon Edmunds* 4.
____HYPNOTISM MADE EASY *Dr. Ralph Winn* 3.
____HYPNOTISM MADE PRACTICAL *Louis Orton* 3.
____HYPNOTISM REVEALED *Melvin Powers* 2.
____HYPNOTISM TODAY *Leslie LeCron and Jean Bordeaux, Ph.D.* 5.
____MODERN HYPNOSIS *Lesley Kuhn & Salvatore Russo, Ph.D.* 5.
____NEW CONCEPTS OF HYPNOSIS *Bernard C. Gindes, M.D.* 5
____NEW SELF-HYPNOSIS *Paul Adams* 4
____POST-HYPNOTIC INSTRUCTIONS—Suggestions for Therapy *Arnold Furst* 3
____PRACTICAL GUIDE TO SELF-HYPNOSIS *Melvin Powers* 3
____PRACTICAL HYPNOTISM *Philip Magonet, M.D.* 3
____SECRETS OF HYPNOTISM *S. J. Van Pelt, M.D.* 3
____SELF-HYPNOSIS A Conditioned-Response Technique *Laurance Sparks* 5
____SELF-HYPNOSIS Its Theory, Technique & Application *Melvin Powers* 3
____THERAPY THROUGH HYPNOSIS *edited by Raphael H. Rhodes* 4

JUDAICA
____HOW TO LIVE A RICHER & FULLER LIFE *Rabbi Edgar F. Magnin* 2
____MODERN ISRAEL *Lily Edelman* 2
____ROMANCE OF HASSIDISM *Jacob S. Minkin* 2
____SERVICE OF THE HEART *Evelyn Garfiel, Ph.D.* 4
____STORY OF ISRAEL IN COINS *Jean & Maurice Gould* 2
____STORY OF ISRAEL IN STAMPS *Maxim & Gabriel Shamir* 1

JUST FOR WOMEN
____COSMOPOLITAN'S GUIDE TO MARVELOUS MEN Fwd. by *Helen Gurley Brown* 3
____COSMOPOLITAN'S HANG-UP HANDBOOK Foreword by *Helen Gurley Brown* 4
____COSMOPOLITAN'S LOVE BOOK—A Guide to Ecstasy in Bed 4
____COSMOPOLITAN'S NEW ETIQUETTE GUIDE Fwd. by *Helen Gurley Brown* 4
____I AM A COMPLEAT WOMAN *Doris Hagopian & Karen O'Connor Sweeney* 3
____JUST FOR WOMEN—A Guide to the Female Body *Richard E. Sand, M.D.* 4
____NEW APPROACHES TO SEX IN MARRIAGE *John E. Eichenlaub, M.D.* 3
____SEXUALLY ADEQUATE FEMALE *Frank S. Caprio, M.D.* 3
____YOUR FIRST YEAR OF MARRIAGE *Dr. Tom McGinnis* 3

MARRIAGE, SEX & PARENTHOOD
____ABILITY TO LOVE *Dr. Allan Fromme* 5
____ENCYCLOPEDIA OF MODERN SEX & LOVE TECHNIQUES *Macandrew* 4
____GUIDE TO SUCCESSFUL MARRIAGE *Drs. Albert Ellis & Robert Harper* 5

___ HOW TO RAISE AN EMOTIONALLY HEALTHY, HAPPY CHILD *A. Ellis*		3.00
___ IMPOTENCE & FRIGIDITY *Edwin W. Hirsch, M.D.*		3.00
___ SEX WITHOUT GUILT *Albert Ellis, Ph.D.*		3.00
___ SEXUALLY ADEQUATE MALE *Frank S. Caprio, M.D.*		3.00

MELVIN POWERS' MAIL ORDER LIBRARY

___ HOW TO GET RICH IN MAIL ORDER *Melvin Powers*		10.00
___ HOW TO WRITE A GOOD ADVERTISEMENT *Victor O. Schwab*		15.00
___ WORLD WIDE MAIL ORDER SHOPPER'S GUIDE *Eugene V. Moller*		5.00

METAPHYSICS & OCCULT

___ BOOK OF TALISMANS, AMULETS & ZODIACAL GEMS *William Pavitt*		4.00
___ CONCENTRATION—A Guide to Mental Mastery *Mouni Sadhu*		3.00
___ CRITIQUES OF GOD *Edited by Peter Angeles*		7.00
___ DREAMS & OMENS REVEALED *Fred Gettings*		3.00
___ EXTRA-TERRESTRIAL INTELLIGENCE—The First Encounter		6.00
___ FORTUNE TELLING WITH CARDS *P. Foli*		3.00
___ HANDWRITING ANALYSIS MADE EASY *John Marley*		3.00
___ HANDWRITING TELLS *Nadya Olyanova*		5.00
___ HOW TO UNDERSTAND YOUR DREAMS *Geoffrey A. Dudley*		3.00
___ ILLUSTRATED YOGA *William Zorn*		3.00
___ IN DAYS OF GREAT PEACE *Mouni Sadhu*		3.00
___ KING SOLOMON'S TEMPLE IN THE MASONIC TRADITION *Alex Horne*		5.00
___ LSD—THE AGE OF MIND *Bernard Roseman*		2.00
___ MAGICIAN—His training and work *W. E. Butler*		3.00
___ MEDITATION *Mouni Sadhu*		5.00
___ MODERN NUMEROLOGY *Morris C. Goodman*		3.00
___ NUMEROLOGY—ITS FACTS AND SECRETS *Ariel Yvon Taylor*		3.00
___ NUMEROLOGY MADE EASY *W. Mykian*		3.00
___ PALMISTRY MADE EASY *Fred Gettings*		3.00
___ PALMISTRY MADE PRACTICAL *Elizabeth Daniels Squire*		3.00
___ PALMISTRY SECRETS REVEALED *Henry Frith*		3.00
___ PRACTICAL YOGA *Ernest Wood*		3.00
___ PROPHECY IN OUR TIME *Martin Ebon*		2.50
___ PSYCHOLOGY OF HANDWRITING *Nadya Olyanova*		3.00
___ SUPERSTITION—Are you superstitious? *Eric Maple*		2.00
___ TAROT *Mouni Sadhu*		6.00
___ TAROT OF THE BOHEMIANS *Papus*		5.00
___ WAYS TO SELF-REALIZATION *Mouni Sadhu*		3.00
___ WHAT YOUR HANDWRITING REVEALS *Albert E. Hughes*		2.00
___ WITCHCRAFT, MAGIC & OCCULTISM—A Fascinating History *W. B. Crow*		5.00
___ WITCHCRAFT—THE SIXTH SENSE *Justine Glass*		3.00
___ WORLD OF PSYCHIC RESEARCH *Hereward Carrington*		2.00

SELF-HELP & INSPIRATIONAL

___ DAILY POWER FOR JOYFUL LIVING *Dr. Donald Curtis*		3.00
___ DYNAMIC THINKING *Melvin Powers*		2.00
___ EXUBERANCE—Your Guide to Happiness & Fulfillment *Dr. Paul Kurtz*		3.00
___ GREATEST POWER IN THE UNIVERSE *U. S. Andersen*		5.00
___ GROW RICH WHILE YOU SLEEP *Ben Sweetland*		3.00
___ GROWTH THROUGH REASON *Albert Ellis, Ph.D.*		-4.00
___ GUIDE TO DEVELOPING YOUR POTENTIAL *Herbert A. Otto, Ph.D.*		3.00
___ GUIDE TO LIVING IN BALANCE *Frank S. Caprio, M.D.*		2.00
___ HELPING YOURSELF WITH APPLIED PSYCHOLOGY *R. Henderson*		2.00
___ HELPING YOURSELF WITH PSYCHIATRY *Frank S. Caprio, M.D.*		2.00
___ HOW TO ATTRACT GOOD LUCK *A. H. Z. Carr*		3.00
___ HOW TO CONTROL YOUR DESTINY *Norvell*		3.00
___ HOW TO DEVELOP A WINNING PERSONALITY *Martin Panzer*		3.00
___ HOW TO DEVELOP AN EXCEPTIONAL MEMORY *Young & Gibson*		4.00
___ HOW TO OVERCOME YOUR FEARS *M. P. Leahy, M.D.*		3.00
___ HOW YOU CAN HAVE CONFIDENCE AND POWER *Les Giblin*		3.00
___ HUMAN PROBLEMS & HOW TO SOLVE THEM *Dr. Donald Curtis*		3.00
___ I CAN *Ben Sweetland*		4.00

	I WILL *Ben Sweetland*	3.00
	LEFT-HANDED PEOPLE *Michael Barsley*	4.00
	MAGIC IN YOUR MIND *U. S. Andersen*	5.00
	MAGIC OF THINKING BIG *Dr. David J. Schwartz*	3.00
	MAGIC POWER OF YOUR MIND *Walter M. Germain*	4.00
	MENTAL POWER THROUGH SLEEP SUGGESTION *Melvin Powers*	3.00
	NEW GUIDE TO RATIONAL LIVING *Albert Ellis, Ph.D. & R. Harper, Ph.D.*	3.00
	OUR TROUBLED SELVES *Dr. Allan Fromme*	3.00
	PSYCHO-CYBERNETICS *Maxwell Maltz, M.D.*	2.00
	SCIENCE OF MIND IN DAILY LIVING *Dr. Donald Curtis*	3.00
	SECRET OF SECRETS *U. S. Andersen*	4.00
	SECRET POWER OF THE PYRAMIDS *U. S. Andersen*	4.00
	STUTTERING AND WHAT YOU CAN DO ABOUT IT *W. Johnson, Ph.D.*	2.50
	SUCCESS-CYBERNETICS *U. S. Andersen*	4.00
	10 DAYS TO A GREAT NEW LIFE *William E. Edwards*	3.00
	THINK AND GROW RICH *Napoleon Hill*	3.00
	THREE MAGIC WORDS *U. S. Andersen*	5.00
	TREASURY OF COMFORT *edited by Rabbi Sidney Greenberg*	5.00
	TREASURY OF THE ART OF LIVING *Sidney S. Greenberg*	5.00
	YOU ARE NOT THE TARGET *Laura Huxley*	4.00
	YOUR SUBCONSCIOUS POWER *Charles M. Simmons*	4.00
	YOUR THOUGHTS CAN CHANGE YOUR LIFE *Dr. Donald Curtis*	3.00

SPORTS

	ARCHERY—An Expert's Guide *Dan Stamp*	2.00
	BICYCLING FOR FUN AND GOOD HEALTH *Kenneth E. Luther*	2.00
	BILLIARDS—Pocket • Carom • Three Cushion *Clive Cottingham, Jr.*	3.00
	CAMPING-OUT 101 Ideas & Activities *Bruno Knobel*	2.00
	COMPLETE GUIDE TO FISHING *Vlad Evanoff*	2.00
	HOW TO IMPROVE YOUR RACQUETBALL *Lubarsky, Kaufman, & Scagnetti*	3.00
	HOW TO WIN AT POCKET BILLIARDS *Edward D. Knuchell*	4.00
	JOY OF WALKING *Jack Scagnetti*	3.00
	LEARNING & TEACHING SOCCER SKILLS *Eric Worthington*	3.00
	MOTORCYCLING FOR BEGINNERS *I. G. Edmonds*	3.00
	RACQUETBALL FOR WOMEN *Toni Hudson, Jack Scagnetti & Vince Rondone*	3.00
	RACQUETBALL MADE EASY *Steve Lubarsky, Rod Delson & Jack Scagnetti*	3.00
	SECRET OF BOWLING STRIKES *Dawson Taylor*	3.00
	SECRET OF PERFECT PUTTING *Horton Smith & Dawson Taylor*	3.00
	SOCCER—The game & how to play it *Gary Rosenthal*	3.00
	STARTING SOCCER *Edward F. Dolan, Jr.*	3.00
	TABLE TENNIS MADE EASY *Johnny Leach*	2.00

TENNIS LOVERS' LIBRARY

	BEGINNER'S GUIDE TO WINNING TENNIS *Helen Hull Jacobs*	2.00
	HOW TO BEAT BETTER TENNIS PLAYERS *Loring Fiske*	4.00
	HOW TO IMPROVE YOUR TENNIS—Style, Strategy & Analysis *C. Wilson*	2.00
	INSIDE TENNIS—Techniques of Winning *Jim Leighton*	3.00
	PLAY TENNIS WITH ROSEWALL *Ken Rosewall*	2.00
	PSYCH YOURSELF TO BETTER TENNIS *Dr. Walter A. Luszki*	2.00
	SUCCESSFUL TENNIS *Neale Fraser*	2.00
	TENNIS FOR BEGINNERS *Dr. H. A. Murray*	2.00
	TENNIS MADE EASY *Joel Brecheen*	2.00
	WEEKEND TENNIS—How to have fun & win at the same time *Bill Talbert*	3.00
	WINNING WITH PERCENTAGE TENNIS—Smart Strategy *Jack Lowe*	2.00

WILSHIRE PET LIBRARY

	DOG OBEDIENCE TRAINING *Gust Kessopulos*	4.00
	DOG TRAINING MADE EASY & FUN *John W. Kellogg*	3.00
	HOW TO BRING UP YOUR PET DOG *Kurt Unkelbach*	2.00
	HOW TO RAISE & TRAIN YOUR PUPPY *Jeff Griffen*	2.00
	PIGEONS: HOW TO RAISE & TRAIN THEM *William H. Allen, Jr.*	2.00

The books listed above can be obtained from your book dealer or directly from Melvin Powers. When ordering, please remit 50¢ per book postage & handling. Send for our free illustrated catalog of self-improvement books.

Melvin Powers
12015 Sherman Road, No. Hollywood, California 91605